THE UNCONSCIOUS LIFE
OF ORGANIZATIONS

The Unconscious Life of Organizations

INTERPRETING ORGANIZATIONAL IDENTITY

Michael A. Diamond

QUORUM BOOKS

Westport, Connecticut • London

Library of Congress Cataloging-in-Publication Data

Diamond, Michael A.
 The unconscious life of organizations : interpreting
organizational identity / Michael A. Diamond.
  p. cm.
 Includes bibliographical references and index.
 ISBN 0–89930–833–3 (alk. paper)
 1. Organizational behavior. 2. Psychology, Industrial.
3. Corporate culture. I. Title.
 HD58.7.D53 1993
 302.3'5—dc20 93–6766

British Library Cataloguing in Publication Data is available.

Library of Congress Catalog Card Number: 93–6766
ISBN: 0–89930–833–3

First published in 1993

Quorum Books, 88 Post Road West, Westport, CT 06881
An imprint of Greenwood Publishing Group, Inc.

Printed in the United States of America

Copyright Acknowledgments

Excerpts in Chapter 3 reprinted with permission from *Political Psychology*. Copyright © 1991.
Diamond, Michael A. (1991). "Dimensions of Organizational Culture and Beyond." *Political
Psychology*, 12(3).

Excerpts in Chapter 4 reprinted by permission of Sage Publications, Inc. Copyright © 1992, 1992,
1988. Diamond, Michael A. (1992). "Hobbesian and Rousseauian Identities: The Psychodynamics of
Organizational Leadership and Change." *Administration and Society*, 24(3). Diamond, Michael A.
(1992). "Treating the Parataxic Organization: An Example of Intervention Strategy." *Administration
and Society*, 24(1). Diamond, Michael A. (1988). "Organizational Identity: A Psychoanalytic Exploration of Organizational Meaning." *Administration and Society*, 20(2).

Excerpts from Chapter 5 reprinted by permission of Jossey-Bass, Inc. Copyright © 1991. Diamond, Michael A. (1991). "Stresses of Group Membership: Balancing the Needs for Independence and Belonging." In M. F. R. Kets de Vries et al. (eds.), *Organizations on the Couch:
Clinical Perspectives on Organizational Behavior and Change*, pp. 191–214. San Francisco:
Jossey-Bass.

To Deb, Tova, and Simone,
with love . . .

CONTENTS

PREFACE

In this book, I introduce the reader to numerous snapshots of unconscious organizational life hidden behind the official organization. On the basis of contemporary psychodynamic thinking, I explore the unconscious dimension of knowledge, power, and social relationships in work organizations. Governing these relationships, I find *organizational culture*, the values that shape people's actions at work, and *organizational identity*, the network of emotional relationships that define who they are in a work group and, ultimately, who they are as organizational members. By probing for the deeper layers of organizational meaning and images held by individual members, we can bring to light the reasons and motives for their collective actions, and exploring these depths can make their problems better understood. This understanding of organizational life goes to the origins of the psychology of work.

The book transcends the technical rational approach to the study of behavior in organizations by isolating and then analyzing the nonrational side of administrative behavior. In it, I attempt to show how the different characteristics of organizations emerge from the dynamics of shared and projected emotions between leaders and followers, between managers and subordinates, and among peers. These complementary unconscious feelings anchor the definition of organizational membership in interpersonal relationships at work. The result is the emotionally grounded structure of organizations, what I call the organizational identity.

What distinguishes this book from other psychodynamic approaches to organizations are the following: (1) an up-to-date synthesis of object relations, self psychology, and interpersonal psychoanalysis based primarily but not exclusively on the work of Melanie Klein, Donald Winnicott, Heinz Kohut, and Harry Stack Sullivan; (2) a discussion of psychoanalytic organization theory and the application of psychodynamic concepts in organizational behavior; (3) a psychodynamic critique of organizational culture, the structure of values and rituals at work, and the introduction of the structure of organizational emotions, what I call organizational identity, as the unconscious foundation of organizational culture; (4) a psychoanalytic explanation and typology of regressive behavior in work groups; (5) a discussion and illustration of the role of language and communication in organizational consultancy; and (6) a variety of case studies drawn from over ten years of organizational research and consulting.

This book attempts to present and elaborate upon psychoanalytic organization theory and practice. Hence, I have not constructed a complete psychoanalytic organization theory. However, I offer the organizational theorist and consultant a variety of psychodynamic· tools to apply in understanding and positively changing organizations.

My purpose in writing this book is to encourage organizational members to confront institutional forms of oppression. This is not possible, I believe, without a willingness to confront ourselves as producers of and collaborators in our own oppression. No doubt it is easier to talk and write about organizational change than to produce it. People experience pain and anguish in trying to alter their work bonds and organizations. It cannot be done without grief. Planned organizational change is rare. Most often organizational change occurs in response to crises. People typically avoid dealing with problems in their organizations, and not because their problems are of an incidental nature. The problems denied and suppressed at work are often the unmentionable and taboo issues such as the intimidating boss, the lateral transfer experienced as a demotion, the lack of direction provided by organizational leaders, the unwillingness to share information across divisional boundaries, and the eccentric or sadistic manager. These and other unmentionables are hidden behind the organizational mask and are commonly the most crucial problems and barriers to organizational resilience.

Organizational psychodynamics go beyond the norms, values, mission, and structure of organizational culture. It takes us to our feelings about membership in the organization and the subjective meaning of our everyday relationships at work. In this book, I challenge the notion, found in some of the organizational literature, that subjective and emotional data are irrelevant and unimportant to our understanding of organizational behavior. I suggest that this assumption is false and represents a defense against anxieties about the true nature of life in contemporary organizations, a resistance to lifting the organizational mask and locating the organizational identity. Finally, I argue (along with Howell Baum) that collaboration and problem solving within organizations are unattainable without intimacy at work—by which I mean authentic caring and mutual respect among workers.

The book is organized into three general parts. In Part I, which follows the Introduction, where I define psychoanalytic concepts for organizational studies, I discuss what I call *psychoanalytic organization theory*. Subsequent chapters consider the psychodynamics of organizational defenses, organizational culture, organizational identity, regressive work groups, and the psychodynamics of language and communication in organizational consultations. Part II presents case illustrations. Here, I offer examples of how I work with organizations and the ways in which I think about organizations psychodynamically. Part III summarizes my thoughts on the psychodynamics of organizational change, reflecting upon Hobbes' *leviathan* and Rousseau's *general will* as organizational metaphors—the former symbolizing the modern defensive organization and the latter signifying positive change and what I call *organizational resilience*. One might say this book is about how to understand and overcome defensive organizations so that organizational resilience may be realized.

ACKNOWLEDGMENTS

Working across traditional disciplines in academics requires a network of supportive people. I am fortunate in this regard to know some extraordinarily kind, intelligent, and talented individuals. I wish to thank my friends and advisers on this project: Guy B. Adams, Seth Allcorn, Howell S. Baum, and Ralph P. Hummel, all of whom read the manuscript, some more than once, and offered helpful comments and suggestions. I am grateful for their support and encouragement. I want to thank James M. Glass, my dear friend and intellectual mentor. In addition, Manfred Kets de Vries, Harry Levinson, and Howard Schwartz have been immensely helpful and encouraging over the years and I thank them. I also want to thank all of the members of the International Society for the Psychoanalytic Study of Organizations (ISPSO) for providing me with an annual forum unlike any other. In addition to Seth Allcorn, Howie Baum, Howie Schwartz, Harry Levinson, and Manfred Kets de Vries, I wish to acknowledge other influential members of ISPSO: Gilles Amado, Harold Bridger, Eugene Enriquez, Roderick Gilkey, Laurence Gould, Leopold Gruenfeld, Larry Hirschhorn, Laurent Lapierre, Donald M. Levine, Susan Schneider, Glenn Swogger, and Abraham Zaleznik. I also owe a debt of gratitude to Chris Argyris, whose thinking and whose support of my work have had a significant and lasting influence on me. I also want to thank Penny St. John, my administrative assistant, for her help, and my colleagues in the Department of Public Administration, Guy B. Adams, the late Stanley Botner, John Forrester, Brenda Gardner, Charles Sampson, and Sheilah Watson. Robert Denhardt, Ed Jennings, and Jay White, former colleagues at University of Missouri–Columbia, were always encouraging and enthusiastic. Mark Heidenry, my research assistant, was quite helpful. I also wish to thank Dean Bruce Walker for his support.

Finally, I wish to express my admiration, love, and affection for my wife, Deborah, and our beautiful daughters, Tova and Simone.

THE UNCONSCIOUS LIFE
OF ORGANIZATIONS

INTRODUCTION

FREUD'S INFLUENCE ON CONTEMPORARY PSYCHOANALYTIC THEORY

Any presentation of psychoanalytic theory must begin with certain fundamental Freudian ideas. Although psychoanalysis has changed since Freud, his thoughts on the nature of the psyche and personality are precursors to contemporary psychoanalysis. His theory of instincts is overshadowed today by object relations theory and self psychology; however, his thinking remains influential.

This paradigmatic shift is best described as a movement away from the view of human behavior as primarily biologically driven by the need to diminish instinctual tensions and toward the view of behavior as primarily motivated by relational aims. To appreciate the presentation of psychoanalytic organization theory put forth in this book fully, one must first comprehend Freud's instinct theory and its central features.

In this introductory chapter I do not rehash the controversy between psychoanalytic proponents of metapsychology and clinical theory, instinct theory and object relations, hermeneutics and neopositivism. Rather, I provide the reader with an overview of psychoanalytic concepts for use in organization theory. I begin the presentation with a discussion of Freud's tripartite model.

THE EGO AND THE ID

As late as 1933 in *The New Introductory Lectures*, Freud repeats an earlier metaphorical description of the relationship between the ego and the id. He writes:

> The ego's relation to the id might be compared with that of a rider to his horse. The horse supplies the locomotive energy, while the rider has the privilege of deciding on the goal and of guiding the powerful animal's movement. But only too often there arises between the ego and the id the not precisely ideal situation of the rider being obliged to guide the horse along the path by which itself wants to go. (1933: 68–69)

For Freud, the ego has the most difficult of tasks. As he puts it, it must cope with three tyrannical masters: "the external world, the superego and the id" (69).

The id is the most primitive and primordial component of personality. For Freud, it comprises the dual drives of sex and aggression, the life and death instincts, and signifies a proclivity for dependency captured in the libidinal bond of baby and mother. In the preverbal state of the id, no cognition of self-other boundaries and no awareness of time exist. The psychic state of the id is premoral. The id, according to Freud, is irrational and implies free energy (1923: 205). It abides only by the "pleasure principle." In sum, Freudian instinct theory assumes that we are driven by the desire to reduce tension: the reduction of tension is pleasurable and the heightening of tension painful. Hence, there is a basic human tendency to discharge excitation immediately.

In contrast to the dominance of the pleasure principle of the id, the ego is associated with what Freud calls the "reality principle." The task of the ego is to present the external world of objective reality to the id. Freud writes: "The ego is after all only a portion of the id, a portion that has been expediently modified by the proximity of the external world with its threat of danger" (1933: 68). Cast from the tumult of the id, the ego, as best it can, is responsible for carrying out the intentions of the id—that activity which is called sublimation results. "The instinct is said to be sublimated in so far as it is diverted towards a new, non-sexual aim and in so far as its objects are socially valued ones" (Laplanche and Pontalis, 1973: 431). Work is an act of sublimation. And work organizations are cultures of sublimated actions—some liberating and productive, others oppressive and counterproductive. The ego is rational and comprises bounded energy.

However, as Freud pointed out in his metaphor of the horse (id) and rider (ego), the ego is often dominated and misdirected by the unconscious demands of the id. And so Freudians would say the management of organizations is often dominated by irrational forces contrary to the aims of productivity and public service. While driven by the pleasure principle of the id, the ego is also constrained by the judging and repelling superego.

The superego is heir to the Oedipus complex. Its formation results from social and parental taboos against the emerging sexual dimension to the child's relationship with the parent of the opposite sex and his or her rivalry toward the same-sex parent. This renunciation occurs in the child's identifying with the superior authority of the restrictive parent. The superego is born out of the id, then regulated by the ego. And so Freudians suggest that relations in organizations are at times ruled by the organizational superego in the externalized form of hierarchy and authority.

The ego ideal represents the idealized image of oneself; the superego, its limitations and constraints. The importance of this distinction will be further examined in discussions of narcissism to follow. The clue to the formation of the superego and the ego ideal, however, is the process of *identification*, which is a "psychological process whereby the subject assimilates an aspect, property or attribute of the other and is transformed, wholly or partially, after the model the other provides. It is by means of a series of identifications that the personality is constituted and specified" (Laplanche and Pontalis, 1973: 205). With the formation of the superego and the ego ideal, the child identifies with the norms, values, morals, and ideals of parents. Superego processes become one's internalized conscience, censor, and judge. Conflict may result. As Freud pointed out: "The tension between the demands of conscience and the actual performances of the ego is experienced as a sense of guilt. Social feelings rest on identifications with other people, on the basis of having the same ego ideal" (1923: 27).

Self-esteem is directly affected by the identification with the ego ideal; the extent of incongruity between one's idealized version of oneself and one's actual self-image will ultimately either diminish or enhance self-esteem. The greater the incongruity, the lower is the self-esteem; the smaller the incongruity, the greater is the self-esteem. Organizational members, for instance, may come to identify with the ego ideal of the department head or corporate leader. Their self-esteem as followers depends upon the degree of respect and the quality of recognition they receive from their leadership.

In Freudian theory, the ego is the object as well as the subject of id and superego demands. Battered by the "tyranny" of the external world, the id and superego, the ego becomes the seat of anxiety and the initiator of defensive actions.

For the psychodynamic organization theorist, individual and interpersonal experiences with anxiety and their subsequent defensive actions are critical moments, which produce a window of potential insight into the unconscious life of organizational members. Accordingly, we now examine the concept of anxiety as a signal of real, perceived, and fantasized danger in addition to many of the defensive actions for coping with anxiety.

ANXIETY AND DEFENSIVE ACTIONS

Rapid heart rate, rising blood pressure, sweaty palms, and panic are common sensations of fear and anxiety. Some fears and anxieties are realistic: Being confronted in the street with an oncoming car at a high rate of speed or a strange gang of weapon-carrying youths is cause for alarm. Anxiety is here realistic and flight seems an appropriate lifesaving response. But all anxious actions are not the effect of objective danger. Sometimes a person's anxiety seems inappropriate, excessive, and unfounded in reality. An adult who acts anxiously, for example, when visiting strangers, going to the movie theater, or traveling certain distances from home is said to experience neurotic anxiety. In contrast to realistic anxiety, neurotic anxiety involves action and experience that simply do not fit the objective situation. But like realistic anxiety, it signals danger that triggers a flight response. The basis for the neurotic, anxious experience lies not in reality but in unconscious fantasy—in psychic reality. In contrast to those of realistic anxiety, the reason for and meaning of neurotic anxiety are a mystery.

Flight from a dangerous situation, whether real or fantasized danger, is a form of defensive action; defensive actions are intended to diminish the anxiety and do away with the perceived danger. They are protective measures. Psychoanalysts acknowledge the following defensive actions: regression, repression, reaction formation, isolation, undoing, projection, introjection, turning against the self, reversal, and sublimation (which includes displacement of instinctual aims) (A. Freud, 1966: 44). I add to this list the primitive defensive processes of splitting and projective identification, which are accentuated by psychoanalyst Melanie Klein and object relations theory. These Kleinian concepts are closely associated with acts of projection and introjection noted by Anna Freud. As you will see in the contents of this book, the concepts of projection and projective identification are central to understanding what and how people place meaning and parts of themselves into organizations.

It's time we treat organizational psychodynamics as an emerging paradigm. That way, we are forced to define central concepts and, in so doing, admit to particular biases.

In this next section, I discuss defensive actions. I pay special attention to those defensive acts most commonly found in organizations, which include repression, regression, projection, projective identification, and splitting. I must stress at the outset, however, that the categories of defensive actions are not mutually exclusive. They overlap a great deal in the literature, and consequently the task of defining the concepts adequately for application to organizational phenomena is imperfect. I begin with the concept of repression, one central to the foundations of psychoanalytic thinking.

Repression

Without the concept of repression there would be no theory of unconscious processes. Freud puts it simply: "The essence of repression lies simply in turning something away, and keeping it at a distance, from the conscious" (1915). Anxiety connotes a dangerous situation where certain socially taboo desires, evoked in the private or public realm of the psyche, require action. The fantasy of gratifying such desires, on the one hand pleasurable, provokes greater anxiety for the individual, on the other hand.

Anxiety can be diminished, and relative pleasure restored, by shutting the initial idea out of awareness and behind a barrier of repression, entrusting the idea to the unconscious process. Repression is the most powerful defense. Resistance to thoughts, images, and actions first initiates and then maintains once conscious processes in the form of unconscious memory traces. Consequently, the initial idea appears to have vanished; only the working through of resistance, as it occurs in psychoanalysis, or the weakening of defensive ego functions, will allow for the "return of the repressed."

In psychoanalytic organization theory, the repression (often suppression) of critical incidents in organizational history, intraorganizational conflicts between key personnel, changing task environments and poor performance, is often rendered unconscious. Psychoanalytic organization consultants and researchers speak of confronting psychological resistance to change and learning (Diamond, 1986) by the process of working through resistance (Diamond, 1986; Kets de Vries and Miller, 1984) to insight and change in the status quo. Resistance and repression are formidable psychological barriers to organizational analysis and renewal. They represent both the hiding and the withholding of data that are crucial to diagnosis and interpretation of what I call *organizational identity*.

Regression

In contrast to repression, regression is not as viable or efficient a defensive activity. Anxiety persists after regression only at a more primitive stage of ego functioning. As Laplanche and Pontalis write: "In the formal sense, regression means the transition to modes of expression that are on a lower level as regards complexity, structure and differentiation" (1973: 386). *Regression* is a metaphorical return to earlier modes of human relations where stage appropriate conflicts reemerge in the present. To put it simply, adults take on childlike roles.

For example, regression may be viewed as a reaction against environmental circumstances that are perceived as threatening to organizational members. Within organizations, self-esteem may be compromised by political change and organizational uncertainty brought about by conditions of retrenchment, leadership transitions, suspicious publics, unclear or ambiguous objectives, ambiguity of authority and leadership. Regressive action serves the defensive function of protecting individual organizational members from perceived annihilation (separation anxiety) by constructing unconscious fantasies of withdrawal into a safe and secure inner space—a space-in-time symbolized by the "holding environment" of infancy (Winnicott, 1971). In response to the anxiety of uncertainty, organizational participants often construct regressive (work group) subcultures where leader-follower relationships resemble relations between parents and children.

Individual developmental themes of attachment, separation, loss, and anxiety are often reenacted in authority relationships at work. Individuals' unconscious expectations of organizational authorities and subordinates parallel the demands of caretakers during infancy (for example, see Levinson's [1981] categories of ministration, maturation, and dependency needs). Organizational hierarchies (as noted) may provoke unresolved conflicts with parents and other authorities from childhood by way of transference between superior and subordinate, or between executive and staff. Similar developmental themes are reenacted. As we will discuss in later chapters, Winnicott's (1971) notion of the "holding environment" of baby and mother may be a useful metaphor for the often regressive, unconscious psychodynamics in organizations.

In a regressive fashion, individuals unconsciously project incomplete and frustrated basic needs onto the image of organizational membership, affecting their expectations and interpersonal relationships at work. Next, we explore the primitive psychological act of projection.

Projection

Projection is another defensive strategy for coping with anxiety. Laplanche and Pontalis write:

Freud makes projection (along with introjection) an essential part in the genesis of the opposition of subject (ego) and object (outside world). In so far as the objects, which are presented to it are sources of pleasure [the ego] takes them into itself, "introjects" them (to use Ferenczi's term); and, on the other hand, it expels whatever within itself becomes a cause of unpleasure (the mechanism of projection). (1973: 352)

In other words, one throws out what one refuses either to recognize in oneself or to be oneself (1973: 354). *Projection* is the defensive act of getting rid of an unwanted part of the self, and a mental process of placing the bad part into someone else.

Projection is a way of getting rid of "bad me" images (or introjects) of oneself, which are anxiety-producing. This is accomplished by containing them (bad parts) in someone else. The process first involves denial of certain aspects of oneself and (what Melanie Klein and others call) splitting of good (accepting) and bad (rejecting) images. Anxiety is then alleviated by expelling the negative affects and holding onto the positive. "One denies that one feels such and such an emotion, has such and such a wish, but asserts that someone else does" (Rycroft, 1968: 126).

For instance, reacting to weak leadership and failing institutional support, a health care department split into two persecuted subcultures. The opposing subcultures, then, attempted to defend themselves against the experience of annihilation anxiety by internally splitting "all good" and "all bad" images of the respective groups. This, of course, polarized the organization into two antagonistic camps. Each persecuted subculture viewed itself as perfect and ideal and projected hostility and blame onto the other. Primitive defenses of projection and psychological regression were observed at the group level, leaving the organization in paralysis. Differences between projective actions and those of projective identification are elusive but significant. Let's turn to the concept of projective identification to elaborate.

Projective Identification

Projective identification is a term introduced by Melanie Klein. It is "a mechanism revealed in phantasies in which the subject inserts his self in whole or in part—into the object in order to harm, possess or control it" (Laplanche and Pontalis, 1973: 356). The subject imagines his or her self to be inside the other. As Sandler points out,

> the element of control of the objects (into which parts of the self have been projected) . . . is central to the concept. The urge to control the object is evident in the process of "living through another person"— Anna Freud's "altruistic surrender" (1936) can be taken as a good example of this process. (Sandler, 1987: 20)

Projective identification differs from projection in that the one who projects part of his or her self into the other is able empathically to experience that split-off part vicariously in the other as the object of projection—a combined act of projection and introjection. A senior deputy director, for example, is unconsciously fearful of assuming authority and responsibility. He avoids it at all costs and is unaware of his tendency to do so. Unwittingly, he projects his fear on to the new director, who in turn becomes fearful of making difficult and necessary budgetary decisions. The deputy director who cannot experience directly his fear of authority encourages and supports the new director's willingness to do nothing. The deputy not only identifies with his new director's choice to avoid responsibility and potential conflict, he rationalizes his boss's actions to others who inquire why the director is not taking some action. Through the vehicle of projective identification, the deputy covertly controls his boss, the director, and, at the same time, keeps his own anxieties under wraps. The deputy finds a welcome container for his bad feelings in his superior, maintaining the organizational status quo at a time of great administrative vulnerability. It is as if the deputy created a "screen character" for himself in the body of the director. He can manipulate and observe it, be entertained and even "moved" by it, but his experience of himself in the other (screen character) is far enough removed from the screen to make it an emotionally safe and relatively detached defensive act.

Both acts of projection and projective identification involve the processes of splitting, which I turn to next.

Splitting

Splitting is an essential component of projective identification; it involves the separation of a whole psychic (self or other) structure into two part structures. The part structures represent contrary and opposing attitudes toward self or other, which coexist side by side. According to

Melanie Klein, splitting (along with projection and introjection) is the most primitive defense against anxiety. "The tendency to perceive objects as either ideal (all good) or persecutory (all bad) is the consequence of early defensive operations of splitting. *Splitting* [emphasis added] is the active separation of good from bad experiences, perceptions, and emotions linked to objects" (Kernberg, 1980: 25). In later development, splitting tends to diminish, except in severe psychopathologies such as borderline conditions.

Projection and splitting affect human relations in groups and organizations. Splitting of self and other occurs in psychological responses to stress and anxiety at work. What happens? Individuals experience critical incidents (change in the organizational status quo) very personally—that is, as damaging to their core sense of self (their self-identity). In some instances, otherwise whole, integrated self-images split into two opposing views of self: good versus bad, loved versus hated, accepted versus rejected, idealized versus despised self-images. For example, under the pressure of takeovers, cutbacks, leadership transitions, and the like, organizational participants may experience annihilation (separation) anxiety that causes them to regress psychologically (cognitively and emotionally). They may feel persecuted and, consequently, need to rid themselves of these negative feelings, whereupon they come to view themselves and their work groups as all good and others and others' work groups in the department as all bad. This (projection via splitting) enables them to maintain good (loving) feelings about themselves and project bad (hateful) feelings elsewhere. It also encourages them to locate a scapegoat and blame others for the circumstances, avoiding responsibility as members of the organization. Splitting may be a primitive psychological defense but we find it occurs often among "normal" individuals in organizations undergoing extraordinary levels of stress and uncertainty.

Introjection

Introjection is the opposite of projection; it entails the "taking in" of the external world. In psychoanalytic theory, internal and external worlds are differentiated by boundaries between self (subject) and other (object), and the parameters of the inside and outside of the body (often called body-ego). Introjection involves the taking of the object into the self, making the object a part of one's self—the so-called internal object. In defense against anxiety, introjection serves several purposes and occurs in several forms. Internalization of important objects (parents and significant others) in the child's fantasy world (the "introjects" or "selfobjects") provides one with inherent security by the reassuring (introjected) presence of the other (Sandler, 1987: 10). Introjection of a loving, nurturing "good mother," for example, may reinforce object constancy (a reassurance of parental presence and nurturing) in the child, a prerequisite to self-esteem. In later development, the child introjects the parental superego and ego ideal "(modified by projections and other fantasy distortions)" as his or her own (1987: 10). By means of identification with and introjection of parental and other significant persons, the child constructs a sense of ideals, conscience, internal judge, and censor.

During the course of organizational socialization, for instance, members adapt by assuming organizational values and ethics. In so doing, they come to introject the superego and ego ideal of their executive (organizational leadership), taking the image of the chief officer into themselves, so to speak, and then identifying with the internal object.

On the other hand, the character of the leader's introjected childhood superego will affect the manner in which one executes one's role of authority in adulthood, and the manner in which he or she uses and abuses power. Introjection of an abusive and punitive (parental) superego, the result of (what Anna Freud calls) "identification with the [introject] aggressor," may therefore produce an intimidating and authoritarian manager. The abused child becomes the abusive adult as a consequence, in part, of introjection.

Reversal or "turning against the self" is yet another defensive strategy against anxiety.

Reversal

Reversal is a defense that simply takes advantage of the possibility of turning an impulse or action around into its opposite. This is often described in shifts from activity to passivity, and vice versa. Most typical of reversal is the metamorphosis from sadistic to masochistic behavior, and voyeuristic to exhibitionistic activity (Rycroft, 1968: 143). Reversal from activity to passivity may also be called *turning against the self*.

The example of a manager who, as a child, experienced his or her parents as abusive and punitive illustrates reversal. The child introjects the abusive and punitive superego as a defense against anxiety. In adulthood, the same child becomes a manager who mistreats his or her employees, actively reversing an earlier psychological insult that was passively experienced (G. S. Klein, 1976). Initially the child felt helpless and powerless to the psychological mistreatments of his or her parents. In this case, reversal into the opposite is "the transformation of passivity into activity, or a turning round from the self on to the other person" (Laplanche and Pontalis, 1973: 399–400).

Similar to reversal, reaction-formation is a way of turning around an experience into its opposite.

Reaction-Formation

Reaction-formation is a "psychological attitude or habitus diametrically opposed to a repressed wish, and constituted as a reaction against it (e.g., bashfulness countering exhibitionistic tendencies)" (1973: 376). Two managers competing for the same executive position may act as if they are mutually supportive and trusting team members, when, in fact, they unconsciously wish the other great harm. Passive-aggressive behavior typifies reaction-formations.

There also exists the defensive capacity to distance ourselves from what has occurred by processes of undoing and isolation.

Undoing and Isolation

Both performing defensive maneuvers of *undoing* (what has been done) and *isolating* its affects are characteristic of obsessional thinking and compulsive behavior, or obsessional neurosis. For Freud, undoing (what has been done) or causing past thoughts, words, gestures, or actions to vanish is a magical feat of mind (1926/1959a). The defensive intent of undoing is to destroy any cognitive and emotional trace of the anxiety-producing event completely. This psychic obliteration is accomplished by making use of thoughts or behavior having the opposite meaning. The act of splitting or dissociating one's self from the feelings connected to the anxiety-producing acts is a form of isolation. "Among the procedures used for isolation are: pauses in the train of thought, formulas, rituals and, in a general way, all those measures which facilitate the insertion of a hiatus into the temporal sequence of thoughts or actions" (Laplanche and Pontalis, 1973: 232).

As I discuss at great length in Chapter 2, ritualistic action is a common attribute of bureaucratic organizations, where authority structures and practices often promote symptomatic rituals among members. These rituals perpetuate denial (or what Sullivan called "selective inattention") and dissociation in the service of defense against anxiety, anxiety over loss of control and the potential disintegration of self-other boundaries. Similar to the rigid defensive structures in obsessional neuroses, ritualistic behavior in the organization reestablishes equilibrium, securing the status quo by successfully diminishing anxiety (Diamond, 1985b: 663–79). Bureaucratic organizations framed by ritualistic activities may be viewed as social defense systems.

As noted in Chapter 2, ritualistic actions are indicative of nonrational administrative behavior attributed in the organizational literature to vicious circles, self-sealing processes, single-loop learning, and generalized displacement of goals (e.g., Merton, Argyris, Crozier). These organization theorists have identified such ritualistic phenomena in bureaucracy as decisive to dysfunctional consequences, ineffectiveness, and organizational pathology (1985b: 663–79). As a result of an overreliance on formalized structures and procedures, organizational actions are often rendered meaningless and purposeless, distorting their original human intentions. Ritualistic defenses are common examples of acts of undoing the self-alienation that occurs in organizations and isolating the affects.

Next, I come to the least neurotic of all defensive actions, what is called sublimation.

Sublimation

Sublimation, according to Anna Freud, is the act of displacing instinctual aims in conformity with higher social values. This action "presupposes the acceptance or at least the knowledge of such values," and the existence of the superego (1966: 52). Hence, the superego is viewed as the psychic agent of civilization, which is imposed upon the child through identification with the restrictive parent, his ideals and values. The ability to work and be productive calls forth some degree of displaced libidinal gratification. Sublimation is a prerequisite for work.

Sublimation and displacement, however, are not sufficient for creative and meaningful work. Psychoanalysts Kris (1952) and Greenacre (1959) emphasize that "the psychic energies utilized for creative work are not well neutralized or sublimated. Both libidinal and aggressive drives are used in such activity, which is often plainly observable in the agitation and drivenness during the creative period. In some creative people the sexual and aggressive strivings are often very conspicuous in their overt behavior during such periods. In others they are discernible in the products of their creativity. Greenacre goes so far as to state that people who sublimate very well may be very capable but do not turn out to be creative. She also points out that creative people have a lower tolerance for repetitive work than do noncreative ones" (Greenson, 1978: 344). The case example of a public agency in Chapter 8 provides a good illustration of "displacement" at work.

Sublimation and displacement are common adaptive and defensive practices, and they are necessary for work productivity. Some degree of sexual and aggressive frustration, and some element of internal tension between superego constraints and the pleasure seeking aims of the id, is required for creative and innovative thinking and action at work.

However, excessive superego constraints, whether privately or publicly driven, are repressive. They tend to block the play of imagination from which unconscious and preconscious thoughts reach consciousness. Publicly driven superego constraints on creativity and imagination may stem from the execution of bureaucratic strategies and structures that inhibit the free exchange of ideas and feelings (Diamond, 1984; 1985b).

Some individuals may unwittingly exchange their internal superego and conscience for formal organizational authority and hierarchical relations, producing excessive sublimation and authoritarianism, and divorcing them from taking the blame for their actions.

Among others, particularly narcissistic personalities, privately driven superego constraints are nearly absent, possibly a consequence of ongoing internal conflicts with dependency, separation, and autonomy. In fact, these same individuals may appear to lack a sense of boundaries between self and others. They may view themselves as omnipotent and grandiose, tending to exaggerate and inflate the image of self and others.

Compromise-Formation

For Freud, neurotic symptoms are manifestations of *compromise-formations*, which are products of conflict that signify both parties (the repressed impulse and the repressing agency) to the conflict. Laplanche and Pontalis describe compromise-formation as a

form taken by the repressed memory so as to be admitted to consciousness when it returns in symptoms, in dreams and, more generally, in all products of the unconscious: in the process the repressed ideas are distorted by defense to the point of being unrecognizable. Thus both the unconscious wish and the demands of defense may be satisfied by the same formation—in a single compromise. (76)

Joining and participating in organizations involve ego adaptation and adjustment. The individual must strike a compromise between the unconscious requirements of his or her personality and the demands of the organization. Such compromises are worked out in role performances where the individual reshapes his or her assigned role to fit unconscious organizational demands more closely. At the heart of this conflict that eventuates in a compromise is the problem of narcissism—the state of perfection and symbiosis from which we begin life, first inside and then outside the womb.

Narcissism

The term *narcissism* originates in the myth of Narcissus and, generally, refers to love directed toward the image of oneself (255). In psychoanalytic thought, it is used to describe the state of merger between the infant and the mother—that time of life when being at the center of the universe is not only acceptable but required. Infantile narcissism is reflected in the baby's demands for affection and recognition and its need to idealize the parent and feel idealized in return. Through mutual idealizations, the child comes to feel more secure and self-confident. Healthy narcissism and self-esteem are thereby the effects of this "good enough" parenting.

When the baby does not receive adequate *narcissistic supplies*, low self-esteem results. Narcissists are then torn or *split* between a despised and an idealized self-image. They may then demand that others mirror their idealized image so that they may successfully project the bad, despised part elsewhere. Such demands often take the form of requiring others to love and admire them. Feeling weak and vulnerable, narcissists defend themselves by reinforcing an omnipotent and grandiose self-image. Projecting superiority and perfection, they tend to surround themselves with others who are willing to indulge them. Frequently in organizations, one observes narcissistic superordinates holding onto staff who admire and idealize them, while rejecting those who question their superiority and godlike qualities.

In this introductory chapter, I have tried to review some central psychoanalytic concepts for application in organizational behavior. My intent is to make the reader more comfortable with the language and its use in interpreting the unconscious life of organizations and, ultimately, in changing counterproductive and unhealthy organizational dynamics. In the next chapter, I introduce the reader to what I call psychoanalytic organization theory.

Summary

Human behavior in organizations is the outcome of characteristic relational conflicts and patterns between and among participants. It is the result of distinctive organizational identities, which stem from superior-subordinate relationships and collective defensive practices. These defensive practices are encouraged by traditional organizational norms and values, perpetuating a vicious circle that ensures suppression and denial (or selective inattention) at the expense of reflection and personal responsibility.

Traditional methodological approaches to organizational behavior do not consider unconscious actions. Proponents claim to present factual statements of detached and objective observers. Consequently, they may adequately describe formal and to some extent informal structures and procedures, but they cannot explain with any authority the cognitive and emotional dimensions of organizational behavior—the truly subjective and personally meaningful attributes of organizational dynamics.

Psychoanalytic organization theory, the topic of the next chapter, is a derivative of psychoanalytic organizational consultations and research, and clinical practice. Acquisition of knowledge is intended to enhance our understanding of human relations in organizations, both rational and nonrational, and our methods of intervening with and changing organizational cultures.

Now, let us turn to the question, What is psychoanalytic organization theory?

I

THEORY

1

PSYCHOANALYTIC ORGANIZATION
THEORY

In the individual's mental life someone else is invariably involved, as a
model, as an object, as a helper, as an opponent; and so from the very first,
individual psychology, in this extended but entirely justifiable sense of the
words, is at the same time social psychology as well.

Sigmund Freud
Group Psychology and the Analysis of the Ego[1]

It may at first seem hard to imagine how psychoanalysis can inform
organization theory. After all, psychoanalysis is a method of interpreting
the unconscious life of the individual. It is customarily practiced one-on-
one, between analyst and patient, with the latter reclining on a couch and
the former sitting on a chair outside the direct vision of the patient. Thus,
the organization theorist must ask, How can the analyst's tools for interpreting the hidden meanings of a patient's neurotic symptoms, such as free
associations, dreams, and transferences of emotion, be of any use in
exploring organizations?

Free association requires the patient to say what comes into his or her
mind, uncensored, while the analyst applies "evenly suspended attention."
The willingness of the patient to free associate signifies a degree of trust
in the analyst, which is essential to gaining insight and therapeutic change.
Dream reporting is a treasured vehicle for reaching the unconscious. In
using it, the analyst searches for latent meanings in the patient's communication of the dream's manifest content. So-called transference of emotions between the analyst and patient elicits insightful data about the

patient's world of relatedness to others. Transference (discussed later in this chapter) signifies the patient's treating the analyst as if she or he were some significant other, such as a mother, father, sibling, or spouse. The analyst must also be aware of his or her emotional responses to the patient that trigger familiar reactions in the analyst—countertransference. For example, a patient expresses his fears and anxieties associated with losing a loved one. While commenting on how this affects his relationship to his wife, the analyst herself experiences unconscious separation anxiety, which results in a negative, and potentially compromising, counterreaction toward the patient. At the same time, the analyst may point out to the patient how their therapeutic relationship reproduces familiar conflicts and anxieties for the patient. Awareness of transference,[2] countertransference, and the latent content of dreams and free associations is crucial to gaining insights into the patient's inner world of conflicts and experiences, his or her psychic reality.

Taking that into consideration, how is it possible, then, to apply psychoanalysis to organization theory? And what can be gained from it?

THE PSYCHODYNAMICS OF ORGANIZATIONAL BEHAVIOR: A REVIEW OF THE LITERATURE

Applying psychodynamic theories to organizations, unlike psychoanalyzing patients on the couch, is not intended to change the personality of individuals as a consequence of insight and intervention. Rather, the primary intent is to offer the opportunity to alter key relationships between and among organizational members. Such changes result, to some extent, from the members' gaining insight into the reasons and motives for their actions, and to a greater degree from expanding their awareness of problematic relational patterns at work and, ultimately, their willingness to take responsibility for those actions.

Psychoanalytic organization theory is not only a framework for understanding organizational dynamics: It is a theory for practicing organizational change and development. That is, it is concerned with changing the culture of organizations.

Psychoanalytic organization theory is a model of action research in that it builds and renovates its theory as an outcome of attempts to gain insight, heighten relational awareness, and change actual organizations. It is ultimately a theory drawn from practice and, thereby, cannot be set apart from its application to organizational consultation and intervention. This does not mean we cannot generalize from our findings in the workplace. On the contrary, we must do so in order to improve and appropriately revise the theory and our assumptions about people in organizations on basis of the clinical data.

In the following section, I present some prominent illustrations of psychodynamic approaches to organizations. My objectives are to present the reader with an overview of a number of psychoanalytic applications to organization and management theory and to suggest some commonalities and distinctions between them. I begin with a discussion of Harry Levinson's *Executive* and follow with *The Neurotic Organization* by Manfred F. R. Kets de Vries and Danny Miller. Then I review Howell S. Baum's *The Invisible Bureaucracy* and Larry Hirschhorn's *The Workplace Within*. My rationale for selecting these books, among others, is that they best represent the scope of psychodynamic approaches to organizational life and, thereby, offer the reader a more accurate view of this expanding disciplinary matrix. Finally, these are merely summaries of each work and are not intended to substitute for more thorough readings of the texts themselves.

Levinson's *Executive*

Many psychoanalytic organizational writers stress the importance of leadership. Rather than focusing on diagnosing the personality of the leader per se, as do Kets de Vries and Miller, Levinson utilizes the tenets of psychoanalytic ego psychology to improve managerial performance. He believes that responsive management lies in a teaching role for managers. One of management's primary failures, according to Levinson, is that of unawareness of human needs at work. Executives and their managerial staff must become better mentors to those who will eventually replace them, and to do so they must become more knowledgeable about what motivates their employees. They also must become better diagnosticians of personnel problems in the workplace. For Levinson, the framework for more responsive management and problem diagnosis is psychoanalytic ego psychology.

Psychoanalytic ego psychology stresses the function of the ego in maintaining internal adjustments and external adaptations. Its foundation is in Freud's tripartite model of the psyche: the id, ego, and superego (or ego ideal). The ego's primary function is, of course, that of balancing the demanding impulses of the irrational and free flowing id against the censoring, punitive, and restrictive authority of the superego. The ego represents that which is most rational and controlled in the human psyche. The ego also must adapt to the external demands of others and the environment. Any imbalance may provoke a sense of uncertainty and lack of control; consequently, anxiety may signal potential danger. Ego defenses will then emerge to control the anxiety and reinstitute some equilibrium in the individual. Herein lies the centerpiece of Levinson's application.

In what way does Levinson use psychoanalytic ego psychology to teach managers to be more responsive and better stabilizers of the social system? Let's take a look.

The executive is, figuratively speaking, the agent of the organizational ego; his or her role is to respond to the internal organizational needs of employees and the external demands of the organization's task environment. Management's executive (ego) function is that of homeostasis.

Levinson tells managers to pay attention to three primary needs: ministration, maturation, and mastery. Ministration takes into account needs for gratification, closeness, support, protection, and guidance; maturation needs comprise fostering creativity, originality, self-control, and reality testing; mastery needs encompass the demands for ambitious striving, realistic achievement, rivalry with affection, and consolidation (Levinson, 1981).

Levinson's categories have a developmental sequence: Ministration must be adequately served before maturation, and maturation must be satisfied before acquisition of mastery. Speaking metaphorically, the sequence parallels that of the parent meeting baby's primary needs for sustenance, security, safety, and contact comfort, which are precursors of ego identity and self-esteem.

Ministration, comprising healthy attachments and dependencies, must take hold before maturation, including separation and individuation, occurs. Adequate guidance and support of employees are as essential to good management as constant nurturing and loving of infants are to good parenting.

After establishing secure attachments between organization and employee, managers must encourage maturation through individuation. The employee—like the maturing child—must now find the necessary space to experiment with his or her relative independence. When management establishes closeness, guidance, and protection between itself and the employee, imagination can thrive. The seeds of innovation and creativity in organizations may blossom when there is a nurturing climate for employee growth and development.

A sense of mastery must occur. The employee must come to terms with his or her "real self" in the workplace. Along with maturity and relative independence comes responsibility for oneself and the direction of one's life ambitions and ideals. In addition to the integration of a strong ego comes the identification with an ego ideal, the employee's ideal image of himself or herself. In the workplace, the open communication of ambitions, expectations, and ideals is crucial to effective management-employee relations. An employee may not always be conscious of his or her ambitions, for example, and responsive managers must encourage an ongoing dialogue with subordinates about how they see themselves at their future best.

Exceptional executives, for Levinson, are those who respond to the ministration, maturation, and mastery needs of employees and who take seriously the roles of educator and mentor. They are also capable of analyzing problems in human relations because of their psychological knowledge of human needs and motivations. Levinson proffers a psychoanalytic framework for problem diagnosis to assist managers that contains the following psychological components: "(1) the dimension of a person's ego ideal and the degree to which he feels he has lived up to this ideal; (2) the way in which he handles affection; (3) the way in which he deals with feelings of aggression; and (4) the way in which he reacts to dependency" (1981: 33). According to Levinson, these are always factors and should, therefore, be taken into account in identifying and solving problems.

In contrast to Levinson, Kets de Vries and Miller have come up with a different manner of diagnosing organizational problems. Let's take a look.

Kets de Vries' and Miller's *The Neurotic Organization*

At first glance, *The Neurotic Organization* may seem a primarily negative psychoanalytic account of human behavior in organizations. After all, it is a book about sick organizations, and, unlike that of Levinson's *Executive*, its concern is less explicitly with enhancing management's development of human resources than with diagnosing neurotic styles and then repairing organizational dysfunctions. In the final analysis, however, it is as much a book about organizational well-being and effectiveness as Levinson's text. Like Levinson, Kets de Vries and Miller draw on cases from consulting experience and present a framework for change.

In contrast to Levinson's use of psychoanalytic ego psychology, Kets de Vries and Miller apply psychoanalytic object relations. *Object relations* refer to a person's mode of relation to his or her world; this relation is the outcome of a particular personality, and of an apprehension of others that is to some extent or other fantasized (Laplanche and Pontalis, 1973: 277). Kets de Vries and Miller identify five neurotic organizational styles: paranoid, compulsive, dramatic, depressive, and schizoid. Each has potential strengths and weaknesses and does not necessarily signify organizational pathology—what the authors call organizational dysfunctioning. Their major premise is that individual pathology, defined by excessive use of one neurotic style, and organizational dysfunctioning are parallel phenomena. Individual pathology in the leader contributes significantly to inappropriate organizational strategy, structure, and culture (Kets de Vries and Miller, 1984: 22–23).

Neurotic fantasies of key organizational members produce shared fantasies that in turn influence the "dominant organizational adaptive style," which affects "decisions about strategy and structure" (1984: 20). Fantasy is an internal representation of self and other relations. It is a private theater in which experience is subjectively organized. It is our so-called psychic reality and therefore influences our perceptions and attitudes about the external world, self, and others. For example, a paranoid style generates a fantasy characterized by the attitude "I cannot really trust anybody. A menacing superior force exists that is out to get me; so I had better be on guard." Typical of a compulsive fantasy is the statement "I don't want to be at the mercy of events—I have to master and control all the things affecting me." A dramatic style may be described by the fantasy "I want to get attention from and impress the people who count in my life," and a depressive fantasy may sound like "It is hopeless to change the course of events in my life. I am just not good enough." Finally, a schizoid fantasy might include "The world of reality does not offer any satisfaction to me. My interactions with others will eventually fail and cause harm, so it is safer to remain distant" (23). With each predominant leadership fantasy one can imagine a consistent set of organizational strategies and structures to match. Such fantasies are not always dysfunctional and maladaptive; at times, organizational environments may require such attitudes for survival.

We are all familiar with these fantasies and may express them from time to time; their significance in organizational pathology rests in their impact on leaders (executives, managers, supervisors), particularly when these fantasies are excessive. In those instances, the neurotic style of key organizational members represented by their predominant fantasies will influence organizational strategy, structure, and culture. Consequently, an organizational neurotic style will emerge and because of its rigidity and maximum defensiveness will produce dysfunctional and maladaptive consequences. Organizational change will seem impossible.

In centralized authority structures, leaders have inordinate power and control over subordinates. Thus, individual pathologies (neurotic excesses) among leaders influence overall organizational character and operations. Moreover, organizational members themselves reinforce their leaders' excesses by acting submissively and indulging the whims of their bosses. For Kets de Vries and Miller, transference of emotions between superior and subordinate partially explains the persistence of these organizational problems.

Thus, any effort to change organizational culture will meet with serious resistance and psychological defenses among organizational members. Neurotic styles develop over time, taking root in the transference between the executive and staff. It is therefore unrealistic to expect organizational members to welcome change. Neurotic styles are, after all, characterized by inflexibility and conservatism. Changing the status quo is anxiety-producing and perceived as dangerous by participants, especially in changing and highly stressful organizations.

Transforming organizational structure and strategy and attempting to change key personnel who are emotionally wedded to routine patterns of interacting and relating are extraordinarily difficult tasks. Resistance to change is realistically anticipated. For Kets de Vries and Miller, the organizational consultant must first generate insights into the organizational problems. This involves acts of confrontation between consultants and clients, and between and among members. It also demands clarification of mutual problems, expectations, and meanings and interpretation of the sources and reasons for problems. Finally, a process of emotionally "working through" resistance to change must occur. Change means loss, and the processes of organizational change center on grieving the loss. Letting go of old patterns of relating and taking on new ones give rise to mourning—a subject we will return to later in the book.

Kets de Vries and Miller offer a map for analyzing organizational dysfunctions and an outline for organizational therapy. Their explicitly clinical categories, such as paranoid, compulsive, depressive, dramatic, and schizoid, are intended to enable the organizational consultant (interventionist or therapist) to identify pathological tendencies in organizational leadership. The application of such categories may then assist the consultant in understanding organizational problems of strategy, structure, and culture.

A psychotherapeutic application of the processes of confrontation, clarification, interpretation, and working through should prove helpful to the organizational consultant and interventionist.

Both approaches (Levinson, 1981; Kets de Vries and Miller, 1984) apply select components of psychoanalytic theory and practice to problems of management and organization. In so doing, they provide organization theorists with insights into problems of motivation, dysfunctional processes, and change.

Levinson calls for a new managerial role, that of mentor and teacher, and provides a framework for enhancing the manager's awareness of unconscious developmental processes. Paying attention to human needs for ministration, maturation, and mastery is crucial to developing satisfied and valuable employees. Acknowledging the impact of drives for affection, aggression, dependency, and the nature of the ego ideal will assist managers in diagnosing and solving problems among staff.

Levinson's work is a prescription for executives who wish to be perceived as responsive to their employees. Based on psychoanalytic ego psychology, it stresses the value of adaptation and adjustment. The manager becomes the organizational ego—its stabilizing force. Homeostasis is seen as profitable. Managers become educators and mentors to those subordinates who will eventually replace them—hence, perpetuating the system.

Kets de Vries' and Miller's text is a diagnosis of neurotic styles and organizational dysfunctioning based on psychoanalytic object relations, which emphasizes the role of neurotic fantasies in fostering relational problems. Neurotic leadership styles, it is believed, inevitably lead to dysfunctional organizations. Here, adaptation to the organizational environment is of greatest value. Leaders and their organizations are either functional or dysfunctional neurotics.

Baum's *The Invisible Bureaucracy*

Somewhat in the spirit of Talcott Parsons' and Robert Merton's separate studies of bureaucracy and personality, Howell S. Baum looks at the psychological structure of bureaucratic organizations—what Baum calls *the invisible bureaucracy*. Ultimately, Baum is concerned with difficulties in problem solving and collaboration among planners and public administrators. This psychological structure of bureaucracy, Baum submits, has the following determining attributes: (1) *hierarchy* in which responsibility is dispersed while authority is centralized; (2) *work* that is appraised and rewarded by superordinates who are infrequently visible or accessible; and (3) *responsibilities, authority, and relationships* among bureaucrats that tend to be ambiguous (24). Consequently, workers feel anxious and ambivalent. They are anxious about that which they cannot control, that which they are held responsible for, and the anonymity of their superior's authority.

Baum tells us, further, that this social structure of alienated vertical and horizontal relationships produces decisions and actions based upon unconscious fantasy and imagination. Horizontally, bureaucrats experience fragmentation and a lack of purpose; vertically, they feel ambivalence to authority and confusion about power. The relative autonomy of superiors, he claims, is bridged by untested assumptions based upon unconscious interpretations of others. That empty psychological space between superiors and subordinates is filled with reverie.

Relying on extensive interviews with planners and public administrators, Baum discovers that responsibility and authority are unevenly matched and cause much ambiguity among bureaucrats. Workers come to feel anxious about aggressive action and insecure about recognition and the assumption of responsibilities where there is little formal authority.

Baum's central focus of concern is the subordinate's predicament. He writes that subordinates respond to two images of bureaucratic authority— the image of "moral paragon" and the image of "superiority in competence and strength." Both images trigger different types of anxiety: the former produces guilt anxiety and the latter provokes shame anxiety.

How do subordinates cope with the insult to their integrity and the sense of incompetence evoked by the invisible bureaucracy? Baum proffers several dramatic cases in which bureaucrats unwittingly design alternative images of the organization through the psychological mechanisms of escape and compensation, which are, in effect, colorful illustrations of compromise formations—or neurotic symptoms.

In contrast to Levinson and Kets de Vries and Miller, Baum argues that neurotic symptoms are a consequence of the clash between bureaucratic structure and personality—what he calls the psychological structure of bureaucracy. Ambivalence and ambiguity, shame and guilt, escape and compensation are the result of an authoritarian structure of autonomous superiors imposing their will upon powerless subordinates.

Hirschhorn's *The Workplace Within*

Similar to Baum, Hirschhorn focuses upon the psychological connotations of contemporary organizational structure. However, Hirschhorn moves us beyond the divisive structure of bureaucracy and toward the more structurally integrated and technologically advanced, and more hopeful, future of the postindustrial society.

Similarly to Kets de Vries and Miller, and in contrast to Levinson and Baum, Hirschhorn applies Kleinian object relations theory[3] to interpret the experience of his clients and to predict the psychological prerequisites of future organizational membership. He writes:

The psychodynamics of work life in the coming decades will be shaped by four factors: (1) the postindustrial job structure in which

once divided roles, units, divisions, and organizations are increasingly integrated; (2) people's wish to limit anxiety they feel; (3) the
strength of their reparative desires; and (4) the degree to which a set
of coherent economic values helps people to understand the purpose
of their work and the value it creates for others. (11)

For Hirschhorn, the postindustrial milieu needs workers capable of confronting their anxieties over complexity and change at work.

From the vantage point of an organizational consultant (in the Tavistock
and A. K. Rice traditions), Hirschhorn reports on the psychological nuances of the changing workplace. He tells us, for example, that greater
integration at work results in complex roles for workers, who will thereby
need to know more of what their fellow workers are doing. Information
sharing and communication become critical. Bureaucratic divisiveness
characterized by specialization and a detailed division of labor is giving
way to an interdependent system of integrated roles.

What does Hirschhorn claim is the psychological effect of this
transition into the postindustrial milieu? And what does he suggest is
required of people for this to occur? To begin with, he submits that
anxiety will reemerge as defensive social systems are transcended for
less routinization and more risk taking. I will say more about defensive
social systems in Chapter 2. Taking a role, Hirschhorn writes, will
mean working at its boundary in order to promote improved linkages
and coupling with other roles, units, divisions, and organizations.
Applying Kleinian object relations theory, Hirschhorn optimistically
predicts that the reparative desires of workers allow integrative and
participative actions to occur. These reparative inclinations originate
with the individuals' efforts (beginning during their infancy) to "repair" damaged psyches (part objects) and make them whole again.
Reparation stands for a person's need to repair the world and others,
and to view others more humanely and realistically. That involves, for
example, the recognition of others as both good and bad, loving and
hating, accepting and rejecting, constructive and destructive.

Hirschhorn suggests that by the activation of the clients'/workers'
depressive positions, and their desire to mend emotional injuries (which
are the source of part objects), development and change of organizational
cultures are possible. In Kleinian theory, the depressive position refers to
the stage of emotional development when the baby mourns and then
accepts the loss of total dependency upon the mother and rejects any
illusions of the mother as either all good or all bad. The child comes to
accept contradictory views and feelings of self and others.

In Part II the reader will see many case examples of reparation and the depressive position in the process of organizational change and consultation. In fact, all of the cases presented in this book and the concluding discussion in Chapter 11 should make clear the overriding importance of these psychological dynamics of organizational change.

The four books discussed here represent various forms of action research in which the application and reconstruction of psychoanalytic organization theory derive from the authors' experiences as psychoanalytically informed organizational consultants and researchers, which is the topic I turn to next.

Psychoanalytic Consultation as Action Research and Theory Construction

Most psychoanalytic views of organizations are written by action researchers, those who study social systems by changing them (Argyris, 1985: 8). Thus, organizational research and consultation are combined, and theory construction is closely linked to social intervention (1985: 4). It is, therefore, difficult to divorce psychoanalytic organization theory from the fieldwork of organizational consultants and interventionists.

Like psychoanalysts, they encounter resistance to insight and change in the workplace. Since most of their data come from organizations in turmoil, it is not surprising they find people's defenses maximized. Organizational members may rely on fantasies, denial, and other defensive activities to escape realities at work. Some may feel personally vulnerable and uncertain of their futures. Thus, it is easy to see why organizational consultants are often seen by participants as "invited intruders" (Baum, 1987).[4]

Suspicion and mistrust can obstruct the organizational consultant's work. Attempts to uncover and interpret the motives for defensive actions among organizational members are anxiety-provoking. Such challenges to participants' confidence and sense of competence are unwanted: self-esteem, organizational members unconsciously feel, may be damaged as a result of seeing themselves more "authentically" and (one might say) more "deeply."

Understanding oneself more authentically and more deeply implies the acknowledgment of a dialectic in oneself, others, and the external world—a confrontation between the good and bad (loving and hating) parts of self and others, the contradictions and inconsistency of human actions, and the "reality principle"—what (as discussed earlier) Melanie Klein calls the act of *reparation* experienced in the *depressive position* of early development.

Mechanisms of denial, suppression, narcissistic fantasies, and grandiose expectations of oneself and others at work, however, provide some measure of self-protection against an unwelcome reality.

Organizational members, and the rest of us for that matter, take seriously the interruption of such defensive operations. They often feel guarded despite any agreement they may have between consultant and client to learn from their exploration and attempt to gain insight required for productive change and effectiveness. Intervention can, at least momentarily, cause regressive tendencies among organizational participants, forcing them into childlike roles.

Thus, people's relationships in organizations are analyzable, but not without confronting defensive resistance between and among them. There is always the possibility that opening up the system's membership to critical self-examination will go no further than initial steps of in-depth interviews and data collection. Such resistance among participants is the effect of anxiety (Diamond, 1986).

Reflective learning and change present organizational members, generally, with challenges to self-competence, and many change efforts represent a public test of subordinates' willingness to assume power and delegated authority where appropriate and, in some instances, include a scrutiny of the sincerity of executives' intentions to relinquish unproductive control over others. In fact, actual resistance among participants may appear to the consultant to contradict the clients' espoused commitment to change. When the organizational consultant confronts the issue of commitment, expressing his or her puzzlement, clients' anxiety about and resistance to change accelerate. Contrary to most approaches, a psychoanalytic approach insists on the consultant's exploring, individually and collectively, the source of members' anxiety. The key to unlocking insight and releasing the potential for organizational change is thereby located in the organizational consultant's and clients' attending to, and rendering public, defensive and resistant activities between and among themselves. This leads directly to the significance of the next topic: personal responsibility and claimed action.

Personal Responsibility and Claimed Action

Many participants and analysts mistakenly view the organization not as a human construct but as some structure or design devoid of human origins. People speak of the "system" as if it descended from the heavens—hence, they surely cannot take responsibility for it. On the contrary, they experience themselves as alienated and disconnected from it. Disclaimers of action and responsibility for problems in the workplace among adults exemplify faulty reasoning and are reminiscent of a three-year-old's reaction to his mother's obvious displeasure with him for breaking a treasured object. "I didn't do it; my hand did it!" he exclaims. Similarly, organizational members often see their actions as belonging to the "system" and, thus, as the responsibility of the "organization." That frame of mind, combined with excessive role conformity, contributes to many commonly known incidents of amoral and inappropriate behavior among personnel in modern organizations.[5]

Nevertheless, organizations are human, social constructs. We are the originators of their form—their structure, procedures, rules and regulations—and are ultimately responsible for the outcome of our collective actions. We are the producers and the beneficiaries of organizational actions, and sometimes the outputs are undesirable and amoral. Regardless, organizations are products of the human mind and human actions.

Willingness to take responsibility for one's actions is as essential to the success of psychoanalytic treatment as it is to the succeeding application of psychoanalytic principles to organization development and change. If organizational systems are viewed by their inhabitants as separate entities, detached from their decisions and actions, neither psychoanalysis nor any other form of intervention can be of value.

However, a contemporary psychoanalytic approach to organizational insight and change is advantageous to other methods, because the consultant recognizes that while the client is unconscious of many counterproductive, relational patterns in the organization, he or she does not use that information to justify clients' actions. Instead, the consultant views disclaimed action and an unwillingness to assume personal responsibility as indicators of resistance to insight and learning, and as a signification of the clients' unawareness that arises from repression, suppression, and a host of possible defensive activities discussed in the Introduction. This "unawareness" has nothing to do with the level of individual or collective intelligence; it has more relation to the absence of opportunities to examine deeply the meaning of work and working relationships in the organization. Psychodynamic consultation helps to reveal the intersubjective dimension of organizational life.

Organizations mean different things to different people, whether as consultants, members, workers, clients, executives, middle managers, supervisors, or subordinates. Organizations are meaningful to both those who inhabit them and those who are served by them. Organizational meanings reside in the experiences and expectations of participants' feelings. When we join an association we do so for a purpose: It is anticipated that our membership will satisfy certain needs, whether for income, security, companionship, knowledge, aggression, spirituality, or identity.

Organizations are social settings where people can, ideally, express their true selves; however, they are often authoritarian cultures that promote false and inauthentic actions. Whether or not organizations facilitate genuine and productive human relations depends upon the values, ambitions, ideals, talents, and skills of key participants, members of powerful organizational coalitions, and their host political culture. If one acknowledges the influence of personality on power relations and decision making in organizations, then one must look beyond traditional organization theories.

Why We Need an Alternative Organization Theory

Organizations are produced and perpetuated by people who come together in order to accomplish something that they cannot achieve alone. Whether their purpose is to defend national boundaries; govern and collect taxes; build homes, roads, and schools; or provide health care and education, complex organizations are permanent fixtures of contemporary life. Thus, an in-depth understanding and evaluation of organizational life can be of great value.

Organizational sociologists, economists, and political scientists typically pay attention to the structural dynamics of management-worker relations, coalitions of power and authority, hierarchies and markets, or power strategies for interdependence between and among organizations. This is valuable. However, they also assume that people make only conscious choices and interact only on the basis of self-interest and cost-benefit exchanges. From the vantage point of observing and participating in large, complex organizations, that assumption is incorrect. Furthermore, social and behavioral scientists typically apply technical and instrumental rationality in their investigations and descriptions of organizational behavior. Their studies may be methodologically rigorous and statistically sophisticated. But are they relevant to the world of practice, a reality that is uncertain, unpredictable, and unique from one moment to the next? Do they unwittingly discourage reflectivity and critical awareness? Can they account for, and explain, incidents of irrationality and irresponsibility?

What, then, do psychoanalytic organization theorists look at? What can they teach us? And how do their methods apply?

Suppression, Defense, and the Unconscious in Organizations

Analyzing an organization is not the same as analyzing an individual. Granted individuals are complex creatures who may act defensively, anxiously, and even paradoxically. People are not always aware of why they do what they do, nor why they feel what they feel. From one moment to the next, they may forget a thought, idea, or name of a friend or colleague. Certain experiences and relationships may trigger specific anxieties or attributions of which they are unaware. Accepting that individuals are perplexing subjects of analysis (not to mention imperfect and at times irrational), it follows that organizations might be expected to present overwhelming complexity to the prospective analyst.

One does not psychoanalyze the organization as one would an individual on the couch—although there are similarities. Rather, one analyzes patterns of relationships (intersubjectivity) and individual perceptions of organizational experiences—that which constitutes what I call organizational identity. For example, individuals in the organization often forget (some might say, deny and suppress) critical incidents in the organization's history. In fact, it is commonplace for organizational members to push out of awareness (by means of suppression) painful organizational realities such as the effects of retrenchment, leadership transitions, reorganization, shifting budgetary procedures and evaluations, changing task environments, and conflicts among executives, managers, and staff. People may go about their business, despite the turmoil, and often do so with diminishing effectiveness.

Suppressed incidents and denial of reality affect people and their organizational operations. Errors are repeated. Problems are unsolved. Conflicts are avoided. Organizational members are demoralized, and organizational viability is jeopardized. Suppression and denial negatively affect morale and diminish organizational effectiveness. These activities are part of the unconscious dimension of organizational culture—what I call the organizational identity.

Like psychoanalytic patients, organizational members often passively experience critical incidents such as those mentioned. They characteristically feel victimized by constant change and transition. Seeing themselves as powerless and helpless, they suppress their anger and come to rely upon ritualistic defenses and routines at work. That way they can deny and avoid confronting their problems of coping and adaptation and succumb to cynicism. It is this pessimism and negativity that organizational consultants confront in trying to extract pertinent information and facilitate collaboration and change. And, quite possibly, it is this experience that leads many organization theorists and consultants back to Freud.

The Relevance of Freud's Findings to Organization Theory

Freud's discovery of the unconscious coincided with his finding that people repress painful thoughts, ideas, and experiences. People shut out of awareness certain emotionally loaded, anxiety-producing information, rendering it unconscious knowledge. Individuals cope with perceived dangers by defending themselves in this way. They may physically or psychologically flee or withdraw from a relationship or situation viewed as dangerous. However, people are suppressing thoughts, feelings, and ideas and defending themselves against anxiety, not organizations.

While there is unconscious life in organizations, there is no organizational unconscious per se. The intricacy of organizational psychology in contrast to individual psychology seems enormous. Understanding behavior in organizations, however, rests in ferreting out the meanings of interpersonal and group relationships, which collectively constitute the identity of the organization.

Freud's quote at the beginning of this chapter claims that individual psychology is at the same time social psychology. Despite his intense focus on instincts and drives (the aims of bodily stimulus and tension reduction), Freud understood the impact of social and interpersonal phenomena on the construction of personality. To understand the individual, one must comprehend the character of his or her relationship to others and the context of interactions.

Adherents of contemporary psychoanalytic thinking emphasize patterns of relationships, both conscious and unconscious, and view individuals as object-seeking rather than instinctually driven (Mitchell, 1988; Greenberg and Mitchell, 1983). Analysts with the assistance of clients are thereby encouraged to make public the intersubjective meaning of patterns of relationships, values, attitudes, frames of mind, and personality characteristics found to be unique to the organizational culture under investigation.

In order to distinguish the peculiarities from one organization to the next, the consultant must evaluate the nature of leadership and interpersonal and group activities in their cultural, historical, political, and environmental context. Psychoanalytic knowledge of organizations is acquired from the in-depth study of human activities and relationships, whose meaning is communicated through the verbal expression of individual feelings, fantasies, and perceptions of the participants.

It could be further argued that one rarely, if ever, reaches the unconscious life of organizational members; it is more often the case that the application of psychodynamic theories to organizational behavior helps to elicit what is more accurately termed valuable *preconscious data*—the unexamined, undiscussed, avoided, and denied issues of organizational experience. Preconscious data—the result of suppression—are more accessible than unconscious material—the consequence of repression. That is why I referred earlier to the act of suppression rather than repression—organizational participants may deny and suppress problems that were at one time conscious, and of which they may be partially aware. Not surprisingly, acts of suppression and defense occur often in organizations—a fact ignored by mainstream organization theorists.

On the other hand, if one takes seriously the notion that people enter organizations as adults with their personalities complete, then one might assume unconscious processes will influence role performance. That is, one's identity, psychoanalytically speaking, results from the *internalization* of significant interpersonal relationships, particularly those of infancy and childhood. One might assume, therefore, that early interpersonal experiences unconsciously affect interactions at work. That is why the concept of transference, which we turn to next, is central to the understanding of the psychodynamics of everyday organizational life.

Transference and Organizational Hierarchy

Transference is the unconscious sharing of emotions between two (or more) persons in which one projects feelings and attitudes from past relationships (to parent, sibling, etc.) onto another person in the present. According to Ralph Greenson, "Transference is the experiencing of feelings, drives, attitudes, fantasies, and defenses toward a person in the present that are inappropriate to that person and are a repetition, a displacement of reactions originating in regard to significant persons of early childhood" (1978: 201). Such unconscious reactions are bound to occur in adult life, particularly in the context of authority relations that tend to trigger unconscious expectations.

For example, a subordinate may come to idealize his or her superior as a consequence of frustrated idealization of parents during childhood. Kohut (1977; 1984) stresses the child's need for greatness, strength, and calmness to be found in his or her identification with a parent. If thwarted, the need for idealization becomes exaggerated; if left unfulfilled, it provokes an unconscious search for such traits in adult relationships. The idealizing subordinate, thereby, comes to view his or her boss as superhuman and infallible. Children with parents who are not worth idealizing, for whatever reason, continue searching, often obsessively, for substitutes.

A superior, on the other hand, may require idealizing subordinates as a consequence of frustrated needs for acceptance by parents during childhood. His or her own narcissistic needs were not met. Kohut's (1977; 1984) self psychology stresses the child's developmental need to be the center of his or her parents' universe, to feel loved and admired, and to satisfy exhibitionistic demands. In the case of unresponsive or overly indulgent parents, the child's need for recognition and acceptance (what Kohut calls mirroring) will motivate him or her in the selection and maintenance of adult relationships. The mirror-hungry superordinate, for instance, will require idealizing, loving, and admiring subordinates.

What is most relevant for organizational life in the concept of transference (and countertransference) is not so much the childhood origins of participants' relational conflicts as their awareness of interactional patterns in the present that limit their abilities to change and work effectively with others. Childhood experiences shape individual perceptions of roles in the workplace. "Here-and-now" relational patterns are the result of personalities-in-roles, and hierarchies encourage transference dynamics between and among organizational members—power and authority relations stoke the fire of internal parental images whether real or fantasied. Participants interpret hierarchic positions, tasks, and roles differently and often unconsciously. Gaining insights into the emotional dimensions of their relations can enable them with the help of a consultant to clarify and resolve differences, improve coordination, and thereby consider alternative ways of interacting at work. Psychoanalytic organization theory views feelings as the unconscious foundation from which everything else emerges in the context of organizational culture. Let's conclude with an elaboration of this point.

SUMMARY: WHAT IS PSYCHOANALYTIC ORGANIZATION THEORY?

Psychoanalysis is a theory of interpretation for understanding the significance of human feelings and actions. Its application to examining organizational life moves us beyond the scientific search for observable facts and truths; rather, it offers a theory and practice for ascertaining the meaning of human relations and experiences at work—meanings found in the unconscious and latent processes of social systems.

Psychoanalytic theorists attempt to locate the intent of human experience by focusing on psychic reality in contrast to objective reality. Acquisition of psychic reality is at the center of psychoanalytic work—referring to subjective and, especially, unconscious meaning. "Its usefulness resides in its reminding us that psychoanalytic explanation depends on our knowing what an event, action, or object means to the subject; it is the specifically psychoanalytic alternative to descriptive classification by a behavioristic observer" (Schafer, 1976: 89). Here, one finds the relevance and contribution of psychoanalysis for organization theory.

Psychoanalytic organization theorists want to know the significance of, and the reasons for, the private images people hold of organizational life—the participant's psychic reality. That includes unconscious fantasies, expectations, attributions, assumptions, fears, and anxieties about themselves and others in their mutual organizational roles. Psychoanalytic organization theorists work to understand the meaning of critical incidents and the collective patterns of response to those events. Psychoanalytic organization theorists believe the mysteries of organizational life reside in the intersubjective world of organizational members' experience—what I call their organizational identity.

People use their organizations for unconscious reasons such as defending themselves against certain anxieties, renewing a sense of lost omnipotence, enhancing their self-esteem, and resolving incomplete developmental issues; as targets of aggression; and as a psychological space for play and imagination, to name a few. The personal meaning of organizational experience, discovered in organizational identity, helps to explain the unconscious intentions of those who plan and structure organizational action. How people, particularly those in power, use their experiences with and fantasies about organizational membership affects their relationships, and ultimately their collective image of organization. Awareness of the structure of intersubjectivity and the relational patterns organizing experience and action helps to explain human behavior.

Organizations, however, are not analyzable as a single entity, an organism with its own psyche, but as a consequence of interpreting the patterns of human interactions and perceptions of members in their respective roles and groups. Collective patterns of private images and interactions may differ from one organization to the next, rendering coherent what otherwise seems chaotic and unreasonable. Organizations are more than the sum of members' collective projections: that is, organizations are psychological containers for members' individual and shared experiences, fantasies, and expectations. Organizational images, psychoanalytically speaking, are neither real nor fantasy: they are the product of imagination, and in this potential space between reality and fantasy the riddles of organizational life reside. This is not meant to deny the objective reality of organizations, but to emphasize the psychodynamic position that the understanding of organizational dynamics rests in the psychic reality of organizational participants. Interpreting their individual stories, images, experiences, and perceptions of organizational reality is what matters.

Drawing upon ideas from psychoanalytic theory and practice helps organizational theorists to understand the experience of organizational members—experiences held in members' private images of organization. Meaningful private images result from one's internalization of events before and after entry into an organization. These intra- and interpersonal, group, and organizational events are incorporated into preconscious thoughts and, if repressed, reside as unconscious memory traces.

In the next chapter I discuss, somewhat critically, the interaction of ritualistic organizational defenses and the self-system at work. Here, I portray ritualistic behavior and excessive defensiveness, rooted in obsessive-compulsive individual proclivities among workers, as a central problem of modern organizations.

NOTES

1. See p. 1 of Freud's introduction to *Group Psychology and the Analysis of the Ego.*

2. Transference and countertransference phenomena are emphasized more heavily by contemporary psychoanalysts than techniques of free association and dream analysis. In psychoanalytic organization theory and consultation, this is also true. However, free association and dream analysis offer many untapped resources for exploring individuals and groups in organizations. For example, free association encourages openness and uncensored communication, and dream analysis proffers a technique for discovering latent meaning and motives of human behavior. The intent of these analytic tools is consistent with the objectives and values of psychoanalytic organization theory and consultancy.

3. In her treatment of children Klein found that it is not the patient's relationship to the real parents that is transferred to the analyst but the relationship to internal fantasy figures, the inner parents. Hence she emphasized the importance of early internal object relations in normal and pathological development in children and adults (Moore and Fine, 1990: 106). See also Segal (1988).

4. In *The Invisible Bureaucracy*, Baum (1987) elaborates on the scapegoating ritual with a case illustration in which an adviser to a public organization is blamed for the problems he was invited to help solve.

5. Consider how officials rationalize and distance themselves from responsibility in the following contemporary cases: funding decisions at the Department of Housing and Urban Development, denial of critical feedback at NASA and the space shuttle disaster, Hooker Chemical and the authorization to dump toxic wastes into Love Canal, the Iran-Contra affair and the diversion of funds. For an in-depth psychodynamic view of how officials disconnect themselves from the consequences of their actions and appear normal outside their professional and organizational roles, see Lifton (1986), *Nazi Doctors.*

2

RITUALISTIC ORGANIZATIONAL
DEFENSES AND THE SELF-SYSTEM

It is ironic that while psychoanalytic theory and techniques may prove useful in interpreting organizational paradoxes, the values inherent in the "psychoanalytic attitude"[1]—insight and change—are contrary to those common to many organizational cultures—efficiency and control. Given that the object of psychoanalytic work is the liberation of painful emotions and thoughts rather than their containment, its unsung value to organizations lies not in mere interpretation, but in its potential as an antidote to organizational norms.

In this chapter, I discuss the psychoanalytic critique of organizations, more specifically of bureaucratic organizations. This critique presents organizations as social constructs with a deep psychological function—that of externalized ego defense. In particular, I try to show how these particular organizational cultures originate and are then perpetuated by ritualistic defenses that limit the processing of anxiety-producing information and thereby minimize the potential for learning and change while maximizing the probability of authoritarian behavior and role conformity. In these bureaucratic institutions, information and feedback that run contrary to the status quo of norms, policies, and procedures and data that contradict planned schedules and routines are typically censored by collective individual and organizational defenses—what I call *externalized self-systems*. The organizational stories presented in Part II exemplify the tangibility of externalized self-systems and ritualistic organizational defenses that obstruct organizational learning and problem solving.

Ritualistic organizational defenses literally can act as blinders to reality—defensive screens that conceal problems and deny conflicts. Human energy (cognitions and emotions), which might otherwise be channeled into the correction of errors and actual problem solving, is often displaced by the influence of anxiety onto substitute objects[2] promoting the illusion of safety and security without substantive reflection and change. Under the stress of uncertainty and anxiety, form (procedures, regulations, impersonal rules, red tape, etc.) takes precedence over organizational mission and substantive output (problem solving, provision of services, personal responsibility, and the quality of product).

Resistance to environmental and personal demands for change in organizational objectives (characteristic of management's dependence on traditional styles of organizing and planning) signifies the presence of overactive self-system operations among members. Denial of the impending state of organizational decline suggests a dependency on defensive organizational cultures, resulting in management's inability to test the reality of organizational environments accurately. Particularly in times of unusual stress due to political changes, cutbacks, retrenchment, and overall decline, acknowledgment of ritualistic defenses illuminates the extent of our emotional investment and overdependency on externalized self-systems. Resistance to change is psychological at its roots, and political and structural attempts at change often ignore the psychological anchors of attachment to prevailing forms.

Many prominent organization theorists, as I will show, either implicitly or explicitly characterize organizational behavior as ritualistic and defensive. A more complete appreciation of the role of ritualistic behavior in organizations recognizes its origins in the ego defenses of human personality—what I refer to here as the self-system. "The culture of the [social] system reflects . . . the types of people the organization attracts" (Burke, 1982: 76). Psychoanalytically speaking, ritualistic behavior in organizations arises from unconsciously motivated obsessional thinking and compulsive behavior aimed at defending one's self from anxiety over losing control, uncertainty, and conflict (Diamond, 1984; Zaleznik and Kets de Vries, 1975; Sperling, 1950). Ritualistic defenses are intended to contain the anxiety—anxiety from momentary loss of psychological boundaries between oneself and others and, ultimately, one's sense of identity.

First, organization theorists need to delineate dysfunctional, meaningless, and conformist activities from functional, meaningful, and adaptive activities. In this regard, a distinction between cultural ritual and ritualistic behavior can be established.

CULTURAL RITUAL AND RITUALISTIC BEHAVIOR

A major distinction exists between socially useful cultural rituals and what become obsessional and compulsive features of ritualistic behavior by workers. *Cultural rituals* are systems of rites, ceremonial acts or actions, and customarily repeated acts or series of acts (Merriam-Webster 1974: 604). From a psychological standpoint, cultural rituals (such as religious and magical ceremonies) serve to confirm and accept human emotionality (Kafka, 1983). These acts are meaningful and life confirming. In contrast, *ritualistic behavior* is often a dysfunctional and obsessional practice such as the habitual observance of an established form or process for doing things and the repetition of such acts. Cultural rituals control the unknowable, and make it appear knowable, and are valuable to the collective (Siggins, 1983). Ritualistic behavior, in contrast, is experienced as meaningless routine that serves to suppress and deny genuine feelings.

When organization theorists discuss ritual in the social context of organizations, they are more precisely describing ritualistic behavior in which rationally organized and routinized actions acquire an obsessional-compulsive defensive nature. Among organizational participants, obsessive thoughts and compulsive behavior (obsessive rituals) are characteristic. To clarify, obsessional thoughts differ from normal thoughts in that they are experienced as unspontaneous, distracting, repetitive, ruminative, and as coming from elsewhere than oneself, whereas compulsive behavior is repetitive, stereotyped, ritualistic, and superstitious.

In his article "Challenge and Confirmation in Ritual Action," Kafka (1983) makes an important distinction, for our purposes, between the terms *ritual* and *ritualistic*. Social rituals, he tells us, "can produce a feeling of completeness—a whole act, a finished sequence, the achievement (at least for a while) of satisfaction, satiation, perhaps serenity. But sometimes as in 'ritualistic behavior,' they may instead generate a feeling of mechanical repetition or the absence of a meaning achieved, a sense of being enmeshed in a endless series of aborted sequences" (1983: 31). Organization theorists often similarly describe the experience of organizational members (Baum, 1987; 1990; Diamond, 1984; 1988; Schwartz, 1990).

In sum, cultural and social rituals differ significantly from ritualistic behavior by both confirming and challenging everyday reality. Ritualistic behavior functions to deny the presence of a reality principle in life and death, love and hate, conflict and growth. Cultural rituals, such as the celebration of puberty rites, represent the healthy adaptive recognition and affirmation of human development and change. In contrast, ritualistic behavior signifies the emergence of psychological defenses, as illustrated in organizational performances of symptomatic repetition, which exaggerate the importance of rationality, routinization, stability, and control. Ritualistic behavior represents the attempt to overcome by repression the ambivalent feelings that threaten one's self, in contrast to some cultural rituals that encourage tolerance and awareness of ambivalence (Kafka, 1983). However, from a developmental perspective, one finds the positive contribution of ritualistic behavior to psychological well-being in early development, while, in the context of adult behavior in work organizations, ritualistic acts take on negative attributes. Next, let me say something about the positive characteristics of ritualistic behavior in early childhood before elaborating on the obsessive-compulsive nature of ritualistic work patterns.

The Psychological Origins of Ritualistic Behavior

R. D. Laing (1966) describes "primary ontological security" as the existential position of a person with a "centrally firm sense of his own and other people's reality and identity." According to Laing, it is precisely the lack of this security that distinguishes the psychotic from others. In the cycle of human development, ritualistic behavior in the child integrates the self by differentiating self and other. Erik Erikson (1966) notes that the earliest ritualization (ritualistic behavior) occurs in the mother-infant greeting and recognition behavior. According to Erikson, a "sense of basic trust" or "mistrust" emerges out of the interpersonal experiences of the first year of infant development (1968: 96). Hence, if the parents are emotionally healthy and the emotional bonding between parents and infant is good, then a primary sense of security and trust originates from the earliest ritualistic act. More specifically, if the necessary "trust" and sense of personal security are established during the first two years, the baby comes to trust with minimal anxiety the parents' periodic absence. In the ritualistic performance one observes playful interactions between parents and their children as an exercise in learning to cope with their mutual absence and presence. These playful interactions may take on a rather serious quality, if we acknowledge their necessary ego function in challenging and confirming the child's sense of security and awareness of its separateness from the parent. Consider for a moment the popularity of games like peek-a-boo and hide-and-seek among babies and toddlers.

Ritualistic behavior in the form of greetings and recognition between parents and infants carries great implications for the crucial psychological foundations and genesis of self. Initially, ritualistic behavior symbolizes a decisive moment in the early object relationship between mother and infant, wherein the psychodynamic processes of separation and individuation, the necessary establishment of boundaries between self and other(s), make their appearance.

Thus ritualistic behavior in its earliest manifestation is both purposeful and meaningful. It shares much with cultural rituals as meaningful celebrations and ceremonials with a common aim to control and make manageable that which appears life-threatening. Siggins (1983: 3) states that ritual acts serve common personal needs "to control, to make manageable that which is unknown, frightening, overpowering." "The more helpless one feels," she writes, "the more one calls upon outside magical aid." Surely, cultural rituals in society and ritualistic behavior in infancy have this in common.

On the other hand, individuals engaged in ritualistic acts (obsessional symptomatic rituals) may also wish to satisfy these personal needs for control and manageability, but institutionalized actions may lack meaningfulness, purposefulness, and human intimacy. As Siggins writes:

> In the structured situation, ritual is an integral part of the organization. When a person or group revolts against the confines of the structure and wishes to be free and unfettered, he wants to be part of an individualized community based on personal intimacy, which tends to be antiritualistic. (10)

She continues, "This is one aspect of the paradoxical relationship between form and freedom that continually occurs in human life and institutions" (10). The organizational critique presented in this chapter and much of the book leads us to this antiritualistic position.

What then do we need to know about the relationship between the self and the organization to safeguard us against excessive reliance on the ritualistic defense?

The manner in which individuals receive, process, and interpret information has great significance for the study of organizational behavior and administrative decision making. The distorting effects anxiety imposes on cognitive processes suggest that previous interpersonal experience and cultural environment influence present attitudes toward self, others, and the organization.

The Organizational Context of Ritualistic Behavior

Formal characteristics of modern organizations tend to neutralize the otherwise personal, emotional, irrational, and often political behavior of their members. As Max Weber understood, bureaucracy offers the civil servant job security and compensation along with a high degree of certainty of expectations and performance in return for the relinquishment of independence and autonomy of action. To meet the human needs of predictability and certainty, organizations and their management emphasize control and efficiency of operations in rationally defined, instrumental, means-ends administration.

Bureaucratization emerges in part from defensive psychodynamic processes that occur as a consequence of the person's crucial need to maintain self boundaries (identity) and ego integrity just before and after entry into the formal organization. In ritualistic behavior, routine and repetition serve no organizational purpose. Yet, that behavior plays a decisive role for the recruit in managing self boundaries and defending against anxiety felt during entry into the complex organization. At the moment of interface between the individual recruit and the organization, signal anxiety is felt in response to a fear of losing one's self boundaries and identity. At this decisive moment, any recruit must decide whether to affiliate with (by becoming a part of) the organization or to remain separate from (and not part of) the institution.

This choice, regardless of how seemingly rational or irrational, invokes some dissonance and affects the integrity of the ego. The existential and psychological foundations of self are momentarily uprooted. Primitive human needs for attachment, merger, and dependency are reawakened. Such initial human motives encourage the organizational member to locate his or her identity outside the self in the external quarter of hierarchy. Along with the decision to join and accept membership in the formal organization, a renewed attachment is formulated by hierarchical arrangement. A *merger relationship* between superordinate and subordinate that contains ambivalent feelings with organizational practices and ritualistic behavior is established.

At the outset, ritualistic behavior ensures the management of self and other boundaries for the newcomer. Psychologically regressive dynamics of repetition and routine (reminiscent of primary process thought essential to the child's need for object constancy and his or her development of focal attention) emerge in service to the vulnerable adult self. As Kafka notes: "Ritualistic" action represents striving for "object constancy" and "reality-anchoring" that appears to defend one against "massive confusion and total disorganization" (1983).

Organization theorists often depict organizational action as ritualistic. A psychodynamic perspective enables us to see the contradictory relationship between the individual and the organization. Organizations as externalized self-systems reinforce defensive human needs for psychological security and self-esteem. They symbolize the unconscious wish to return to the safety of the womb, the original holding environment (Winnicott, 1971). In organizational life, the wish is signified by ritualistic behavior intent on maintaining the status quo, avoiding anxiety-provoking conflict, and denying realities of shifting political pressures and market demands. Exaggerated ego defenses and ritualistic actions perpetuate the organizational culture by encouraging resistance to insight and change. This defensive organization, what I refer to in Chapters 6 and 7 as the *parataxic organization*, censors anxiety-producing information antithetical to the status quo. Next, I present the reader with an overview of how organization theorists represent organizational behavior as ritualistic.

RITUALISTIC BEHAVIOR AND PSYCHOANALYTIC ORGANIZATION THEORY

Many organization theorists examine ritualistic behavior in modern organizations from different but mutually consistent perspectives. Such behavior is explicitly identified as a key factor in perpetuating dysfunctional consequences and ineffectiveness within institutions; at the same time, it achieves a necessary defensive equilibrium for organizational participants by managing self-other boundaries and alleviating anxiety. The following discussion outlines the arguments of prominent organization theorists and attempts to draw parallels and develop a consistent underlying pattern of thought.

In her classic study of a nursing service, Menzies (1960) reports on a nursing staff that utilizes defensive techniques including obsessional rituals (ritualistic behavior) for coping with anxiety:

A necessary psychological task for the entrant into any profession that works with people is the development of adequate professional detachment. He must learn, for example, to control his feelings, refrain from excessive involvement, avoid disturbing identifications, maintain his professional independence against manipulation and demands for unprofessional behaviour. (102)

Menzies points out the degree to which nurses are preoccupied with impersonal norms and acceptable behavior patterns. She suggests that the level of denial and emotional detachment imposed on the newcomers by the experienced professional nurses greatly contributes to the stress and high rate of turnover among nursing trainees. Menzies' study illustrates the extent to which organizational members construct social defense systems characterized by obsessional rituals (ritualistic behavior) to protect the participants against anxiety.

In Menzies' (1960) study nurses of a general hospital are observed relying on "ritual task performance" as a defense against the anxiety of taking responsibility for decision making in nurse-patient relationships. The ritual task performance seems contrary to the patients' needs for recovery and consistent with the nurses' need to minimize the anxiety of intimacy with the patients. Characterized by lists of prescribed actions and rigid routines, the ritual task performance is analyzed as a reaction-formation to the anxiety of losing control and experiencing feelings associated with patients and their illnesses. Nurses awaken their patients to dispense pills during the night, despite the fact that getting rest may be a more significant factor in the patients' recovery. In the stressful climate of a nursing service, acknowledged feelings of empathy for the patients may represent too great a risk to the nurses' identity and professional role.

Cultural rituals that regularly celebrate life (rites of passage) or death (funeral rites) often succumb to dysfunctional, irrational organizational forms of action. In place of celebrating life and acknowledging death, ritualistic behavior facilitates individual attachment to hierarchy and conformity to impersonal rules, regulations, and procedures. Managers function to perpetuate hierarchy and ritualistic behavior by selectively attending to control and accountability of subordinates. Thus, managers treat subordinates as "part" human and one-dimensional for purposes of domination. Hummel illustrates this with the complaints of a "functionary" in the personnel department of the Cleveland, Ohio, Board of Education, who proclaims:

> For a long time, I felt my role within the bureaucracy was to deal with human needs. In recent years, accountability has become so important, however, that I now must spend more and more time completing forms and compiling records. In many instances this work is duplicated by others and there is less time devoted to rendering service. My program director is caught up in this control situation and is constantly seeking new control methods and reactivating dormant rules. We had the sign-in and the sign-out procedure, the daily log, weekly, bi-weekly, monthly and yearly reports; now, we have a management information retrieval system. When similar information about all workers in the program is placed in the system, management can then analyze this [sic] data and attempt to control the daily work schedule and work distribution. Before all this paperwork there was

more productivity. It seems that accountability and productivity are not compatible. (1977: 26–27)

Management's preoccupation with control, accountability, and efficiency often results in duplication and lower productivity. Behavior among organizational participants replaces intersubjectively meaningful, collaborative, and effective social actions (cultural ritual) with meaningless, rigidly conformist, and routine (ritualistic) actions. In my interpretation, Hummel's functionary is a product of organizational ritualism.

In 1940 the sociologist Robert Merton criticized the dysfunctional and purposeless aspects of organizations. He suggested that dysfunctions arise from the bureaucrat's preoccupation with control over subordinates and insistence on the "reliability of response" and predictability of behavior. According to Merton, sentiments of loyalty and conformity can be "more intense than is technically necessary." In a later work, he explains:

> There is a margin of safety, so to speak, in the pressure exerted by these sentiments upon the bureaucrat to conform to his patterned obligation, in much the same sense that added allowances (precautionary overestimates) are made by the engineer in designing the supports for a bridge. But his very emphasis leads to a transference of the sentiments from the aims of the organization onto the particular details of behavior required by rules. Adherence to the rules, originally conceived as a means, becomes transformed into an end-in-itself; there occurs the familiar process of displacement of goals whereby an instrumental value becomes a terminal value. (Merton, 1963: 258–59)

For Merton, the bureaucrat's reliance on impersonal rules and prescribed actions fosters ritualistic attitudes. This results in diminishing effective responses to clients or customers, employees, and the task environment of the agency or company. Such ritualistic attitudes and excessive precautions produce rigidity and a lack of spontaneity necessary to organizational adjustment and development. At the individual and organizational levels such attitudes reflect obsessional processes at work that promote narrow-mindedness, parochialism, and selective inattention.[3] This phenomenon is comparable to the ritual task performance (mentioned earlier) in the Menzies case study of the nursing service. According to Merton, organizational behavior (characterized by the worker's excessive dependency on rules and prescriptions for action) often results in goal displacement. Originally intended to produce rationally organized and

efficient action, modern organizations deteriorate into dysfunctional, in-
efficient, and irrationally organized impersonal actions. Workers emphasize means over ends; form (process) takes priority over substance.

From a critical psychoanalytic framework, one might suggest that ego
integrity, autonomy, and a sense of reality are sacrificed to a collective
wish for certainty and predictability in a changing environment. Managers
tend to emphasize control of workers and their task environment. This is
symptomatic of the ego's need in an obsessional neurosis to control anxiety
from the inside and distort reality from the outside. Managers stress
conformity to impersonal rules and procedures (official behavior). This
results in goal displacement. Unlike cultural rituals that enhance a feeling
of completeness and achievement, ritualistic acts promote mechanical
repetition and suppress feelings from thoughts and behavior. Compulsive
routine and impersonal action among organizational members symbolize
the individual's reliance on formalism, cases, and red tape as a defense
against anxiety about losing control. These defensive actions illustrate
psychological repression and unconscious denial of reality among organizational participants. Many of the cases presented in Part II illustrate the
lengths to which many organizations and their members go to censor
anxiety-provoking data.

For sociologist Michel Crozier in *The Bureaucratic Phenomenon*, a
typical feature of the modern organization is its tendency to produce
"vicious circles" where organizational participants repeat errors and do not
learn from their mistakes because of an overwhelming propensity to
defend themselves against the necessity for and the reality of change. The
bureaucrat's common response to failure is reinforcement and/or expansion of routine structural arrangements and normative assumptions—illustrated by a "more of the same" attitude. In Chapter 8, the case illustration
of a public agency undergoing leadership transition and expansion reflects
this attitude and resistance to change.

Crozier identifies four basic components that the "vicious circle" of
organizational behavior comprises: "impersonal rules; the centralization
of decisions; strata isolation and concomitant group pressure on the
individual; and the development of parallel power relationships around
remaining areas of uncertainty" (1964: 187). The function of ritualistic
behavior in modern organizations, Crozier believes, is both a response to
and a perpetuation of centralization and impersonal norms. *Ritualistic
behavior* is a dysfunctional consequence of peer group pressure intended
to enhance group or unit cohesion and promote power relationships for
bargaining purposes. Such behavior reinforces isolationist tendencies and
defensive attitudes among the strata of organizations, which in turn pro-

mote competition and divisiveness between organizational units and peer groups. Intraorganizational boundaries among units (or departments) become increasingly rigid and protective and communication and coordination become increasingly difficult. For Crozier, this outcome is illustrated by the narrow-minded and parochial (often territorial) ritualistic attitudes among organizational group members.

From a psychodynamic perspective, I believe, these findings suggest that meaningful reality testing is unlikely and that the organization finds itself incapable of responding to environmental demands for change. Peer groups surface as havens in an alienating and depersonalizing organizational climate. As a symbol of the organizational ego, management inadequately functions to balance internal and external systemic pressures. At the individual level, a *bureaucratic personality* emerges among functionaries: those who respect power relationships throughout the organizational strata, but who are predominantly motivated by defenses against anxiety over losing control.

In their books *Theory in Practice* (1974) and *Organizational Learning* (1978), Chris Argyris and Donald Schon detect (what I interpret as) ritualistic and dysfunctional behavior by focusing on what they call *constancy-seeking behavior* and *single-loop learning* in organizations. In addition, I believe that which they refer to as *model 1 theories in use* and *0–1 learning systems* are individual and organizational archetypes, respectively, of ritualistic and, one might say, obsessive-compulsive behavior (1978). For example, model 1 assumptions and governing values promote limited learning, decreasing effectiveness, and promotion of rigidity among members in organizations. The assumptions and governing variables that affect behavior in this way, according to Argyris and Schon, include the tendency to achieve purposes *as the individual perceives them*, the stress among participants on maximizing winning and minimizing losing, the proclivity to minimize eliciting negative feelings, and the affinity to be rational and minimize emotionality (Argyris, 1976: 31). Model 1 strategies include efforts to design and manage the environment so that the individual is in control of the factors relevant to her or him—a climate in which organizational members move to own and control their tasks and unilaterally protect themselves and others from being hurt from negative feedback. Simply speaking, model 1 values face-saving and defensive strategies (31).

The parallel between model 1 theories-in-use and my critique of modern organizations is found in the shared observation of ritualistic defenses at work. The individual in 0–1 learning systems, according to Argyris and

Schon, is seen as defensive and so too is his or her interpersonal and group dynamics. Moreover, defensive norms prevail along with a "low freedom of choice, a lack of internal commitment and no risk taking" (Argyris, 1976: 31). Model 1 and its counterpart 0–1 learning systems result in the inability to double loop learn. That is, workers are incapable of detecting and correcting errors, when their detection and correction require a change in the status quo, such as a conversion of organizational norms, values, and policies. Individual members of these systems perpetuate self-sealing processes and little public testing of individual and organizational assumptions (31).

Hence, ritualistic organizational defenses protect members against the anxieties of uncertainty and unpredictability associated with problem solving and changing the status quo. They further promote the collective repression and denial of organizational and interpersonal change. Ritual- istic organizational practices disavow the pain of emotional loss associated with change through processes of denial and selective inattention. These defenses repress feelings and narrowly focus thoughts on meaningless and repetitive tasks, while functioning to meet the unconscious desire among workers for stability, constancy, and the status quo. Organizational and individual reality testing surrender to a collective fantasy of control and conflict avoidance. The two cases presented in Chapter 10 show the emotional loss associated with change, and the case examples in Chapters 8 and 9 illuminate the extent to which organizational members avoid dealing with conflict.

Finally, in *Power and the Corporate Mind*, Zaleznik and Kets de Vries observe ritualistic approaches to problem solving that arise as a common feature of modern organizations. They discuss how people come together in committees "in the naive belief that the exchange of ideas is bound to produce a solution" (1975: 135). A mere proposal to form the committee to examine a particular problem may, in a ritualistic way, encourage workers to perceive the simple idea of the committee itself as the solution to the problem—a magical formula to alleviate the anxiety of uncertainty. The faith in the committee may, for the moment, serve as the object of a collective wish to be rid of the anxiety-provoking event and a substitute for solving the actual problem.

As I have tried to show, there are many examples of how organizations are viewed by theorists as ritualistic. Moreover, with the exception of Zaleznik and Kets de Vries, these organization theorists are not psychoan- alytically informed: their observations are grounded in organizational sociology and psychology. Next, I explain the linkage between self-sys- tems and ritualistic organizational systems.

THE ORGANIZATION AS PRODUCT OF COLLECTIVE SELF-SYSTEMS

The self-system is the component of personality structured to avoid anxiety—similar to what classical psychoanalysts call defense mechanisms. The self-system contains our experiences in coping effectively with threats of anxiety[4]—anxiety first felt in relation to the parent during infancy. Parents' anxieties are internalized by infants whose self-other boundaries are relatively primitive. Attachments between parents and infants may produce positive self-worth or low self-esteem in the child's mind. Levels of self-esteem then affect the quality and quantity of interpersonal defensiveness in the child's relations to others.

The degree of defensive activities can diminish with more secure and less anxiety-provoking experiences of significant others. A healthy, emotionally supportive juvenile and adolescent set of interpersonal experiences, for example, can counteract narcissistic deprivations of earlier experiences during childhood. These counterexperiences may reduce the need for defensive and paranoid activities and thus in turn enhance a person's ability to process information, knowledge, and, most importantly, novel experiences. Past and present experiences with anxiety distort information-gathering and decision-making activities. The relevance for work organizations is that collective, as well as interpersonal, experiences of key organizational members such as senior executives and high-level managers shape the kinds of information processes that form administrative action among adults.

The self-system encompasses many forms of defensive psychic configurations including selective inattention and parataxic distortions, which will be discussed and illustrated in Chapters 6 and 7. For now, it is sufficient to say that these are defensive activities that censor potential experiences, information, and knowledge, which might stimulate anxiety, loss of self-esteem, and panic among organizational participants. For instance, an environment perceived by organizational members as hostile and threatening may activate psychological defenses and thereby result in some distortion of reality and cognition. By narrowing one's cognitive scope on reality and limiting one's actions to the familiar and routine, anxiety is minimized but not without psychological and organizational costs. Such defensive actions protect people from the psychic effects of change and uncertainty, often at the price of denying reality and learning from experience.

Positive as well as negative changes in the self-system can occur at different phases of a person's life, depending upon experiences with interpersonal (object) relationships. The effects of anxiety and defensive activities such as selective inattention constrict the capacity for processing and storing information. Defensive actions may produce a cognitive inability to learn from experience and past mistakes—symptomatic of what psychoanalysts call *repetition compulsion.*

Organizations are fertile soil for obsessional activities such as selective inattention—exemplifying what I call *ritualistic organizational defenses.* For instance, a compulsive reliance on "files and records" for task activities often ignores social and political changes in the organization's environment. Collecting data for the sake of defending a program, regardless of the relevance or irrelevance of the data as a measure of the quality of a program's output, is also commonplace. In addition, management's preoccupation with scheduled completion dates for projects can encourage rejecting data that require a delay or cancellation in the completion or start of a project's mission. This can occur, as it did in the case of NASA and the space shuttle disaster, despite acknowledged costs for ignoring the negative feedback and error detection. Finally, an abundance of committee meetings with little or no product output reflects significant ritualistic organizational defenses as well.

In particular, *selective inattention* is a psychological process (defensive in character) that intentionally ignores specific information in the interests of protecting oneself from the recurrence of anxiety. The defenses are intended to protect the individual from changes in the self and ego functioning caused by an overload of anxiety-producing circumstances. Simultaneously, this defensive schema limits information processing that might otherwise result in enhanced self-awareness and competence. This inner contradiction illuminates the competing human motives for security and learning in organizational life.

Ritualistic organizational defenses shield organizational participants from the cognitive and emotional realities of the unknown, uncertain, and unpredictable character of organizational environments. Earlier experiences with anxiety can produce highly rationalized, stereotypic, and narrow-minded thinking among workers. Although ego defenses of the self are intended to promote greater adaptability and maintenance of security, they can become quite rigid and inflexible. Consequently, the avoidance of anxiety often takes priority over other human motives and values among organizational members.

In contradiction to social demands for diversity, emotional demands for uniform behavior and a shared system of values, what in Chapter 5 I call *homogeneity,* inspire psychological defenses which function to protect and secure the self. Sullivan wrote, "The origin of the self-system can be said to rest on the irrational character of culture or, more specifically, society" (1953: 168). Self-systems are formed in response to anxiety initially experienced in the preverbal, empathic relationship between mother and child. Defensive (security-oriented) activities of the self-system originate with the infant's initial fear of annihilation and separation. Self-system activities force individual attention toward meeting primary needs for security, which encourage institutional affiliations that provide structure and order, predictability, and equality of treatment and thereby minimal anxiety—hence, the complementarity of ritualistic behavior and organization. The cultivation of a self-system of psychological defenses is an appropriate reaction to an irrational world of interpersonal (object) relationships.

People exert a good deal of energy learning patterns of behavior that minimize anxiety and loss of self-esteem. Defensive actions do not end at the point in time we reach adulthood. Nor are defenses limited to internal objects and object relationships. They extend into that part of our physical environment which we construct for ourselves to accomplish things we cannot do alone—the human organization. Organizations are constructs of the mind: They acquire a reality of their own through the individual's reliance on their structures for protection and security against anxiety. In extreme situations, modern organizations consume individual initiative and will.

SUMMARY

As we have already seen, ritualistic organizational defenses are commonplace. In order to maintain psychological security and avoid anxiety, organizational norms and values may facilitate symptomatic rituals that promote human proclivities of denial and selective attention. Thus, ritualistic behavior serves a common purpose for both the individual and the organization. It functions as a defense against the anxiety of organizational learning and change. Actually, ritualistic behavior is indicative of symptomatic administrative behavior that organization theorists refer to with a variety of labels such as vicious circles, self-sealing processes, single-loop learning, displacement of goals, and magical formulas. These theorists have identified, implicitly and explicitly, such ritualistic characteristics of organizational cultures as fostering dysfunctional consequences, ineffectiveness, and organizational pathologies.

In this chapter, I have attempted to illustrate not only how ritualistic behavior contributes to dysfunctional consequences—goal displacement and the like—but how it is symptomatic of obsessional-compulsive neu-

roses in the self (Freud, 1963) and symptomatic of the individual's need
to control ambivalence and manage boundaries between self and other(s)
(Kafka, 1983; Erikson, 1968).

The management of self-other boundaries and the control of ambivalent
feelings are prominent motivating forces among organizational participants. Modern organizations often facilitate and perpetuate such defensive
actions with a highly structured and often rigid institution designed for
control and accountability.

Both cultural (social) ritual and ritualistic behavior are self-limiting;
however, only cultural ritual is truly self-accepting. In the cultural ritual,
we construct a "consensually validated system of meanings," whereas in
ritualistic behavior group and organizational participants perpetuate a
defensive social system against anxiety that fosters the suppression of
collaborative human action by depersonalization and unilateral protective-
ness. Anxiety is minimized at a high cost to individual, organization, and
society as many of the case examples in Part II illustrate.

Organizational structures may reinforce and support defensive actions
among workers and represent what I call externalized self-systems. Organizations often magnify the structural manifestation of embedded defensive psychological operations of the person. Traditional characteristics of
bureaucratic organizations like hierarchy of authority, functional specialization, and impersonality (along with the functional as well as dysfunctional consequences of those structures) share with the conception of a
self-system, the purpose of defending people from anxiety provoked by
uncertainty of conflict and change. Psychodynamic theory vividly demonstrates a central tragic contradiction between human needs for development and learning and needs for defenses against the anxieties inherent in
development and learning. As the covert result of active social defenses,
organizational members resist and often deny conflict and change, constraining learning and development.

Environmental threats to organizations and interpersonal relations
among senior executives, managers, and subordinates permeate the climates of many organizations. As a result of economic and political
uncertainties, organizational members fall back on familiar and often
psychologically regressive and ritualistic behavior patterns. At the interpersonal level, members under stress depend upon what Bion calls "basic
assumptions" of emotionality or what might be called "shared fantasies."[5]
Defensive activities rise and the participants' reliance on organizational
forms of control and patterns for routine and rationalized behavior are
enhanced. Defensive modes of operation at the interpersonal and institutional levels become more overt and commonplace. Individual workers

become more defensive, turning psychic energies inward in an attempt to thwart insecurities and anxieties caused by a lowering of self-esteem and sense of self-competence.

The psychodynamic critique of organizations focuses in part on the defensive and ritualistic use of social structure, and the consequences of this for organizational performance and human relations at work. It exaggerates the point that organizational structure parallels defensive psychological structures, the self-system and ego defenses, of personality. This approach provides a psychological window for more deeply understanding organizational limitations and resistances to change. However, it is a window that illuminates the contents of only one room of the unconscious psychological structure at work in organizations. In the next chapter, I continue this exploration by examining further, and more generally, the notion of organizational culture from a psychoanalytic perspective.

NOTES

1. See Schafer (1983).

2. In defining *object*, Moore and Fine write: "The object is to be distinguished from the subject, or self, to whom it must be psychologically significant; it may be animate or lifeless, but it is external; its counterpart within the mind of the subject is an *internal object*, sometimes called an *object representation*. However, all external phenomena are represented within the mind; the internal object representation is an amalgam of various attributes of the external object—physical, intellectual, and emotional—whether real or imagined by the subject" (1990: 129). Objects, whether animate or lifeless, are often targets of aggression and negative feelings that the self rejects by way of displacement and projection.

3. The term *selective inattention* refers to cognitive processes that filter out or censor anxiety-provoking data. Such defensive cognitive processes negatively influence the quality and scope of problem solving and planning in organizations. In sum, we may tend to process only that information within our individual comfort zones and ignore or deny data that challenge our assumptions and perceptions. For more on the concept of selective inattention see Sullivan (1954).

4. According to Sullivan, "anxiety is a tension in opposition to the tension of needs and to action appropriate to their relief" (1953: 44). In contrast to fear, anxiety is not the consequence of a clearly definable causal object or event. Its very experience blocks from awareness the origins of the anxiety and distorts the cognitive field of observation. Anxiety is experienced in terror, as a direct threat to the living human organism. As Heidegger describes, anxiety symbolizes "nothingness," "the complete negation of what is" (1975: 246). Unsettling feelings of powerlessness and helplessness, and a disconnectedness from reality, further describe this disturbing psychodynamic phenomenon.

5. See Bion's work (1970) on group dynamics in which "fight-flight," "dependency," and "pairing" are observed as basic assumption patterns of emotionality among group members under stress and anxiety.

3

THE PSYCHODYNAMICS
OF ORGANIZATIONAL CULTURE

What can the concept of organizational culture contribute to our deeper understanding of organizational life? I believe the notion of organizational culture helps us better comprehend institutional forms of tyranny. Organizations are human-made environments. They are produced and reproduced by groups of people as particular ways of relating to each other in order to get work done. Institutionally supported authoritarian and totalitarian acts are organizational, psychosocial, and political phenomena. But psychologically these forms of systemic oppression would not exist without group consensus (or collusion) about a set of unconscious feelings that support specific values, norms, ideas, actions. For example, where an organization prizes unilateral decision making, this value can elicit and reinforce needs for obsessional control and compulsive dominance—all of which are common attributes of ritualistic and defensive organizations discussed in the previous chapter.

Simply stated, people unconsciously create public and private organizations that exert social control over individuals and groups within a governing polity. Allaire and Firsirotu claim that the concept of organizational culture takes us beyond a sociological description of organizational structures, strategies, policies, and processes, to a dynamic comprehension of organizational myths, values, and ideologies (1984).

Culture is not simply another variable or isolatable component of organizations. It is what organizations are (Smircich, 1983; Meek, 1988). Organizational culture is the product of social invention and interaction that are influenced by the following factors, which are discussed in this chapter. They include organizational history, artifacts, physical space, and architectural design; degrees of formality and informality; social control that involves professional and institutional modes of socialization or indoctrination; shared symbols and meanings found in rituals and myths; organizational leadership personalities; espoused and practiced norms and values and management philosophies; groups (units, offices, divisions, etc.) as subcultures; host cultures that include economic and political task environments; and, finally, humor and play at work.

My purpose in this chapter is to look at organizational culture from a psychodynamic perspective. I begin by examining the more global and visible aspects of organizational culture and move toward the less visible and more subtle. Conventional concepts of organizational culture, I believe, are inadequate because they do not sufficiently consider unconscious aspects of organizations. The latter is what I call organizational identity—the unconscious foundation of an organizational culture. I discuss this concept in Chapter 4.

Many organization theorists and psychologists focus attention on organizational culture, leadership, and group dynamics. Organizational psychologists like Edgar Schein (1985) claim, for example, that leaders are in the business of creating and managing cultures within institutions, and that groups are the site of the development, containment, or destruction of cultures. Schein and his contemporaries concern themselves with *explicit culture*, which refers to directly observable patterns of values of which members are aware. Explicit culture includes standards of right and wrong and typical norms of behavior and forms of technology (Theodorson and Theodorson, 1969: 96). In addition, culture analysts concern themselves with what they claim to be the deepest layer of organizational culture that is found within groups, where underlying basic assumptions govern interactions and decision making—what sociologists call *implicit culture* (Theodorson and Theodorson, 1969).

Culture, Schein writes,

can now be defined as (a) a pattern of basic assumptions, (b) invented, discovered, or developed by a given group, (c) as it learns to cope with its problems of external adaptation and internal integration, (d) that has worked well enough to be considered valid and, therefore (e) is to be taught to new members as the (f) correct way to perceive, think, and feel in relation to those problems. (1990: 111)

Organizational culture, for Schein, is a collective adaptive mechanism in which members learn to cope with the internal and external pressures of managing institutions. While attentive to the implicit and tacit dimensions, Schein's definition and analysis of organizational culture rest on a functionalist anthropological framework that is influenced by the rational aspects of systems theory, Lewinian field theory, and cognitive theory. He writes, "The deepest level of culture will be the cognitive in that perceptions, language, and thought processes that a group comes to share will be the ultimate causal determinant of feelings, attitudes, espoused values, and overt behavior (1990: 111). For Schein, these shared cognitions are required for survival and systemic equilibrium and shape the psyche.

Before exploring the many components of organizational culture, I address briefly the intellectual origins of the term *organizational culture*.

ATTRIBUTES OF ORGANIZATIONAL CULTURE

Intellectual Background

Many scholars interested in organizational culture are influenced by the human relations movement of the 1930s. Elton Mayo (1933) along with Chester Barnard (1938) and others stressed the significance of informal social structure to understanding human behavior in organizations more deeply and more realistically. The notion of culture in organizations reappeared in London in the 1950s and 1960s with the Tavistock Institute of Human Relations and, particularly, in a work by Elliott Jaques, *The Changing Culture of a Factory* (1951). He, along with such pioneers of group and organizational analysis as Wilfred Bion, Isabel Menzies Lyth, Eric Trist, Eric Miller, and A. K. Rice, is responsible for sustaining interest in the organizational cultural phenomenon. At the same time, however, in the United States, Harry Levinson (1962) at the Menninger Clinic in Topeka, Kansas, and Abraham Zaleznik and his associates (1965) at Harvard University were also thinking about organizations along these lines. Sociologist Talcott Parsons influenced many with his work *Social Structure and Personality* (1964), in which he stated, "The structure of the society stands between the cultural system . . . on the one hand, [and] the personality system on the other. . . . The focus . . . of interconnections is the set of values institutionalized in the society and internalized in the personality" (297). For Parsons, culture is as much a part of personality as of social structure; it is, in fact, an essential link between individual and society.

This brief intellectual history of the notion of organizational culture provides some background for the exploration of its component parts, beginning with organizational history.

Organizational History

The retelling of organizational histories, like the retelling of individual pasts in psychoanalysis, are what Donald Spence calls *narrative truths* rather than historical truths (1982). Organizational myths and stories proffer meaningful information about individual experience and identification with institutions. When these stories are repeated by participants in discussions with nonmembers, such as researchers and consultants, themes often emerge that tell us how the organization and its leadership respond to critical incidents—patterns develop and a group identity is discovered.

Critical incidents are events in organizational history that are perceived by members as stressful and experienced anxiously. Organizations and their members typically do not reflect on themselves or their processes without reason. Changes in the organizational status quo caused by management cutbacks, retrenchment, leadership transitions, budgetary revisions, audits, expansions in size and workload, and the like, trigger anxieties and feelings of panic. Underlying basic assumptions and group defenses are pushed to their limits and beyond. Consequently, organizational culture, and all that it entails, is both endangered and exposed. Psychoanalytically oriented researchers and consultants find that critical moments are opportunities for reaching the suppressed and denied emotions of organizational members (Diamond, 1988).

The analysis of organizational culture includes an exploration of the unconscious and intersubjective structures of organizational life. Examining critical moments of organizational history contributes to this insight. However, if change is desirable to organizational members, one requires a method of analysis and intervention that is based upon the willingness of members to assume personal responsibility for their actions. The notion of organization identity discussed in Chapter 4 takes the analysis of organizational culture to its deepest interpersonal level, beyond explicit and implicit culture to the structure of intersubjectivity. Before discussing organizational identity, we examine the manifestations of organizational culture closer to the surface, starting with artifacts, physical space, and architecture.

Artifacts, Physical Space, and Architecture

As Edgar Schein (1985) points out, organizational culture encompasses three levels of analysis: artifacts, values, and basic underlying assumptions. Artifacts are material objects and, therefore, are the most accessible and readily observable facets of organizational culture.

Material objects may include newsletters, computers, pens and pencils, and architecture such as office work space and the actual design of buildings. These are components of what we call *explicit culture* in organizations. The availability, quantity, and quality of such objects differ from one organization to another, even though they may have similar tasks and occupational membership across organizational boundaries. The most important aspect of these artifacts is understanding their often deeply held meaning for organizational participants. Knowing their official or avowed purpose does not lead directly to knowing what they mean to organization members and the consequences of their interpretations.

The character of company newsletters, for example, says something about the culture: Are they chatty or serious in tone? What kind of information is provided? To whom are they distributed and how? How well written and printed are they? How often are they printed? These concrete aspects of newsletters draw our attention to their true purpose and meaning.

Material objects such as pens and pencils may mean one thing if they carry the company logo and are freely distributed. They will mean something entirely different if those same pens and pencils are given only to management. Who gets computers and who doesn't in the organization also has meaning, especially in regard to status and prestige.

Office space is often scarce and people also value the office size and physical location as signs of prestige and status. The not so hidden agenda among members is often to compete for space. The competition is also influenced by the availability of other kinds of rewards, status, and prestige in the organization. The layout of offices and who has which office, therefore, signify something about the nature of authority relations and management philosophy (including values). CEOs, for example, often have offices on different floors from other officers and staff and may be seen as inaccessible, hiding behind a fortress of receptionists and administrative assistants. Such an arrangement signifies the grandiosity of the office and its inhabitants.

In an attempt to relocate an entire program unit in one office building, the deputy director of a public agency I consulted to went from office to office carrying a white flag. While this may be a bizarre manner of dealing with his staff, many workers can relate to the potentially explosive nature of rearranging office space. The white flag certainly symbolizes the degree of emotional investment in the disbursement of offices in any large organization. From a psychoanalytic perspective, the white flag served as his attempt at surrendering to, and at the same time deflecting, the aggression of his staff through humor—psychologically distancing himself from their rage. Staff rage is generated by feelings of envy in a culture based on the psychology of comparison. We will explore the subject of humor as a component of organizational culture, and as represented here by the deputy director's act of carrying a white flag, later in this chapter. Next, I turn to organizational climate as a component of organizational culture that influences and is influenced by members' feelings and needs.

Warm and Cold Organizational Climates: Degrees of Formality and Informality at Work

One gets a distinctly different feeling from walking into an office where interactions are rigidly formal as compared to an office in which informal relations are the norm. The extent to which a climate feels cold and constraining or warm and liberating also differs from one institution to another and from one member to another. Each is a little different and is thereby experienced differently by different individuals. However, degrees of formality and informality signify differences among organizations. The manner in which people speak to each other, their style of dress, and protocol are elements of organizational culture.

In my consulting experience, for example, I observed an accounting office in which people addressed each other formally, as Mr. Smith or Mrs. Jones or Dr. Riley, and where the chain of command was rigidly adhered to for communications and authorizations. Dress codes were instituted and obeyed; orderliness and rationality prevailed. In contrast, I observed a social services agency where employees dealt with each other on a first name basis, regardless of rank and position of authority, and where people regularly expressed their feelings and attitudes about things. No dress code existed and their offices were generally cluttered and disorganized. Most organizations fall somewhere between these two extremes of formality and informality.

It is important to note that whether an organizational climate is warm or cold is not necessarily indicative of the degree of productivity, effectiveness, or quality of work. It speaks to what people in the organization, particularly executives, value—and that varies. It also signifies the entrant's finding a fit or misfit as a member of this organization. In other words, some may prefer the warm climate and others the cold one. However, if the recruit is not sure, he or she will confront this issue during the process of socialization—the subject to which we turn next.

Professional and Institutional Socialization/Indoctrination

In *The Ropes to Skip and the Ropes to Know*, Ritti and Funkhouser suggest, "The first problem faced by the new member is that of gaining entry into the men's hut—of gaining access to the basic organizational secrets. A key episode here is the rite of passage. This is more or less an affirmation to the individual that he has been accepted into the men's hut" (1977: 3). The men's hut refers to the ruling norms in a typically patriarchal organization, where socialization of the new member depends upon his or her ability to assimilate the values of the organizational culture (Diamond, 1985a: 665).[1] Ritti and Funkhouser say that "the hut is a symbol of, and a medium for maintaining, the status quo and the good of the order" (1977: 3). The new member who wishes to be accepted by and allowed entrance to the men's hut is forced to "learn the ropes" (Diamond, 1985a: 665). Individuals, eventually, internalize institutional norms and values through acculturation (socialization and indoctrination). The organizational or professional ethic becomes part of the member's identity. This aspect of organizational life partly explains the use by organizational change agents of deprogramming concepts like "unfreezing" and "unlearning" to describe the process of initiating organizational change.

A subset of admittance is the presence of professional groups within bureaucratic institutions that generate subcultures with their own languages, norms, and rituals. Cooperation in the form of sharing information and tasks across professional boundaries becomes problematic as a result. For example, the observer of a public works organization comprising separate groups of accountants, engineers, and architects will find each professional group focusing on different aspects of the same project. Task cooperation and communication among the groups will be difficult as each group will try to impose its distinct values and assumptions upon the others. Accountants, for example, cannot understand why engineers and architects do not drop what they are doing and respond faster to their budget requests. While fiscal responsibility may be foremost in the minds of the accountants, it is not for architects and engineers. Accountants, therefore, do not appreciate the frame of mind of practicing architects and engineers, and the latter do not recognize the different priorities and concerns of the former. This insight was very helpful to me in working as a consultant to the public agency described in Chapter 8, in which professional socialization contributed to diminished effectiveness and conflict in organizations.

Rituals

Organizational life is filled with rituals intended to enhance feelings of recognition and importance, group affiliation, and loyalty. According to Theodorson and Theodorson (1969), ritual is

> a culturally standardized set of actions with symbolic significance performed on occasions prescribed by tradition. The acts and words that comprise a ritual are precisely defined and vary very little if at all from one occasion to another. Tradition also determines who may perform the ritual. Rituals often involve sacred objects, and are usually expected to result in the emotional involvement of the participants. The ritual may be believed to have power in itself to produce certain results. (351)

For example, in one of the two cases presented in Chapter 10, a department director ritualistically rewarded his divisional managers with lapel pins of the departmental logo, thinking to himself that the managers would stop fighting over divisional priorities and their share of the budget, become good team players, and identify with the goals of the department. There was much fanfare in the dispensing of the pins, which made those who did not receive a pin envious and angry. Consequently, those who got them failed to wear them around anyone except the director himself. Managers continued to quarrel and operate their divisions as independent kingdoms. In fact, it could be said that relations in the department were worse than before. Despite these outcomes, the director was convinced that the pins were having the desired effect. Such magic rituals, like myths and stories, are commonplace in organizations.

Myths

Myths are highly symbolic and stereotypic stories of major events within a culture and are often retold and reexamined for their wisdom and inspiration (Theodorson and Theodorson, 1969). Organizational myths and stories are nearly as commonplace as rituals. For example, one often finds stories of mythic heroes, such as past CEOs, "who turned the organization around" or maybe "upside-down." At times there is a messianic quality to such tales and members often recite them in bad times when there is a strong desire for hope. Staff often tell and retell stories of previous executives who ruled like tyrants. These stories unify the group with a common identity—viewing themselves, for example, as "survivors of oppressive administrators and vindictive legislators."

ORGANIZATIONAL LEADERS AND FOLLOWERS

Leadership Personality

Beyond artifacts, degrees of formality, socialization, rituals, myths, and governing values lies a deeper level of organizational culture—the personality of leaders. The degree to which a leader's personality influences organizational culture is to some extent based upon the organizational structure and procedures. Taller hierarchies with centralized authority produce inordinate positions of power at the top, which facilitate greater domination of subordinates and unilateral decision making. Consequently, these authoritarian structures require expansive personalities at the top and self-effacing ones at the bottom (Diamond and Allcorn, 1985a). If hierarchic structure is considered a given, then we must consider how individual personality fits and then affects organizational positions.

Relying on Horney's (1950) neurotic solutions to anxiety, Seth Allcorn and I outline six personality types at work. There are three expansive types: narcissistic, perfectionistic, and arrogant-vindictive. There are also a self-effacing type, a resigned type, and an intentional type (Diamond and Allcorn, 1985a). Each type requires something different from staff and in an authoritarian structure that affects everyone. Briefly, the narcissist requires grandiosity and admiration. The perfectionist demands that everyone meet superior expectations and standards. The arrrogant-vindictive insists upon winning regardless of cost (and for him or her to win, someone else must lose). The self-effacing subordinate tries tirelessly to meet the superior's requirements, and the resigned character, which may be found in superior or subordinate positions, wants to be left alone. Finally, the intentionalist requires mutually shared personal responsibility and collaboration. The intentionalist is someone who is not consumed by stress and anxiety as his or her counterparts are.

Organizational cultures are shaped by the leadership's personality and unconscious expectations and demands. Frequently, leaders espouse one philosophy and practice another.

Espoused and Practiced Theories of Action

Executives and their staff often say one thing and do another. It is common to find managers espousing the humanist and democratic philos-

ophy of Theory Y (or, more recently, Theory Z) management and simultaneously practicing the authoritarian Theory X. In fact, executives and
managers are often unaware of their inconsistencies and contradictions.
Their staff, however, are aware of it and commonly resent it. Unfortunately, in most typically ritualistic and defensive organizational cultures,
the contradiction between espoused and practiced theories of action cannot
be discussed. Consequently, such organizations produce a vicious cycle of
undetected errors and unsolved problems.

Organizational cultures may be distinguished by the degree to which
learning and problem solving occur. Chris Argyris and Donald Schon
(1978) have established two models of organizational learning contrasted
by diminishing versus increasing effectiveness. Model 1 is represented by
governing variables (or values) and untested assumptions that render
problematic the detection and correction of error. Some of the governing
values of behavior include unilateral protection of self and others, win-lose
attitudes, owning and controlling of tasks, rationality, and suppression of
negative feelings. Model 1 organizations are theories-in-use that maximize
interpersonal defenses and minimize learning. Model 1 organizational
cultures are based upon single-loop learning—learning that involves altering strategies but not values and norms.

Model 2, in contrast, is a theory of action governed by values that include
valid information, bilateral protection of self and others, shared tasks and
responsibilities, and acknowledgment of negative feelings. In model 2,
conflict is not seen as negative but as an opportunity to solve problems and
learn. Assumptions and attributions are publicly tested rather than held
privately. Model 2 theories of action promote collaboration, information
sharing, and minimal interpersonal defenses. Model 2 is a reflective organizational culture perpetuated by the capacity of individuals and their systems
to double-loop learn—learning that questions and changes, if necessary,
underlying values and norms. The case examples of organizational consultations presented in Part II illustrate the psychological difficulties inherent in
moving organization cultures from model 1 to model 2 theories of action. In
contrast to Argyris and Schon, from a psychoanalytic perspective, one pays
attention to the resistance to change stemming from anxiety associated with
the tension between personal security and learning, and thereby addresses the
emotional investment of members in defensive organizations. This focus is
further illuminated in the case examples and discussions of organizational
consultation in Part II.

As a result of the complexity of large organizations, which include
multiple layers of authority, responsibility, and tasks, groups emerge as
subcultures with relatively distinct identities, our next topic.

Groups as Subcultures

In addition to a leader's characteristic response to stress and anxiety, organizational cultures and subcultures are driven by underlying basic assumptions. Wilfred Bion's (1959) pioneering work, *Experiences in Groups*, taught us that every work group comprises at least two groups— the explicit task group and the implicit basic assumption group. According to Bion, these groups may or may not be compatible at any given time and, frequently, the unconsciously driven basic assumption group sabotages the more consciously driven task group.

Applying Bion's model of groups, we can identify three possible subcultures within work groups of the organization. They include the following basic assumptions: dependency, pairing, and fight-flight. In the *dependency subculture* members desire a leader to protect and care for them. In the *pairing subculture* members focus on the relationship of two other members whose potential merger represents a sense of hope and rebirth. In the *fight-flight subculture* members search for a leader to take them into flight from or into battle against a common enemy.

Multiple and diverse basic assumption groups, or subcultures, may exist in large organizations. Greater autonomy and independence of each group from the central authority structure contribute to a subculture's differentiation from the larger organizational culture. In most organizations, however, central authority patterns determine group subcultures, and the ways in which groups adapt to critical incidents become highly significant in comprehending the overall organizational culture—what I call organizational identity and discuss at length in the next chapter. Chapter 9, for instance, offers a case in which executives and managers share a common fight-flight basic assumption that promotes conflict avoidance and abdication of leadership responsibilities.

Before concluding our discussion of organizational culture with an examination of humor and play at work, we briefly discuss the influence of an organization's host culture—the sociocultural, economic, and political arena of the organization's task environment.

Host Culture

Organizations are dependent upon their surrounding environments for employees, clients, customers, and so forth. Organizational leadership must effectively adapt to the sociocultural, economic, and political nature of that environment. The prognosis for organizational survival is, in part, determined by executive awareness of organizational culture and its fit with the host culture. The ability of organizational leadership to read changes in the environment effectively and then communicate and discuss those changes with the staff is critical.

The host culture may also define the social class and ethnic origins of employees joining the organization as well as clients and customers it serves. In addition, the host culture represents the character of the political climate of an organization, the degree to which it is friendly or hostile. Leadership sensitivity to the nuances of host culture assures the continued openness of the organization as part of a larger social system.

Often overlooked in the literature on organizational culture is the role of humor and play at work. In the next section, I examine this truly psychodynamic dimension of organizational culture.

HUMOR AND PLAY AS UNCONSCIOUS FEATURES OF ORGANIZATIONAL CULTURE

Let's begin by quoting Freud (1928: 9: 2):

There is no doubt that the essence of humour is that one spares oneself the affects to which the situation would naturally give rise and overrides with a jest the possibility of such an emotional display.

The principal thing is the intention which humour fulfills, whether it concerns the subject's self or other people. Its meaning is: "Look here! This is all that this seemingly dangerous world amounts to. Child's play—the very thing to jest about!" (5)

In his essay "Humour," Freud appears to suggest that humor is a competent and playful defense against anxiety. In Freudian terms, humor works by shifting psychic energy away from the ego and its preoccupation with the external world and reality testing, and toward the parental superego, in effect, liberating the pleasure principle of the id. In the passage quoted Freud describes the comic attitude in which the subject treats himself or herself, others, and life circumstances as if they were "child's play"—what psychoanalyst D. W. Winnicott (1971) calls the potential space between reality and fantasy, and between mother (parent) and infant.[2]

Keeping in mind that child's play is at the same time serious and not serious, Freud seems to have captured the reason why people at work and elsewhere rely on humor to cope with stressful and conflictual situations and to communicate messages of an emotional nature—psychological distance. That observation is confirmed by much of the organizational literature on humor (Kahn, 1989; Roy, 1960; Duncan and Feisal, 1989; Collinson, 1988; Wicker, et al., 1980). Organization members regularly distance themselves, psychologically, from conflict, oppression, stress, and boredom at work by joking with one another. This differs from denial.

Some may assume that Freud's notion of humor and joking represents a denial of reality, and therefore a psychopathology of sorts. My reading of Freud, however, suggests that he views humor as a sign of emotional well-being or, at the very least, as a manner of adaptation to an often frustrating environment. Humor is defined as consisting principally of the recognition and expression of incongruities or peculiarities present in a situation or character. It is frequently used to illustrate some fundamental absurdity in human nature or conduct (646). This definition parallels the ideas of Freud and others on the role of humor in psychologically distancing the subject and object of jest; the individual with a sense of humor steps back from the emotionality of relationships and situations and views them from the observer's vantage point.[3] That way the incongruities, peculiarities, and absurdities can emerge in a hilarious light. Humor is the ability to laugh at one's own absurdities, to be the butt of a joke as well as the comic.

For example, at an executive retreat that concluded several months of organizational intervention, I (the consultant) found myself making a joke via a slip of the tongue. As we opened the final day of a two-day retreat and a relatively successful organizational development effort, I addressed the group that morning by asking each of the divisions to share their findings. I began by addressing the first presenter as the "department of ___." This brought on a loud burst of collective laughter from the participants. To an outsider this response would be incomprehensible. But to my clients it was very funny. Why? I was hired to help them establish linkages, improve integration among units, and develop among the many divisions a shared common identity as one whole Department of Transportation. Their conflicted history was marked by divisiveness and identity with and loyalty to the division, not the department. Each division viewed itself as an autonomous entity, independent of a larger hierarchical entity—what they had referred to disparagingly as "THE DEPARTMENT!" After months of overcoming barriers and resistance between and among them, you can imagine their levity in response to my slip of the tongue. Participant laughter was then followed by playful hissing directed, of course, at me. The jovial interlude released much tension regarding the forthcoming presentations of sensitive problem areas to their director. The presentations turned into dramaturgical performances in a frolicsome climate. Psychological distance from the task was achieved, enabling the participants to communicate ideas they had never before transmitted to a superior.

Psychodynamically, humor is a way of reestablishing ego (self-other) boundaries. It puts necessary distance and protection between oneself and one's internalization of others and the events that may consume them. It enables one to limit anxiety and therefore minimize defensive responses in others. That is why humor is a popular psychological device for coping with conflicts, errors, disappointments, and change in organizations. It introduces an element of play into an often all too somber workplace. Collinson (1988), in "Engineering Humour: Masculinity, Joking and Conflict in Shop-Floor Relations," shows how the "joking culture" not only defines boundaries between groups but also creates divisions within them. Joking becomes a part of the subculture, defining who is in and who is out. For better or worse, humor helps to demarcate groups and stakeholders within a hierarchy.

A sense of humor and the expression of laughter signify a desire to obtain psychological distance from the object of amusement. Joking about oneself, another, or collective circumstances is intended to discourage us from taking ourselves and the external world too seriously. Humor can create an atmosphere of play in a disappointing reality or a necessary emotional detachment from conflict to allow resolution. Or, at the least, it can buy time. While humor in the workplace can promote a shared identity and culture through a sense of belonging to a joking culture—being in on the joke—organization members commonly use it to "defuse psychological threats" to their self-image (Kahn, 1989).

Humor, unlike other forms of communication, makes possible the delivery of affective messages in a way that allows them to be received rather than resisted. Kahn explains, "It enables people to say things that, if said directly, would make others feel hurt and defensive and would threaten relationships" (1989: 50). It also allows people to decide for themselves the meaning of the message. Although humor is intended to limit seriousness, it is often a pretext for delivering a very solemn message.

In his article "Toward a Sense of Organizational Humor: Implications for Organizational Diagnosis and Change," Kahn (1989) lists five uses of humor in organizations: coping, reframing, communicating, expressing hostility, and constructing identities. First, joking on the job helps members to cope with unwelcome circumstances and disappointments. Second, humor can be used to challenge the status quo of thinking and acting in organizations by altering perceptions of roles, for example: what we call *reframing*. Third, humor helps people to communicate affective messages by promoting a degree of amusement and distance from the message, encouraging the receiver to take it less seriously. Fourth, wit and sarcasm are often ways in which individuals express hostility at work, sometimes with "disparaging humor" (Wicker et al., 1980). Fifth, humor is an element of culture in organizations like myths, ideologies, and values; it can promote a joking culture in which what appears funny to those on the inside may not to those outside the institution—hence constructing a shared identity.

Underlying these types of humor at work is the subject's attempt to protect herself or himself and others from the effects of anxiety. Humor is not an ordinary defense against anxiety, however. It has, as Freud points out, "a liberating element" (1928: 2). "Humor is not resigned, it is rebellious" (1928: 3). In his discussion of the use of humor in expressing hostility, Kahn (1989) refers to Hochschild's example of a flight attendant's exchange with a passenger. Kahn intends to show how humor can undermine prevailing group dynamics among organization and identity groups (1989: 52–53). I think it's a good illustration of the rebellious side of humor and its frame-breaking potential.

> A young businessman said to a flight attendant, "Why aren't you smiling?" She put her tray back on the food cart, looked him in the eye, and said, "I'll tell you what. You smile first, then I'll smile." The businessman smiled at her. "Good," she replied. "Now freeze and hold that smile for fifteen hours." Then she walked away. In one stroke, the heroine not only asserted a personal right to her facial expressions but also reversed the role in the company script by placing the mask on a member of the audience. (Kahn, 1989: 127)

Joking in the workplace may contribute to error detection and problem solving. Why? Because humor is a medium for acknowledging mixed messages and incongruities. It pokes fun at human imperfections and absurdities while protecting individuals from psychological insecurities and anxiety resulting from damage to self-esteem and self-confidence. Its indirect and playful nature liberates both subject and object from responsibility for sending and receiving the message. It frees people to decide for themselves whether or not they wish to deal with a problem or issue. Humor can be a valuable defensive action, one that enables people to communicate "difficult to hear" messages.

In my role of organizational consultant, I find that dissatisfaction and disappointment are more readily shared when packaged in humor or sarcasm. One agency executive declared in jest to the consultant and in the presence of his boss that his (the executive's) people were spending their time at work playing sophisticated war games on their recently acquired computers. His underlying message was, Why didn't your (the boss's) staff consult us on our computing needs before they purchased this expensive and useless hardware?

In addition to serving communication, humor assists employees in adapting to routine. For instance, Roy (1960) observes in "Banana Time: Job Satisfaction and Informal Interaction" that humor is a language for sharing feelings about relationships at work and coping with boredom. Roy found that one group of machine operators actually produced a set of joking norms and procedures that structured the workday and helped them cope with potential conflict and stress. These joking events were "ritualized" by one worker's stealing the banana of another to signify the start of a comedic interlude. This would occur every day at nearly the same time—what Roy called "banana time." Elaborating on Roy's observations, Kahn (1989) argues, "The communicating function of humor works partly by acknowledging the existence of various issues without pointing directly at them" (50). For the machine operators, it was "the beast" of monotony. This might be described as discussing that which is undiscussable by not really discussing it: in other words, diplomacy cloaked in jest in which the receiver may decide the intent of the message for himself or herself.

So far I have emphasized that humor in the workplace is a competent and playful defense against anxiety. It aids in the communication of difficult messages by diminishing tension with laughter. There are many situations at work that stimulate joking among members as an avenue of coping with uncertainties, conflicts, and disappointments. Humor operates by distancing the subject and the object of jest from the content of the subject matter itself.

Humor, like other cultural experiences, is what D. W. Winnicott calls a potential space[4] originally located between mother (parent) and infant and is fundamentally a form of play that is as helpful to adults in large organizations as it is for children trying to cope with the anxieties of separation and individuation.

Play at Work: Humor as Transitional Phenomenon

Humor is more than a defense against the stress and anxiety of membership in large organizations. Joking on the job interjects play into work. It is a cultural experience located in Winnicott's potential space between the individual and the environment, and "between the subjective object and the object objectively perceived" (1971: 100). This potential space is where playing and creativity occur. Comedy, like music, art, dreams, and religion, originates from the use that was made of this potential space in early childhood. Winnicott refers to these infantile events, objects, and self-other relationships as transitional objects and transitional phenomena.

Transitional objects are the infant's first possessions:

Winnicott saw their normal development as a sequence of mouthing activities followed by attachment primarily to such soft objects as blankets, dolls, and teddy bears. These attachments usually develop between four and twelve months and indicate the child's capacity to create, however protosymbolically, the mental concept of an object, thereby alleviating the normal developmental stress of separation-individuation. . . . Whereas transitional objects are tangible, portable objects, transitional phenomena are activities or products of activities: mannerisms, behavior patterns, images." (Grolnick et al., 1978: 547–48)

Children commonly use dolls or teddy bears to express hostility. For example, in response to the recent birth of a sibling, the child may say, "Teddy wants to eat the baby!" Or, the child may abuse the doll in play as an avenue to express his or her feelings of rivalry with the new family member.

Humor produces in the comic and his or her audience a potential space for relief from stress and anxiety, and freedom for the play of imagination. People use humor in the workplace, whether wittingly or unwittingly, in a manner reminiscent of a baby's need for his or her teddy bear or security blanket. Humor at work routinely arises at moments of uncertainty, confrontation, and insecurity. Joking and associated laughter diminish anxieties and insecurities at tense moments. Similarly, a baby clutches his or her teddy to cope with separation anxieties and to experiment with independence and individuation.

The adult's sense of humor stems from the character of play in early childhood. Its usefulness in coping with systemic transitions is evident in work organizations undergoing change. For example, a deputy director of a public agency, which underwent a substantial expansion of its budget and personnel, found himself clinging to ineffective routines. Despite the acceleration of projects, he continued to take responsibility for personally reviewing each. His clinging to inadequate procedures within radically changed circumstances and his resistance to change suggested that he was using routines and procedures as transitional phenomena. The deputy director's embrace of the bureaucratic process was an adaptive, transitional act. Once, with the aid of a sarcastic consultant,[5] he stepped back from his resistance to change and viewed it with some sense of amusement and irony, he showed evidence of a readiness for renewal.

Comedy on the job, momentarily, removes oneself and others from the rationalization and routinization of work relations and into a potential space in which organization members can safely experiment with new ideas, feelings, and thoughts. When a work group collectively participates in the construction of that space, an immeasurable opportunity for coping, learning, change, and development arises. Trust among group members, or between subordinates and superiors, is essential to the creation of potential space in organizations. Trust is critical to the establishment of a playful experience in which participants willingly take risks.

Organization members will not form a potential space for the expression of ideas, in comedic form or any other, unless they are certain that their jobs are secure and that they will not be the object of retribution or punishment of any kind. Job security and the structure of power relations at work may be contributing factors as significant to the expression of humor as trust. Like the holding environment of parent and infant, the organization must nurture play and creativity. That can only occur in a climate of trust and mutual respect. The relative success of organization development retreats and consultations in which participants meet outside the workplace is, in part, due to the construction of a potential space for reflection and learning.

SUMMARY

Organizational culture is ultimately a product of the ways in which participants interact at work. Components of organizational culture, both explicit and implicit—artifacts, formalities and informalities, socialization and indoctrination, rituals, myths, espoused and practiced theories of action, leadership personalities, groups as subcultures, host cultures, organizational history, and humor and play at work—contribute to organizational design, strategy, and productivity. Leadership and group dynamics are essential variables in assessing organizational culture. However, the shared meaning of organizational life cannot be adequately captured with conventional treatments of organizational culture. There is more to it than that.

Organizational culture itself originates from unconscious relational patterns (structures of intersubjectivity) between and among organizational members. These unconscious structures are precultural and intrapsychic at their roots. They shape organizational culture and the manner in which leaders and followers cope with internal and external pressures.

By assuming that all relationships which characterize groups and organizations involve the transmission of transference and countertransference dynamics, the observer of organizational culture reaches unconscious layers of experience and, thereby, better understands organizational life. To deepen our appreciation of the psychodynamics of organizational culture, in Chapter 4, I turn to the concept of organizational identity—the foundation of organizational culture.

NOTES

1. See Baum (1990), for a psychodynamic perspective on organizational socialization and unconscious issues surrounding affiliation and membership.

2. Winnicott's notion of the potential space refers to the psychological space between reality and fantasy in which play and imagination occur. It is within this psychological space that the child learns to adjust and adapt to the external world of objects. Moreover, it is within this space that the child first interacts with culture, whether music, art, literature, or the sandbox.

3. Harry Stack Sullivan's notion in *The Psychiatric Interview* (1954) of the role of participant-observer is parallel, as is Anna Freud's conception of the observing-ego. Both frames of mind are viewed as therapeutic, reflective, and signifying mental health.

4. *Potential space* is "the metaphorical space between infant and mother while differentiation of self- and object-representations is incomplete—or, more positively, while the infant is hatching from the dual unity or symbiotic membrane. It is within potential space that the transitional process occurs, and from which emerge transitional objects and transitional phenomena and the capacity for illusion, play, and the creative imagination. Potential space meshes seamlessly with the developmental use of actual space. . . . The terms *intermediate area*, *third world*, and *third area* are earlier versions of Winnicott's more definitive concept" (Grolnick et al., 1978: 545).

5. The consultant, for instance, quipped, "Ever feel like you're sitting on the dock, watching your ship leave harbor without you?" The deputy director laughed and then replied, "Yes, but this time I'm holding the anchor!" In jest, the deputy communicated an appreciation of the need for change, which he had previously resisted, and insight into his role in obstructing that change.

4

ORGANIZATIONAL IDENTITY

This chapter introduces the concept of *organizational identity*, which I generally define as the unconscious foundation for organizational culture. More specifically, it is the totality of repetitive patterns of individual behavior and interpersonal relationships that, when taken together, comprise the unacknowledged meaning of organizational life. Organizational identity is influenced by conscious thought; however, its relational patterns among individuals at work are primarily motivated by unconscious thoughts and feelings. Its foundation rests with the transference of emotions beneath organizational structure.

Organizational identity differs, most sharply, from organizational culture because of the prominent role of transference phenomena. The nature of emotional attachments and connectedness, or disconnectedness, is the footing of organizational life and the essense of organizational identity. The centrality of this emotional substructure is especially crucial when there is demand for organizational change and development. Change depends on members' willingness to assume responsibility for their actions and to depart from the status quo. But this willingness is the result of mutual understanding of shared emotions between superordinates and subordinates, and often among peers in organizations, and is the outcome of their recognition of unconscious expectations and desires. Helping members to become aware of the structure of organizational identity and their place in it is a precondition for freeing them up for organizational change that is strategically sound and productive. Under stress we often get a glance at that which organizational identity conceals and that which it truly comprises. Often the disposition of organizational identity is revealed by acts of management, by intimidation, scapegoating, interpersonal and intergroup conflict, avoidance of organizational problems, and personal responsibilities. These and other signifiers of organizational identity are illustrated in the case examples in Part II.

Coming to know the identity of organizations evokes the personal meaning, experience, and perception of organizational life in the minds of individual members. Gaining access to members' organizational experience helps us better understand individual and collective motives that govern their behavior and enables us to distinguish otherwise similar organizations from one another. Organizational identity defines who we all are in a group and who (or what) we can be as members of groups (role identity). This includes the network of repeated interpersonal strategies for coping with (defending against) interpersonal and organizational events that are stressful and perceived as threatening.

Organizational identity may be found in the difficult to observe interactions within organizations—the intersubjective structure of what Heinz Kohut calls *selfobject* relationships.[1] Discovering it involves finding out how people experience one another and observing how they handle themselves and others under stressful circumstances. It does not assume that people in organizations share the same organizational image. Nor does it assume a collective identity for organizational members. However, it does imply that organizational culture and strategies for managing internal and external affairs are the result of members' individual personalities and experiences that shape organizational meanings and experiences.

The concept of organizational identity is not entirely new.[2] Psychoanalytic organizational theorists and consultants, however, do not always have similar conceptions of organizational identity even when they set their sights on the same phenomenon. Levinson and Weinbaum emphasize the role of the ego ideal in organizational identification, and Larcon and Reitter stress major themes upon which the organizational identity is based (Kets de Vries, 1984). Organizational identity represents the means by which work groups orient themselves toward the organization and from which individuals acquire their own sense of security and identity as members.

Through the lens of organizational identity, I wish to contribute to the organization theorists' and administrative practitioners' ways of thinking about and seizing hold of the intersubjective data they collect in the process of working in and investigating organizations. To understand organizational identity fully, we need to consider the psychological origins of the concept.

PSYCHOLOGICAL ORIGINS OF ORGANIZATIONAL IDENTITY

From Individual to Organizational Identity

Speaking of individual identity, Erik Erikson links psyche, culture, and history with individual fate:

> The key problem of identity, then, is (as the term connotes) the capacity of the ego to sustain sameness and continuity in the face of changing fate. But fate always combines changes in inner conditions, which are the result of ongoing life stages, and changes in the milieu, the historical situation. Identity connotes the resiliency of maintaining essential patterns in the process of change. Thus, strange as it may seem, it takes a well-established identity to tolerate radical change, for the well-established identity has arranged itself around basic values which cultures have in common. (1964: 95–96)

Organizational culture rests upon organizational identity topographically just as the conscious rests upon, and is a compromise formation to, the conflicting claims of the unconscious. Organizational identity is, then, a compromise formation to contradictory aims of organizational participants. It is a product of organizational culture and history, member psychology, and the psychology of past and present leaders and followers. It consists of repetitive structures of intersubjectivity found in relationships between superiors and subordinates, which are primarily driven by unconscious assumptions and expectations that influence organizational decisions and actions. When something goes wrong between people in organizations, it can be traced to the psychological bonds and tensions between them. The case illustration presented in Chapter 9 shows the extent to which an organization's problems are rooted in a conflicted organizational identity with conscious and unconscious dimensions. Getting at the unconscious psychological dimensions of the conflicted organizational identity, however, is essential to restoring fully organizational effectiveness.

Individual feelings about organizational membership are rooted in infancy. Winnicott (1965) speaks of the *holding environment*, referring to the initial bond between mother and child. An explanation of interpersonal relationships grounded in adulthood but with origins in infancy and childhood is similarly offered by Kohut (1977; 1984), who speaks of early grounding in narcissistic or selfobject transferences. In uncovering organizational identity, the interpreter finds transference of emotions a valuable focus for observing and explaining key interpersonal relationships between organizational superordinates and their subordinates, among organizational peers, and between organizational consultants and their clients. Such relationships are grounded in the unconscious ambitions, ideals, conflicts, and fantasies of parties to the relationship.

The Holding Environment of Infancy and Organizational Identity

As noted, the psychological origins of the concept of organizational identity can be traced to the holding environment of infancy (Winnicott, 1965). The childhood holding environment influences behavior in organizations, and, equally significantly, the holding environment of organizations influences human behavior and adult development. The holding environment of infancy may be regarded as the first organizational matrix of the developing self. The infant's life in that environment is its first experience with the human artifact called organization. Both infancy and organizational life engage the individual in a manipulation and negotiation of self-other (self-object) boundaries, answering questions ranging from Who am I? to What needs do others fulfill? Distinguishing and clarifying oneself from others is a central task of infancy and childhood, as it is an ongoing activity, conscious and unconscious, of organizational members. The subjective experience of organizational identity is grounded in the earliest of tensions between the individual (infant) and the organization (parental selfobject): The experiences are need and desire, trust and mistrust, fulfillment and denial, independence and dependence, attachment, separation and loss, to name a few.

The beginnings of organizational identity are rooted in babies' first awareness of themselves as separate from others, an awareness that results in feelings of ambivalence about dependence and self-identity as well as separation anxiety. The degree of success of separation and individuation depends upon the adequacy of the child's original holding environment and the establishment of object constancy—the quality of "good enough" parenting. Babies must feel secure and safe enough in their parents' presence to practice their newly discovered autonomy and independence. Object constancy implies the need for reliability and authenticity of parenting (good enough) during children's transition from attachment to separation to individuation (Winnicott, 1965; Mahler et al., 1975). The importance of these phases of development requires further elaboration.

An adequate or good enough holding environment consists of parental empathy in mirroring and idealizing responses to the needs of infants' nascent self. Parents satisfy infants' narcissistic needs for self-affirmation (mirroring) and merger with greatness, strength, and calmness (idealization) by a willingness and ability to react authentically and compassionately to the babies' preverbal cues. Parents can help infants' cognitive and emotional development by establishing a secure and relatively anxiety-free attachment from which babies can separate and individuate with confidence. Consequently, parental availability for safety and contact comfort facilitates babies' sense of themselves as separate from loving parents, and, therefore, as separate from others and the environment—establishing healthy boundaries between self and others.

In contrast to the positive holding environment, an insecure and unresponsive holding environment will not satisfy babies' primary narcissistic requirements. Infants' needs for safety and security may be unmet. In some unfortunate instances, parents demand that infants respond to their (the parents') previously frustrated narcissism. The parents come to depend upon the child for their self-esteem, rather than the reverse. Narcissistic parents are not emotionally accessible to their children. They unconsciously coerce children, through projective identification,[3] into meeting their exaggerated needs for self-assurance. This set of circumstances sets the stage for an anxious attachment between infants and parents. It further compromises infants' efforts toward separation and individuation, frustrating relative independence and autonomy.

When intense feelings of ambivalence and separation anxiety are experienced, and the relationship between parents and infants becomes filled with uncertainty, differentiation between self and others, self and environment, becomes confused and (self-other) boundaries become blurred. The emerging self is, then, depleted, without the necessary narcissistic supplies for individuation and self-esteem. As a result, a false self emerges that intends to protect the emerging true self, now filled with rage and loss due to frustrated narcissism and separation anxiety.

John Bowlby (1979) describes the prolonged dependency of infancy as *attachment behavior* in which the infant clings to and follows the mother. From the beginning of life, this universal human condition sets the stage for a dynamic and contradictory psychological structure of selfhood. Selfhood encapsulates the dilemma of self identity in that it merges from a dialectical process of separation and individuation, differentiation and integration. The dilemma may be described as the ability, simultaneously, to be intimate and separate from the other. Adult interactions are, therefore, bound to renew feelings of attachment, separation, loss, and anxiety that promote the splitting up or repression of such feelings. These phenomena are often viewed psychodynamically as forms of repetition-compulsion, or simply the compulsion to repeat earlier conditions. The outcome of these adult human interactions is unconsciously affected by the interpersonal quality of the relationship.

For example, a subordinate has unconscious expectations of his superordinate. These expectations may originate in his frustrated need for idealization during childhood, where his need to merge with greatness was unfulfilled. The painful disappointment is pushed out of conscious awareness, repressed, until a significant adult relationship revives the desire to merge with someone of strength and calmness. The subordinate comes to admire his supervisor, perceiving the "superior" as superhuman and infallible. Inevitably, his idealized supervisor makes mistakes and exposes human imperfections. This results in the subordinate's feeling enraged and depressed. The subordinate's desire to merge with greatness is once again frustrated. His rage and depression are linked to his experience as a child, when he perceived the holding environment between parent and child as fragile and insecure.

From the observer's point of view, such reactions seem inappropriate to the present adult circumstances. However, they are legitimate, rooted in past experience that shapes perceptions and expectations of others' roles at work. The individual enters the organization with personality in place and, therefore, carries unconscious demands to be made on others. These are the elements of what psychoanalysts call the transference of emotions, and most clinicians believe the phenomenon is not exclusive to the analyst-patient relationship. As in this case, transference is often an expression of what Heinz Kohut describes as frustrated narcissistic (selfobject) needs or narcissistic injury that results in damaged self-integrity and lowered self-esteem. Organizational hierarchy is the context in which the psychodynamics of transference are triggered at work.

In sum, organizational identity is a framework for interpreting organizational feelings and experiences based upon self and other relations. In addition, it is a theory which guides action researchers[4] in the practice of analyzing self and other relations in organizational settings. Its grounding premise is that the model for understanding unconscious adult actions in organizations may be found in the dynamics of self-other relations in infancy and childhood. Similar to the role of parenting in establishing a safe and what Winnicott calls a good enough holding environment for the emergence of babies' sense of self, the organizational environment of the adult may either help or hurt self-esteem and, consequently, satisfy or frustrate normal narcissistic needs of members. The psychological dilemmas of organizational membership may, thereby, revive infant anxieties.

TRANSFERENCE PHENOMENA IN ORGANIZATIONAL HIERARCHIES

Organizational identity is understood by analyzing transference and countertransference of emotions, vertically between superordinates and subordinates and horizontally among organizational members during group and interpersonal responses to critical incidents. To appreciate fully the contribution of organizational identity to our understanding of organizational culture, three patterns of transference (and countertransference) in organizations need to be examined: (1) mirroring and idealizing, (2) twinship (alterego), and (3) persecutory. I begin with a discussion of understanding organizational identity in action research and then present a description of the various transferences among organizational members.

Understanding Organizational Identity

Attention to the emotional attachments of human relationships, such as that found between superordinates and subordinates, is at the heart of psychodynamic investigations of behavior in organizations. These hierarchic interactions are often filled with many reenactments of the dependency, attachment, separation, and individuation dilemmas of parent-infant relations.

The analysis of transference in organizations involves the assembly of a coherent image of interpersonal patterns of human interactions. Organizational researchers must, momentarily, shift the center of experience away from themselves so that they may truly comprehend the experience of organizational members (Kohut, 1977; 1984). Empathy is acquired through identification. That is, one must place himself or herself in the shoes of organizational members, laced in their experience of themselves and others as part of a shared organizational culture. In this manner, organizational researchers can acquire a meaningful and subjectively valid interpretive understanding of interpersonal and organizational dynamics.

In describing psychoanalytic organizational research, I approach transference and countertransference phenomena in the manner that Heinz Kohut and the proponents of self psychology do. That is, the action researcher applies empathy and introspection as his or her method of establishing a trusting and productive relationship with clients. Consequently, the researcher's position relative to his or her subjects is one of what Kohut calls *experience near* in contrast to the more orthodox psychoanalytic *experience far* position, in which the analyst is viewed as a blank screen for the analysand's projections and displacements.[5] Kohut stresses the importance of working with the subjective experience of the other. In that spirit, I argue that the psychoanalytically oriented action researcher's position is best described as experience near.

Interpretation of individual and collective organizational meanings is the avenue to understanding organizational identity. With respect to transference and countertransference dynamics, psychoanalytic action researchers learn to use themselves (the self as the core of the personality and interpersonal experience) as instruments of organizational study. Empathy and introspection become necessary skills in helping subjects to share feelings and ideas that previously could not be discussed.

The validity of the intersubjective data uncovered by the analysis of transference and countertransference phenomena in organizations also depends upon the psychoanalytic researcher's willingness to test his or her assumptions of the subject's experiences and perceptions publicly. This requires that researchers attempt to confirm or refute interpretations acquired through self-conscious acts of identification and empathy. Psychoanalytic organizational researchers pay special attention to transferences that are repetitive, psychologically regressive, and counterproductive. As Kets de Vries and Miller suggest, "The focus is on clusters of behavior that remain relatively stable over the years, as opposed to simple dimensions of behavior" (1984: 18). Transference dynamics are also observed in the role ambiguities and interpersonal distortions and misperceptions common among organizational members. Invalid and privately held assumptions about superiors and subordinates are often the result of underlying transference dynamics. Organizational researchers need to be present in organizations during critical moments in which emotional connections among members are readily observable and more easily interpreted.

How do transference dynamics contribute to negative and dysfunctional organizational identity? One's perception of the organization and his or her role identity in it is directly linked to the nature of interpersonal relationships between and among organizational participants. Authority and peer relations may rekindle frustrated (infantile, selfobject) narcissistic needs among adults in work organizations. Stressful organizational events such as change in leadership, retrenchment, cutbacks, policy or budgetary revisions, and shifts of political climate can foster psychologically regressive and defensive responses among members. These responses take the form of transference and countertransference relational patterns between and among participants. Reactions to stress are highly individual but, inevitably, are worked through at the interpersonal, group, and organizational levels of experience. Hence, organizational identity is the outcome of a collective compromise formation and analysis of transference between and among organizational members, and compromise formation and transference are the key to understanding these phenomena. At this point, we need to examine the various patterns of transference, such as mirroring and idealizing, twinship, and persecutory self and other relations.

Mirroring and Idealizing Transference in Organizations

Despite recent alterations in organization design, most organizations are hierarchies. In fact, hierarchically channeled human interactions encourage mirroring and idealizing exchanges between superordinates and subordinates. The power of high position may exaggerate individual demands for admiration and feelings of grandiosity. The presence of hierarchies may perpetuate selecting and rewarding individuals with narcissistic proclivities, thereby indulging quests for power and authority by way of positions of public visibility and official importance. Similarly, executives may come to rely on their staff to mirror their larger-than-life view of themselves. Consequently, staff are unconsciously required to idealize the boss, to inflate his or her public image and sustain his or her self-worth.

A mirroring and idealizing transference between leader and followers can, consequently, mold or reinforce the preexisting authoritarian culture of organization. Institutional values, myths, ideologies, and other components of organizational culture are selected and rearranged to reflect narcissistically driven authority relations. Such idealization of organizational leadership produces a culture of organizational perfectionism in which the detection and correction of errors are unlikely. Governed by narcissistic values of grandiosity at the top, these organizations encourage the denial of human imperfections: the "system" comes to be viewed as flawless and ideal. In such instances, the organizational identity becomes a social defense system (or what I call an *externalized self-system*) against the anxiety of confronting problems that must be denied in order to maintain the "perfect state of narcissism." The case of NASA and the space shuttle disaster is an example of organizational narcissism that Howard Schwartz (1991) discusses in his book, *Narcissistic Process and Corporate Decay: The Theory of the Organizational Ideal.* Moreover, the case example presented in Chapter 7 illustrates this phenomenon with a deputy director who demands "perfect performance" from his staff.

Mirroring and idealizing are two sides of the same pattern of human interaction. Mirror transferences derive from infantile needs for acceptance. If these needs are frustrated in adulthood, managers may strive to support their narcissistic deficits by surrounding themselves with admiring and loyal subordinates. Depending upon the degree of narcissistic injury and deficiency of adequate mirroring, mirror-hungry managers may develop leadership styles that are autocratic, paternalistic, and authoritarian. Subordinates are expected to admire their managers and appear to be forced into a position of overdependence upon them. In these circumstances, staff loyalty and admiration encourage idealized images of their managers, which distort staff capacity to recognize limitations. Staff members may respond by becoming false and inauthentic. The superior's overdetermined needs for admiration are then internalized by subordinates in the form of attitudes of conformity—"I will be as you desire me" (Sullivan, 1953).

In such instances, organizational subordinates become preoccupied with meeting the confirmation needs of managers. The childhood parallel of this is found among young children who must respond to their parents' narcissistic needs in the inadequate holding environment, the origins of what Winnicott calls a false self. In adulthood, this sort of role conformity is indicative of human interactions in organizational hierarchies where managers unwittingly perpetuate inauthentic behavior among workers. The organizational costs of this false self-system are great. In particular, organizational members become preoccupied with saving face and camouflage. Consequently, problems are ignored and errors are not detected. Few workers are willing to risk losing the organizational mask that conceals human imperfections.

Transference is reciprocal. For example, the manager takes on the leadership role with extraordinary needs for acceptance and recognition from earlier deprivations. Subordinates respond with admiration and praise, or they are eliminated or marginalized as undesirables. Managers unwittingly seek out staff members with needs for merging with perceived greatness, strength, and calmness—a merger relationship that will satisfy their (subordinates') hunger for idealization. In this instance, organizational identity is predicated on a mirror-hungry leadership style. Managers unconsciously require staff who are in search of some form of omnipotent authority. Such managers encourage and require this idealization. Eventually, staff members psychologically merge with their leaders' imagined power. They are "someone" because they share in the manager's power. In return, leaders receive love, admiration, and loyalty.

Persecutory Transference in Organizations

People in organizations may find themselves operating in hostile settings. Ways leaders and followers cope with unfriendly environments differ. Some are able to recognize the aggressive actions of others as a political reality of organizational life. For instance, public agencies with relatively large budgets find themselves greatly politicized and scrutinized by legislators and their oversight committees. Heads of those agencies are continuously defending themselves and their organizations to those who control allocations and require accountability. Many organizational executives adapt well and understand the political democratic nature of these adversarial relations.

However, in many public organizations, politically appointed officials and civil servant executives never adapt or learn to work effectively under these circumstances. They act as if they never anticipated the suspicious attitudes of legislators and many public interest groups. They come to feel victimized and, in turn, may take out their aggression on their staff. Aggression need not be active; it can take the form of passive neglect. For example, administrators may slight the details of internal management by communicating less frequently with their staff or by leaving decisions and interpretations of key directives up to their staff. If they do communicate with staff, they may do so ambiguously, causing second-guessing and conflicts among staff members. Executives may also become highly distrustful of their staff. Consequently, they may devise strategies for testing loyalties of staff members so that they may distinguish allies and enemies from within the ranks. At the very least, they encourage organizational members to perceive themselves only as victims, thus discouraging personal responsibility. Some members may come to identify with their leader, regardless of the mistreatment and suspicious nature of her or his relationship. Persecuted organizations become fortresses, social defense systems that encourage the troops either to retreat from battle or to engage in a "search and destroy" mission. The fortress mentality is costly. Blame and responsibility always seem to exist outside oneself and often outside the organization. The persecuted organization is nearly always on the defensive.

Twinship (Alterego) Transference in Organizations

People often join organizations seeking friendship and collegiality in addition to a paycheck. Some want to belong to an organization of like-minded men and women. There they also expect to find leaders to whom they can relate and with whom they can identify. On the cultural level, this means leaders and peers who have common interests, values, and goals; on the psychological level, it means organizations dominated by patterns of twinship transference in which organizational participants look to each other as mentors and alteregos, or kindred spirits. The desire to merge with the sameness of the other is the overarching theme of this organization's adaptive response to its environment.

On the positive side of the transference equation, twinship dynamics promote teamwork and a commitment to placing oneself in the shoes of the other. This intermediate area of skills and talents holds together (Kohut, 1984) the *bipolar self*—a continuum in which at one end are located ambitions, which coincide with the mirror transference, and at the other are located ideals, which coincide with the idealizing transference. The twinship (or alterego) transference reaffirms the individual's self-competence and self-confidence, which are crucial factors in the self-esteem of organizational members. Organizations dominated by twinship transferences and alterego relational patterns offer participants greater opportunities for personal and career development. Such organizations tend to be more responsive to changing environments because of their commitment to training and learning.

Yet, there is a negative side. In contrast to the mirroring-idealizing and persecutory transferences, the twinship transference seems to have many positive attributes, such as an investment in mentoring and training. However, the organizational identity preoccupied with alterego relationships must be viewed with caution. Granted, we all need to experience alikeness through affiliation, but the tendency to establish adult relationships based upon the absence of differences is troublesome and counterproductive in the workplace. Organizational members, who tend to merge with like-minded others, may feel pressure and uncertainty about producing organizational subcultures divided by rigid and impenetrable boundaries. These boundaries are often structured around members' shared vocations, professions, functions, or status in the organization. Organizational structure and function come to serve defensive purposes, where boundaries enhance resistance to change and maladaptiveness within and among organizations. The organizational identity becomes a social defense system against the anxiety of differences, separation, and individuality.

Group cohesion becomes an important issue for organizational members. A retreat into "the presence of essential alikeness," momentarily, repairs the perceived deficit in organizational participants' talents and skills—the intermediate area of Kohut's bipolar self (1984). Identification with peers, similarly trained and educated, may momentarily boost self-esteem with collective reassurances of the importance and superiority of the like-minded member's contribution to the organization. However, institutional reinforcement of a member's false self-system is harmful to both individual and organization.

The relevant factor here as in the other transference categories is the degree of flexibility versus rigidity among organizational members. The more extreme and rigid twinship transferences become, the greater is the tendency for ritualistic organizational defenses to dominate performance and shut down organizational learning. In the case of twinship transference, acknowledgment of differences must be combined with awareness of similarities and likeness.

SUMMARY

In my experience, the utility of analyzing organizational problems is greatest when exploring the network of feelings that bind people together at work. I call this network *organizational identity*. Focus on organizational identity goes below the exposition of patterns of values or organizational culture. Organizational identity emerges from the intersubjective experience of individual organizational members. Transference is a clinical device for interpreting the meaning of interpersonal relations between and among organizational participants. Ultimately, I believe, it is the nonrational and unconscious dynamics of human relations at work that influence members' interpretations of their roles and tasks in the organization. Making emotional and cognitive sense of organizational life is essential to the change and development of total systems and people's images of those systems.

In its origin in individuals, organizational identity evolves from the healthy and normal, narcissistic (what Heinz Kohut calls *selfobject*) demands of organizational members for self-esteem and security from anxiety.[6] Its sources in the environment are the coping responses of work groups and organizational divisions to critical incidents and everyday stressors. In psychoanalytic theory, this definition is consistent with "the speculation that the evolution of affects serves the adaptive needs of the group" (Modell, 1984: 184). Group performance in organizations must always be considered in a situational context. Organizational identity is, in part, the product of interpersonal defensive and adaptive strategies for coping with critical incidents. Such incidents may influence power and authority, responsibility and accountability, or may produce greater uncertainty and helplessness. These incidents represent change in the status quo and simultaneously generate anxiety among organizational members.

Thus, organizational identity is a defensive solution to contradictory motives and conflicting aims of organizational participants. Organizational identity is a compromise formation: It is the product of conflict which partly expresses the needs of the parties to the conflict (Rycroft, 1968: 20). These collective defenses organize experience, shape perceptions of oneself and others, and ultimately, influence administrative behavior.

In sum, organizational identity implies that many repetitive and, frequently ritualistic, patterns of interaction within work groups and among participants are, for organizational members, purposeful, but not necessarily conscious, psychological defenses against threatening events and relationships. These defensive patterns, ultimately, result in the construction of rational administrative processes of organizations that regulate threats to personal security and self-esteem by structuring and defining organizational life.

In the next chapter, I examine groups and organizational identity. As I stated earlier, organizational identity is partly the consequence of the means by which work groups orient themselves toward the organization and from which individuals acquire their own sense of security and identity as members. Chapter 5 deals directly with the central psychodynamic dilemma of group members in organizations: striking a balance between their need for affiliation and membership on the one hand and individuality and personal identity on the other.

NOTES

1. With the concept of *selfobject*, psychoanalyst Heinz Kohut refers to the narcissistic (healthy and otherwise) dimension of interpersonal relationships. This includes needs for mirroring (demanding of others to make one feel grandiose and omnipotent), idealizing (worshiping others and satisfying others' needs for aggrandizement), and twinship or alterego (relating to others on the basis of the criteria of essential alikeness).

2. In Kets de Vries (1984), see chapter 12; in Larcon and Reitter, see chapter 16.

3. Projective identification is the act of attributing some personal feeling or desire to someone else and then reacting to the person as if he or she originally owned the feeling or desire. Consequently, the subject experiences the emotion he or she initially rejected through the other. This concept is explained in greater depth in the Introduction.

4. Action research assumes that the legitimate study of social phenomena results from the researcher's attempt to change the status quo and examine the consequences. Action research requires intervention—that is, the disruption of a social system.

5. One might argue that the "experience far" position is typical of traditional organizational research as well.

6. The *selfobject* is one's subjective experience of another person who provides a sustaining function to the self within a relationship, evoking and maintaining the self and the experience of selfhood by his or her presence or activity (Moore and Fine, 1990: 178).

5

INDIVIDUAL AND GROUP REGRESSION IN THE WORKPLACE:

Striking a Balance Between Personal Identity and Group Affiliation

In the "postindustrial milieu,"[1] work groups have a crucial impact on organizational identity. The cognitive, emotional, and behavioral patterns of interpersonal relations, and the subjective experience of these interactions (what is called transference) between and among members, are determining factors of organizational identity. Thus, interpreting work group cultures is an important step to more deeply understanding organizational life.

In this chapter, I look at work groups from the vantage point of individual and group regression in organizations—a central feature of organizational identity. In so doing, I address the following four issues: (1) why people in work groups behave regressively, (2) the factors at work that cause an apparent reduction of intelligence and foresight among group participants, (3) the form these regressive tendencies take in work groups, and (4) the nature of alternative, nonregressive, work groups.

I begin with a discussion of what I believe is the central psychological dilemma for organizational members in work groups. This predicament may be described as the inner conflict generated in a participant in response to the opposing human needs for belongingness and individuality. Then, I explain the psychodynamics of individual regression in groups, which I argue is a common response among organizational members to this deeper psychological dilemma. Subsequently, I consider various types of regressive and defensive work groups. These include the homogenized, institutionalized, and autocratic work groups (see Table 5.1). In addition, I

Another version of this chapter appears in Kets de Vries (1991).

present a fourth work group, the resilient work group, which incorporates all of the regressive potentials of the other three groups. This is not a perfect group. The difference is in its reflective nature. It is capable of acknowledging these nonrational tendencies and intervening in the process to prevent deterioration of work bonds. Finally, I explain the psychodynamic processes that promote regressive as well as progressive shifts in work group cultures (see Figure 5.1).

THE DILEMMA AND VALUE OF GROUP MEMBERSHIP

The central dilemma for the individual in the work group rests in his or her ability to maintain a balance of relative independence (personal identity and self-esteem) and group membership (a sense of belongingness and affiliation) without becoming overly distressed. Establishing a separate identity in a group is essential to ego integrity and emotional well-being. That requirement of independence and autonomy is what distinguishes us from each other. However, group affiliation draws upon individual narcissism—both healthy and pathological. Individual requirements for self-esteem and reassurance differ. Some need more reinforcement than others, and some must find others who make them feel more powerful and safe. Regardless, all of us need others and therefore require some degree of affiliation. In the case of psychological regression in work groups, I am talking about an excessive demand for affiliation—a merger with the other and a loss of self-other boundaries. That is a compulsive yearning to belong and to be a part of something. The transference categories discussed in Chapter 4 are variations of merger relationships. Group membership can give many a feeling of omnipotence—being part of a group gives individuals a sense of being larger, greater, and more ideal than they really are. That is, group membership is a way of fulfilling the demands of the ego ideal—that near-perfect sense of oneself at his or her future best. Therefore, some affiliation with others is important in that it provides not only a defense, but also a sense of being greater than one.

Consequently, people may often go to great lengths in order to maintain their affiliation with the group, to the extent that sometimes they will do things within the group that they would not consider doing outside it. Robert J. Lifton's study *The Nazi Doctors* exemplified this in what he called the doubling phenomenon. Nazi physicians, who engaged daily in the supervision and selection of humans for extermination, became devoted and loving fathers and husbands with their families in the evenings at home. Psychologically, they were capable of carrying out these extremely contradictory sets of actions. As members of groups and organizations, individuals appear capable of actions that are split off from their self-identity. Authoritarian behavior and other potentially dangerous acts of psychological regression in work groups, I believe, arise out of the individual fear of group rejection. The mere possibility and uncertainty of rejection are then experienced unconsciously as the potential for self-annihilation. Ironically, the threat of self-annihilation which triggers regressive behavior is often the consequence of that regressive (and defensive) response to anxiety.

So while autonomy may be an important need for individuals in work groups, membership and affiliation requirements are important as well. In fact, regressive and defensive actions in groups arise to ward off (what is often called) annihilation anxiety triggered by fears of separation, abandonment, and loss of affiliation. Critical organizational events often ignite anxiety and aggression that, in turn, spark regressive and defensive group responses. Regression, for our purposes, is defined as an extreme and counterproductive reaction to environmental and organizational incidents, which are perceived by group members as threatening to their sense of self. In order to understand this more fully, I next provide some background to the psychodynamics of individual regression in groups.

Individual Regression in Groups

Freud's (1921) *Group Psychology and the Analysis of the Ego*, Melanie Klein's (1959) "Our Adult World and Its Roots in Infancy," Elliott Jaques' (1955) "Social Systems as a Defense Against Persecutory and Depressive Anxiety," W. R. Bion's (1959) *Experiences in Groups*, I. E. P. Menzies' (1960) "A Case Study in the Functioning of Social Systems as a Defence against Anxiety," and Otto Kernberg's (1980) *Internal World and External Reality* all make clear that regressive and primitive defensive actions are critical psychodynamic components of the interpretation of the meaning of group and organizational behavior.

What is individual regression? Rycroft writes:

The theory of regression presupposes that, except in ideal cases, infantile stages of development are not entirely outgrown, so that the earlier patterns of behaviour remain available as alternative modes of functioning. It is, however, not maintained that regression is often a viable or efficient defensive process; on the contrary, it is usually a question of out of the frying-pan into the fire, since regression compels the individual to re-experience anxiety appropriate to the stage to which he had regressed. (1968: 139)

The regressive work groups presented in this chapter are categorized into a developmental sequence as well (see Table 5.1).

Individuals act regressively when they experience annihilation (separation) anxiety resulting from an unstable, inconsistent, insecure, or hostile public (fantasied or actual). Winnicott's notion of the holding environment, a metaphor originally meant to represent the mother-infant relationship as the first and, developmentally, most influential object relationship, may symbolize other significant emotional bonds in one's life, such as that between the individual and the family, the individual and the work group, and the individual and the organization. These emotional bonds represent various selfobject relationships that may or may not facilitate personal identity, self-esteem, and ego-integrity, and which may or may not provide adequate freedom and psychological space within their social structure to provide for both adequate individuation and affiliation.

Regardless, some individuals enter the work group and the organization with excessive demands for association that actually represent a compensatory need for a sense of self and *identity* that is otherwise lacking. Their unconscious expectations are for a group and organization that can provide them with the stable and all-loving holding environment discussed in the previous chapter. Whatever the degree of individual need for membership may be, organizational and environmental stress triggers some level of annihilation anxiety. Kernberg puts it this way:

> Group processes pose a basic threat to personal identity, linked to a proclivity in group situations for activation of primitive object relations, primitive defensive operations, and primitive aggression with predominantly pregenital features. These processes, particularly the activation of primitive aggression, are dangerous to the survival of the individual in the group as well as to any task the group needs to perform. (1980: 217)

Individual regression, therefore, is likely to occur when uncertainty regarding self, others, and environment is experienced, and, concomitantly, where weak ego defenses fail to protect the self from the onslaught of anxiety, anxiety that arises from threatened personal identity.

Within organizations, the balance between personal identity and group affiliation is threatened by change and uncertainty brought about by conditions of retrenchment, decline, management cutbacks, leadership transitions, suspicious publics, unclear or ambiguous objectives, ambiguity of authority and leadership, and unwillingness to delegate authority, to list a few of the more common stressful events at work. Hence, given the

Table 5.1
Work Group Cultures

PSYCHODYNAMIC FEATURES	GROUP TYPES			
	Homogenized	Institutionalized	Autocratic	Resilient
Authority	Leaderless	Hierarchical	Charismatic leader	Collaborative and participative leadership
Structure	Fragmented/polarized	Bureaucratic	Autocratic and patriarchal	Sophisticated work group
Transference	Persecutory	Persecutory	Idealizing and/or mirroring	Twinship/alterego
Psychic Structure	Id	Primitive ego	Superego dominance/ego ideal	Ego strength and self-cohesion
Psychosexual character	Oral	Anal	Phallic and Oedipal	Post-Oedipal
Self-object relation	Schizoid (dedifferentiated)	Paranoid (differentiated)	Depressive (differentiated)	Individuated (differentiated)
Psychosocial dilemma	Trust vs. mistrust	Autonomy vs. shame/doubt	Initiative vs. guilt	Industry vs. inferiority through integrity vs. despair
Political model	Isolationist laissez-faire	Totalitarian and state bureaucratic	Dictatorial and authoritarian	Democratic and pluralistic
Work relationship	Nearly incapable of performing work; no learning	Capable of work; emphasis on quantity, routinization, and control; little delegation; single-loop learning	Capable of work; emphasis on quality; stable leadership; support of work capacity; single-loop learning	Work of high quality and collaborative, meaningful, and purposeful; reflective practice; double-loop learning capability

climate in which most contemporary organizations operate, stress, change, and proclivity in groups for psychological regression are constant factors.

Why is regression a typical group response to environmentally imposed stress and change? Because the imposition of stress and change in the status quo removes the psychological safety and security people find at work in the certainty and predictability of technically rational and routine actions.[2] Regressive action serves to protect and preserve one's self from perceived (psychological) annihilation by withdrawing (in response to the stressors and imposed changes) into a safe and secure inner space. Melanie Klein refers to this state of regressed withdrawal as the need to save the ego by internal object-relations, to withdraw "inside" and out of the external world (Guntrip, 1969: 82).

For example, some individuals' experiences may lead them to isolate themselves from society (as much as possible) in order to avoid (what they perceive as) further persecution and disappointment. Persecuted work groups, cults, ethnic groups, and entire nations have been known to insulate themselves from an external world they view as hostile and dangerous. Alternatively, an individual or group may emotionally retire by denying or taking flight from reality, in which case distorted perceptions and fantasies are substituted for reality. The work group responds to preserve itself but in so doing enters a collective fantasy or delusion.

In the final analysis, individual regression in groups stems from annihilation (or separation) anxiety arising from each individual's fear of rejection from the group and loss of affiliation. This anxiety threatens the very core of one's self-identity. Hence, the unconscious fear of self-disintegration is a motivating factor in group membership and affiliation. Individuals regress to protect themselves from the anxiety of *uncertain* interpersonal relationships, which are brought on by the organization's external stress and imposed need to change. Thus, work groups are often characterized by unconscious actions and shared fantasies, which stem from the sum of individual regressed and primitive coping defenses.

Individual regression and other primitive defenses are observable at the group level of analysis and lend themselves to description as a group culture (or organizational subculture). In classical Freudian terms, these defenses belong to specific stages of psychosexual development: projection, denial, and splitting belonging to the oral stage, and reaction-formation, isolation, and undoing to the anal stage of development. Thereafter, "identification with the aggressor" is a common defense associated with superego development and object love in the Oedipal and puberty stages (A. Freud, 1966).

The psychodynamics of individual and group regression are more fully appreciated when viewed in an operational context. The development of the following types of work groups illuminates the full impact of regressive and primitive defensive actions on work groups and organizational identity.

Regressive and Defensive Work Groups

The assortment of regressive and defensive work groups in Table 5.1 is based on participant observations from organizational consultations, self psychology, and the psychoanalytic object relations framework. It is not my intention to refute previous psychoanalytic frameworks (Freud, Bion, etc.) for interpreting group dynamics, but to enhance comprehension of group processes in complex organizations with greater elaboration and precision. The application of contemporary psychodynamic theory to the analysis of groups in organizations enhances our comprehension of collective human behavior.

The group categories in Table 5.1 are based on the assumption that groups exist in organizational settings and that the meaning of their behavior can be interpreted separately from, but not independently of, individual behavior of group members (Freud, 1921; Bion, 1959; Rice, 1969; Kernberg, 1980). The categories are an attempt to sort out various levels of group member responses to annihilation anxiety. Each work group represents a predominant coping pattern observed in groups as members attempt to contain their anxious feelings of potential rejection and loss of affiliation. Three regressive and defensive groups are presented: the homogenized work group, the institutionalized work group, and the autocratic work group. A fourth nonregressive and nondefensive group, the resilient work group, is also presented.

The Homogenized Work Group

The homogenized group is the most primitive and regressive collective flight from annihilation anxiety. It is characterized by an absence of self-other differentiation. Developmentally, it is a forerunner to the separation-individuation phase of infancy (Mahler et al., 1975; Kernberg, 1980; Frosch, 1983). That is, individuation seems absent here. Similar to the newborn merged with the (love-object) mother, homogenized group members act as one. They do not distinguish between self and other.

Homogenized group members isolate themselves from others outside the group and become detached and withdrawn. An unconscious, collective wish to return to the safety of the womb produces a welcome avenue of flight from (what they perceive is) a hostile environment of destructively aggressive relationships (Guntrip, 1969). Psychic safety is thereby realized, if only momentarily, by group members within their delusional subculture, a subculture of sameness in which members experience similar feelings and act uniformly. But the safety is short-lived; withdrawal from an external world of perceived persecution and self-annihilation results in a schizoidlike group capable of unusual social denial and, therefore, incapable of reality testing. Primitively regressed group members (similar to the schizoid personality) unconsciously operate in an internalized world of introjected bad objects (internalized bad parent) that threaten to devour the group self.

When viewed from the perspective of individuation, differentiation of one's self from others is feared because of the apparent (if not actual) threat of primitive group violence directed toward any deviant individual. A sense of panic about the possible loss of control over group members' aggression exaggerates annihilation anxieties among them. Consequently, group members fear both differentiation (of selfobject) by other group members and potential group hostility if others openly express their individuality. Under these circumstances self-disintegration is defended against by psychic splitting of self and others into "all-good" (accepting) and "all-bad" (rejecting) part images. Group members typically introject all-good selfobject representations into themselves and project all-bad selfobject representations onto others, typically, outside the group. Group and organizational polarization and fragmentation are commonplace.

The homogenized work group exhibits the symptoms of the schizoid problem described by Guntrip and the British object relations school. Individual members of the homogenized group experience primitive aggression, which Guntrip describes as: "an oral sadistic and incorporative hunger for objects [that] sets up intolerable anxiety about their safety" (1969: 30). This "hunger for objects" is believed to take the form of a fantasy in which the subject desires to devour others perceived as threatening and hostile. Eventually, individual members withdraw and deny their violent thoughts and feelings. They may also deny their terror of fellow group members, wishing, conversely, to devour them. Hence, homogenized group members fear, and eventually retreat from, their own aggressive tendencies.

In *Group Psychology and the Analysis of the Ego*, Freud (1921) argues that "libidinal ties" join group members to one another by means of identification with a common ego ideal represented by their collective leader, who ultimately gives the group an identity and its members a sense of belonging and commonality. In the homogenized group, libidinal needs for other(s) are present but viewed as dangerous and potentially destructive. Love itself is perceived as destructive (Guntrip, 1969). Group members fear that which they need most, the good lost object—the "all-protecting," "all-loving," and "perfect" mother-infant dyad. In their search for this "good lost object," group members are confronted by annihilation anxiety—a sense of depersonalization and fear of total destruction of the self.

Anxiety results in the schizoid problem for homogenized group members who identify with each other's feelings of self-annihilation and persecution. Thus, homogenized group members engage in a *persecutory transference*[3] with each other. The subject of the persecutory transference feels that others, like the subject's abusive and hurtful parents, are out to destroy him or her. Persecutory transference reactions encourage cognitive and emotional splitting among group members to whom relations between oneself and others are defined by all or nothing, black or white, absolutist thinking. For instance, group members may see themselves as ideal and all-good, and other groups (divisions or offices) as persecutory and all-bad.

A critical attribute of the homogenized group is that it is apparently leaderless. In fact, the homogenized work group is often a consequence of an absence of group and organizational leadership during difficult times. Homogenized work groups are quite commonly observed in circumstances of very weak and ambivalent leadership. Ironically, the probability that an individual who aspires to be a visionary leader will emerge from the group with this proclivity is very low. Homogenized group members refuse to acknowledge individual differences, such as race, gender, class, perceptions and emotions, talents and skills. Their aggressive feelings and the concomitant anxieties preclude this.[4]

Under these primitive conditions group members are nearly incapable of accomplishing work. The primary unacknowledged task is individual and group survival. But the severely suppressed and resigned quality of the homogenized subculture produces a form of group paralysis in which group members find themselves on the horns of a dilemma. They experience themselves as neither in nor out, neither willing to commit themselves to group participation nor willing to commit themselves to a separateness from the group identity. Guntrip's (1969) description of the schizoid retreat, which he calls *the in and out programme*, illustrates the paradox of the homogenized work group (36): "This 'in and out' programme, always breaking away from what one is at the same time holding on to, is perhaps the most characteristic behavioural expression of the schizoid conflict."

The homogenized work group emerges as a response to the lack of organizational commitment to group member objectives. The absence of commitment, for example, may take the form of diminishing allocations of financial and human resources, perhaps the result of an ambiguous and temporary authority structure in which leaders are discouraged from leading. This type of situation results in uncertainty, distress, poor morale, low self-esteem among group members, and feelings of persecution. Ultimately, homogenized group members are driven by annihilation anxiety and the unconscious desire to protect themselves from the consequences of their aggressive feelings.

This schizoid withdrawal into homogenized subcultures was exhibited by a university department that found itself operating in a hostile environment. In response to very poor understanding and financial support from the dean of the school, departmental members retreated, psychologically, into a schizoid space. The dean had been obliged to appoint a nontenured assistant professor to chair the department. It was viewed as impossible to recruit a chairperson because of the department's poor fiscal situation. Departmental members viewed the dean's decision as further evidence of the school's lack of support and recognition, and the individual appointed was both ineffectual and unacceptable. Department members felt leaderless and persecuted. Their binding organizational identity as a whole department became fragile and many conflicts were unresolved. Splitting occurred in response to members' anger and powerlessness. The combination of positive and negative emotions and thoughts could no longer be tolerated. They required a relatively safe externalized target for their aggression. Instead of collectively targeting the dean, however, they aimed their bad feelings at one another. This action resulted in a bifurcation of the department into two antagonistic subgroups tied together by similar credentials and in a mechanism for coping with their rage and hostility. Each camp viewed the other as all-bad and at fault for their current predicament. Two homogenized subcultures had emerged within the department and paralyzed their ability to deal effectively with the situation.

The Institutionalized Work Group

As I have shown, the threat to group membership and affiliation in the homogenized group produces sadistic defenses such as splitting and withdrawal. In so doing, participants obliterate individuality, project aggression and hostility onto others, and withdraw into a suppressed state. In contrast, institutionalized group members respond to the presence of annihilation anxiety by producing *paranoid social defenses* that encourage submission to a formal hierarchical structure and impersonal authority. Rather than denying aggression and fear of disintegration by resignation and withdrawal into an internal world, institutionalized group members act to contain anxiety by constructing depersonalizing and controlling social structures (Kernberg, 1980; Menzies, 1960; Jaques, 1955).

Underlying paranoid feelings in the group produce primitive infantile aggression and hostility among members. These feelings are in turn contained by defensive social structuring of interpersonal relations in the group. In Chapter 2 I referred to this bureaucratic state of affairs as ritualistic organizational defenses that are produced by the externalized self-system. Kernberg writes:

> The study of large-group processes highlights the threat to individual identity under social conditions in which ordinary role functions are suspended and various projective mechanisms are no longer effective (because of the loss of face-to-face contact and personal feedback). Obviously, large group processes can be obscured or controlled by rigid social structuring. Bureaucratization, ritualization, and well-organized task performance are different methods with similar immediate effects. (1980: 218)

One underlying reason for constructing rigid social structures like bureaucracies is the reaction-formation (anal defense) against the "overwhelming nature of human aggression in unstructured group situations" (218). Whereas homogenization is an oral sadistic response to unstructured group situations that perpetuate the threat to group membership, institutionalization represents an anal sadistic response that calls for a predominance of anal defenses, such as reaction-formation, isolation, and undoing. As noted in Chapter 2, ritualistic behavior in bureaucracy arises from unconsciously motivated obsessional thinking and compulsive behavior aimed at defending one's self from anxiety over losing control. This defense serves to contain anxiety, which is the unpleasant experience of a momentary loss of self and other boundaries or self-identity.

Bureaucratization and ritualization are institutionalized forms of control that promote dependency on rigid and routinized impersonal structures. Group affiliation needs come to dominate contrary demands for personal identity and autonomy. Discussing the role of anality, Frosch (1983) comments:

> The analysis, as is often the case with obsessional patients, highlighted the issue of maintaining control. This issue was reflected in

the way he brought up material, in the transference, in his work, and in his relations with others. Like most obsessionals, he couldn't really delegate work, as people were seen as extensions of himself, whom he had to control. (72)

A special instance of *projective identification* is operating in the institutionalized group. Members react defensively by splitting their perceptions of self and others into good and bad categories and identifying a bad object within the group self. Group members' obsessive-compulsive preoccupation with control of sadistic aggression fosters a paranoid position with respect to group members' action. Not surprisingly, persecutory transference dominates the character of interpersonal relations in the institutionalized work group as well. However, in contrast to the homogeneous work group, the institutionalized work group reinforces submission to oligarchical and hierarchical authority. Although self and other boundaries do become confused, they are not seemingly obliterated as in the case of the homogenized work group. Anxiety and aggression are contained by institutionalized repression fueled by fear and paranoia.

Kernberg elaborates further:

An important part of nonintegrated and unsublimated aggression is expressed in various ways throughout group and organizational processes. When relatively well-structured group processes evolve in a task-oriented organization, aggression is channeled toward the decision-making process, particularly by evoking primitive-leadership characteristics in people in positions of authority. Similarly, the exercise of power in organizational and institutional life constitutes an important channel for the expression of aggression in group processes that would ordinarily be under control in dyadic or triadic relations. Aggression emerges more directly and much more intensely when group processes are relatively unstructured. (1980: 218)

In summary, institutionalized group members rely on structure to control aggression and annihilation anxiety. Rigid routines and impersonal office authority perpetuate an illusion of stability, equality, and dependability—a social defense system. Dependence on rules, regulations, and procedures, and reliance on hierarchic impersonal authority, evoke "disclaimed action" (Schafer, 1976; 1983) and lack of personal responsibility (Diamond and Allcorn, 1984; Diamond, 1985b). Institutionalization also results in a rigid structuring of boundaries, an insistence on loyalty and role conformity, and a general obsession for control of subordinate behavior—all of which are indicative of a *paranoid regressive trend* and *perse-cutory transference* underlying the group's actions and structuring of itself and the organizational identity.

This group accomplishes work in a routine and rational fashion. Procedures, rules, and regulations may take priority over quality of work, substance of product and service, and overall meaning and purpose of task accomplishment. Intra- and interorganizational bound-aries are rigid and relatively inflexible. Bureaucratic administration replaces leadership. An emphasis on the control of subordinate behav-ior renders delegation of authority unlikely. Paradoxically, the procliv-ity of the institutionalized work groups to operate as closed systems fosters perpetual insecurity and paranoia and an obsession with protec-tion from others' aggression. Of course, this overcompensation is a defensive denial of individual sadistic tendencies, which takes the form of projective identification. Many politically unpopular public agen-cies often operate under these regressive and defensive arrangements because of the politics of overzealous subcommittee oversight or overambitious political appointees in positions of authority.

For example, a public agency had defensively overstructured itself into a professional bureaucracy that no longer effectively coordinated its specialized staff and units to accomplish its primary tasks. In response to persistent legislative criticisms and investigations, the division's leader-ship had produced an institutionalized group to control its product in an effort to prevent criticism, and the resulting culture made the coordination of tasks and communications across interdisciplinary organizational boundaries exceedingly difficult. Secrecy and withholding of information were characteristic defensive responses to fear of both the public and organizational leadership. Excessively layered and complex hierarchic channels of communication had to be negotiated for minor authorizations and approvals. This virtually paralyzed otherwise competent members of the system, who consequently felt powerless, angry, and fearful of the leadership, a reaction which, in turn, only reinforced the paranoia and mistrust. These feelings further reinforced the need for defensive strategies and rigid structures to achieve control, despite their frustrations and diminishing self-competence. Individuality was minimized; obedience to authority and managerial control of subordinates were accentuated.

The Autocratic Work Group

In the autocratic work group, participants also find themselves forfeiting their independence and separate identity for group membership. In contrast to the homogenized and institutionalized groups, autocratic work group members identify with an all-powerful charismatic leader from whom they derive omnipotent control of their aggression and anxiety. Guilt arising from feelings of ambivalence and hostility toward the idealized person also develops. In comparison to the institutionalized work group characterized by too much organization and distant and impersonal leadership, the autocratic group is characterized by the personal authority of one leader, or sometimes the family headed by a patriarch. Group members exchange their own personal ego ideal and internal authority for that of the group leader (father), who then, wittingly or unwittingly, comes to dominate the group conscience.

The autocratic group is, therefore, constructed on the foundation of a combined mirroring and idealizing transference. Members grow to feel guilty about their vacillation between affectionate and aggressive desires toward their idealized leader, whom they both love and fear. The autocratic group is similar to Freud's classic portrayal of the primal horde in *Group Psychology and the Analysis of the Ego* (1921):

> Human groups exhibit once again the familiar picture of an individual of superior strength among a troop of equal companions, a picture which is also contained in our idea of the primal horde. The psychology of such a group, as we know it for the descriptions to which we have so often referred—the dwindling of the conscious individual personality, the focusing of thoughts and feelings into a common direction, the predominance of the affective side by the mind and of unconscious psychical life, the tendency to the immediate carrying out of intentions as they emerge—all corresponds to a state of regression to a primitive mental activity, of just such a sort as we should be inclined to ascribe to the primal horde. (54)

Autocratic group members endow their leader with primitive, sadistic, and omnipotent qualities. Group members are guilt-ridden and submissive. They either turn their anger and aggression back against themselves, evoking a depressive and ambivalent quality to the group climate, or project their aggression outside group boundaries. Reminiscent of the *depressive* position described by Melanie Klein and the British object relations school, the autocratic group offers members a prototype of infantile feelings of guilt, atonement, and forgiveness.

> Guilt derives from the ambivalence and hostility toward the object, with its possible destruction. Atonement is achieved by the ego taking

itself as a weak, hateful object and placing the superego in the role of parents whose forgiveness has to be sought by abject behavior. We find here a double identification: the ego as bad parent and the superego as the good one. Ultimately forgiveness may be achieved through fusion with the superego. (Frosch, 1983: 184)

Inevitably group members are disappointed with their "godlike" leader, who cannot possibly meet their fantasied expectations nor control their hatred, aggression, and basic anxiety. The primitive crime of the primal horde's symbolic murder of the father-leader is reenacted. The leader is replaced from time to time. Each reenactment is followed by a period of remorse and mourning. Members who sense their capacity to love and hate the same object must work through their ambivalent feelings in order for the group to progress and develop toward (what I call) the resilient group culture.

In contrast to the oral sadistic defenses of the homogenized group and the anal sadistic defenses of the institutionalized group, the autocratic group relies upon an "identification with the aggressor" (A. Freud, 1966). Identification with the aggressor is a common Oedipal defense against the anxiety of an external threatening object associated with superego development during puberty. In further contrast, the institutionalized group represents a manner of containing the anxious, violent, and explicitly sadistic social organization of the primal horde, and the homogenized group offers a solution to annihilation anxiety and aggression by schizoid withdrawal, where thoughts and feelings are severed indefinitely.

Finally, the autocratic group is capable of carrying out work. The presence of a stable identifiable leader serves to direct and coordinate the work capacity of the group. A utopian climate is created when group members identify with the leader. However, their fear and disappointment with their idealized leader and the group's unconscious wish to replace the leader produce a sense of guilt. As a result, the group's work is affected by shifts in climate from a utopian elation to a depressed position filled with mourning and guilt.

Although most common to family-owned businesses characterized by the norms and authority of a patriarchal system ruled by the "law of the father," the autocratic group also appears in the traditionally conservative and patriarchal culture of many public agencies under the domination of career bureau chiefs in government. For example, units or offices within a complex public organization may operate as (semiautonomous) kingdoms where subordinates come to idealize their autocratic boss, and in which intergroup (interoffice) boundary disputes over jurisdictional authority and the status and prestige of each unit relative to one another are commonplace, while loyalty and deference to authority are strongly encouraged among members *within* these units.

For example, agencies within a governmental department were managed by bureau chiefs who had fifteen to twenty years' experience. Subordinates often publicly expressed their loyalty to and admiration for the chiefs, and obedience to authority and social cohesion were characteristic traits of the units. However, in private consultations with staff from which bureau chiefs were absent, negative feelings and otherwise undiscussable agency problems were acknowledged. In the presence of bureau chiefs, on the other hand, staff members consistently deferred to the chiefs' authority and suppressed personal ideas, feelings, and thoughts. *Identification with the aggressor* (the bureau chief) was a predominant regressive and defensive group strategy. This illustrates a common theme of regressive work groups in organizations under pressure: group membership and affiliation take precedence over the autonomy and independence necessary for self-identity.

ANALYSIS OF REGRESSIVE WORK GROUPS

The three work groups described—homogenized, institutionalized, and autocratic—are regressive solutions to annihilation anxiety and feared aggression. The institutionalized and autocratic groups, however, represent defensive alternatives to the primitive homogenized group. That is, the institutionalized and autocratic work groups are compromise formations against the ultimate regressive schizoid withdrawal of the homogenized group. In contrast, the institutionalized and autocratic groups, regardless of their paradoxical and psychoneurotic features, facilitate interpersonal relations. Members of homogenized groups withdraw from the potential intimacy of interpersonal relationships. Members escape potentially intimate feelings. The institutionalized group culture with its underlying paranoia and the autocratic group culture with its charismatic leader and underlying depressive position are group constructions derived from qualitatively different interpersonal relationships. In contrast is the homogenized group, whose members flee one another in an attempt to escape intimacy.

Regardless of how disturbed and distorted interpersonal relationships in work groups are, intimacy and human relatedness, with its potential for consensual validation and intimacy, persists in the institutionalized and autocratic work groups. In fact, the autocratic work group offers members the opportunity to repair self-other relations that are split apart, thereby promoting more holistic and reality-based work bonds. Although personal identity, independence, and autonomy take a back seat to affiliation and membership in the institutionalized and autocratic work groups, the individual can emerge more readily in these work group cultures than in the homogenized group.

The primary motivational aspects of group behavior are consistent for all three groups, but the regressive and defensive actions are characteristically different. The descriptive validity of the work group typology rests on the underlying developmental characteristics of self and other relations described by contemporary psychoanalytic object relations theory and observable in work groups responding to organizational and environmental pressures.

Psychoanalytic interpretations of group behavior in organizational settings are not entirely negative and pessimistic. In fact, an understanding of the regressive qualities of groups in organizations can provide us with a more holistic and balanced view of effective work groups. The *resilient work group* incorporates all of the regressive potentials of the homogenized, institutional, and autocratic subcultures. The difference is that it is capable of recognizing its nonrational and typically unconscious dynamics that promote defensive and regressive actions under pressure.

THE RESILIENT WORK GROUP

In contrast to the previous groups, in which unconscious actions and covert goals are dominant, the resilient work group is first and foremost a *task work group*. The resilient group is distinguished from the previous three work groups by a reflective process that promotes membership awareness of fantasies and covert actions. Participants realize the necessity of insight as a learning skill that, in turn, supports the emotional well-being and competence of all group members. Twinship or alterego transference seems to play a prominent role in the psychodyamics of the resilient work group.

The *twinship transference* is an emotional bond between people that is based upon their need to be seen and understood by others who are essentially like them. On the positive side, empathy and mutual understanding, which are essential ingredients in collaboration and cooperation, stem from the inherent values of the twinship transference. Moreover, the psychodynamics of twinship and alterego transferences promote the practice of mentoring, the acquisition and strengthening of talents and skills that enhance self-competence and self-esteem among group members. This can, in effect, reduce the proclivity for grandiosity and idealization among members and, thereby, minimize mirroring and idealizing tranference dynamics among them. It can also limit persecutory transference dynamics as a consequence of its members' commitment to taking responsibility for their actions. This means that feeling victimized will lead to some acknowledgment by the worker of his or her role in the victimization process rather than an impulsive turning to scapegoating behavior. On the negative side, the twinship transference may produce work groups of individuals who merge (overidentify) with each other and their leader(s). This can create problems. *If unacknowledged and uninterrupted*, the twinship transference between leaders and followers may deny them their individuality and differentiation. This may, in turn, encourage regressive dynamics of a homogenized nature.

The resilient work group is, therefore, not a utopia. It is capable of all the potentially regressive and defensive actions that characterize the other three work groups. Members may resort to regressive and primitive defensive actions in response to perceived danger and annihilation anxiety. In fact, transference dynamics are not absent: they are simply more cognitively accessible to members and thus potentially less counterproductive. Resilient work group members recognize that progress and change are unlikely without occasional regression into the defensive patterns characteristic of the other three organizational subcultures. They also acknowledge that change without individual and group resistance to that change is unlikely. Resilient workers are, therefore, sensitive to acts of resistance and defense as opportunities for learning and developmental change. They endeavor to learn from experience and are capable of recognizing defensive regressive actions. To reiterate, they are conscious of their individual and collective regressive tendencies.

It should be noted that the relations of the resilient work group differ from traditional "humanistic" views of sophisticated "collaborative" work relations in the emphasis on the need to attend to participants' regressive and defensive tendencies under stressful circumstances. These psychological proclivities underlie all group and organization dynamics. The character of the resilient work group represents a qualitative difference from more traditional prescriptions for collaborative work groups, in that it emphasizes the necessity for understanding and explaining (processing) cognitive and affective work group processes in order to achieve work group effectiveness and intentionality.

In sum, resilient work groups may emerge from organizational change efforts that focus on learning from experience by attending to unconscious group process, particularly leader-follower transference relations and regressive and defensive group actions. The social construction of resilient work groups is possible within facilitative organizational cultures that value collaboration and participation, and where sociotechnical and political factors do not function as serious constraints on change and development.

For example, a relatively autonomous unit in a public bureaucracy learned with the help of a consultant to identify transference dynamics between the supervisor and his staff. After a lengthy and painful exploration into how the group reacted to environmental circumstances, such as expanded work roles, the group members improved their ability to process the emotional nature of their work relationships so they could avoid counterproductive behavior. This involved clarifying and then redefining the interdependent nature of their roles required to complete shared tasks. Once the unit members associated their thoughts and feelings with group tendencies under stress, they realized the need to explore their reactions to constant change in the environment regularly. That realization altered their work group culture and facilitated the emergence of a more reflective and consciously aware group process. Their heightened awareness of collective transference tendencies enabled them to work more effectively in a setting that required innovation and creativity. The driving force behind their ability to overcome their excessive dependency on the consultant, a mere reflection of their dependency on the supervisor, was their desire for mutual understanding and validation of their frustrations. Finding that which they had in common as human beings helped them see and appreciate each other. Awareness of their idealization of the supervisor and its counterproductive nature helped them to be a more cohesive group and more respectful of each other's individual talents and skills. The idealizing transference gave way to a more constructive and productive twinship transference among the staff and with their supervisor.

What are the psychodynamic processes at work that promote such a progressive shift in work group culture? Let's explore that question in the next section.

THE PSYCHODYNAMICS OF GROUP TRANSITION

Striking a balance between personal identity and group affiliation is the central dilemma. Each of the four work groups represents one possible solution to the problem of anxiety and aggression produced by the central dilemma that is inherent to all groups under stress. However, the three regressive work groups solve the problem of annihilation anxiety by overemphasizing group membership and underplaying—and in some instances destroying—personal identity and autonomy. Any of the four work groups can, momentarily, resolve anxiety and control aggression.

However, these groups are not static, nor do they fit into rigid categories that exclude the potential for change. A group's change from one of these types to another is always, however unwittingly, a collective (or collusive) option. In order for these transitions to occur, the leader-follower relations that are critical to shifts in group culture must change. In other words, the nature of transference between superordinate and subordinate must be transformed (Figure 5.1).

For example, the homogenized work group is nearly leaderless because of a subculture that is antagonistic to the individuation necessary to allow any leader to emerge within the work group. A sufficient combination of power, authority, personality, and risk taking in one member would be necessary to move the group from schizoid withdrawal and repression into a state of object (self and other) relatedness (paranoid or depressed) found in differing degrees in the other three types of work groups. This is not to say the leader is pursuing an intentional process of assuming leadership and leading. While this may be true to some degree, it must be acknowledged that the leader may be identified, wittingly or unwittingly, by the group as displaying the social characteristics best suited to the role of leadership. We can never forget the fact that leadership is reciprocal, a relationship founded upon unconscious assumptions and expectations. Therefore, the leader can only exist as long as the emotional and ideological leanings of her following provide the basis for her empowerment. In the homogenized case, the "best suited" person may be the most schizoid in character. The nascent leader influences his or her followers first by gaining their attention and then by manufacturing an alternate defensive and seductively attractive fantasy.

Transference phenomena capture the underlying psychodynamics of group transitions. Awareness of transference dynamics helps consultants to illuminate subtle shifts in leader-follower interactions that foster transformation of organizational subcultures. The actual transition itself represents a resort to a new *compromise-formation* in the group's search for a collective defense against annihilation anxiety. The categories of work groups (see Table 5.1) help to identify different levels of maturity in object (self and other) relationships and varieties of compromise-formations.

For the homogenized work group, for example, to leave the comfort and protection its members find in schizoid withdrawal and isolation would require fight-oriented leadership and redirection of its aggression toward an object (someone or something) and an identifiable target outside the group boundary. A move from the homogenized subculture to the institutionalized work group would not require a change in the persecutory transference as much as a commitment to a new unconscious mission for

Figure 5.1
Group Transition

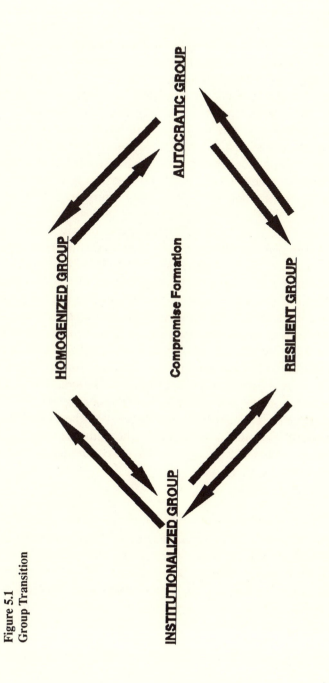

HOMOGENIZED GROUP

AUTOCRATIC GROUP

Compromise Formation

INSTITUTIONALIZED GROUP

RESILIENT GROUP

dealing with annihilation anxiety and feelings of victimization. Members would turn from resignation to overt aggression, targeting the individual or group to blame for their problems. In so doing, they would establish a "we-they" mentality that would further enable group members to depersonalize and dehumanize the other.

Once a leader who has the necessary agenda (an unconscious leader-follower fit), whether impersonal or charismatic in nature, is identified, group members unify and then follow either in retreat from their current predicament or in search of a common enemy. The emergence of a shift in transference dynamics signals a readiness to accept a new organizational subculture. The new work group emerges (either institutionalized or autocratic) out of a compromise-formation produced by changing transferences and emotional attachments between leaders and followers. The collective escape from the most primitively regressive homogenized work group begins with the often unconscious establishment of leader-follower ties. The homogenized work group, it should be stressed, represents the ultimate unconscious fear of group rejection and loss of group membership and affiliation. Its hostility toward independence and autonomy demonstrates the likelihood of its members' vulnerability to schizoid withdrawal.

Both institutionalized and autocratic work groups are capable of regressive action in the direction of homogenization, on the one hand, and progressive action in the direction of resilience, on the other. *In actuality, group and organizational action is in constant motion and, at any time, may be found somewhere along a continuum between regressive homogenization and progressive resilience.* In terms of the nature of transference and the character of self-other relations, the institutionalized and autocratic work groups represent a middle point on the continuum between regressive and progressive actions.

SUMMARY

In this chapter I have attempted to identify and explain regressive psychological trends in work groups. The secret to emotionally healthy and organizationally effective work groups, I argue, may be uncovered in the individuals' attempts to strike a balance between needs for independence and belonging. Regressive work groups, I observe, are characterized by an imbalance that favors group membership and affiliation over personal identity and autonomy. This may be true of the most progressive resilient work group as well, though to a much lesser degree than of the others. In fact, critical organizational incidents trigger regressive group responses, which suppress and, in some cases, nearly destroy the self-identity and independence of members. When autonomy is forfeited for group membership, schizoid withdrawal becomes a dangerous probability. Three primary defensive group responses to annihilation anxiety (homogenized, institutionalized, autocratic) may be provoked by organizational and environmental stressors; a fourth, less defensive response (resilient) is observed as well.

An understanding of regression in work groups, I submit, can enhance reflectivity and self-observation among group members and, thus, increase the group's opportunity for learning and effectiveness. More importantly, the resilient work group that values analysis of group process is capable of intervening in and turning around regressive and often destructive patterns.

Finally, the resilient work group does not perceive itself as superior but as human and psychodynamic. Its commitment to analysis of the group self does not obliterate regressive action but, rather, produces group awareness through a reflective process that creates the opportunity for change and development.

In the next chapter, we explore the role of language and communication in organizational consultancy. Here, I show the benefits of paying attention to the use of language and communication in the process of organizational change.

NOTES

1. In Chapter 1, I discuss Larry Hirschhorn's (1988) *The Workplace Within*, which defines the environment and culture of the contemporary work organization as the *postindustrial milieu.*

2. The overwhelming majority of writings on organizational change, such as those which call for shifts from bureaucratic to entrepreneurial organizations, consistently ignore the psychological factors of defense and resistance that unconsciously perpetuate the status quo.

3. In the previous chapter, I defined the *persecutory transference* in organizations, which signifies patterns of interpersonal relationships based on the perception of oneself as victim. Whether or not the label of self as victim is justified is irrelevant. The important psychological fact is that the individual feels like a victim and this influences his or her perception of others and the nature of emotional bonds he or she establishes. In the case of the persecutory transference, the subject of persecution typically resigns before getting too deeply involved, perceiving relationships as potentially dangerous.

4. Instead they may create a fantasied image of themselves in which they rationalize their actions by claiming to promote a state of equality and social justice. Actually, members of homogenized groups exist in an infantile schizoid position of regression that is "premoral" (Guntrip, 1969).

6

THE PSYCHODYNAMICS OF
LANGUAGE AND COMMUNICATION
IN ORGANIZATIONAL CONSULTATIONS

Special attention to the unconscious exchange of feelings at work between and among organizational participants, and between clients and consultants, distinguishes the psychoanalytic perspective from more traditional ones. Psychodynamically oriented organizational researchers explore worker assumptions and attributions that often take the form of defensive projections[1] and distorted images. These projections harm the delivery and content of communication and thus task accomplishment.

In this final chapter of Part I, I wish to conclude the theory section and provide a transition to the section on practice in Part II. In so doing, I present a theory of the psychodynamics of communication and language in organizational change efforts.

The role of communication and language in successful change efforts, I have found, depends upon the degree to which organizational members convey intersubjective meaning and experience pertinent to work activities and relationships. Typically, in organizations, people suppress ideas and feelings about ongoing problems at work, behavior often viewed as politically useful and adaptive. Paradoxically, successful efforts at organizational change and development rely upon participants' genuine expression of feelings and ideas. Nevertheless, sincerity may challenge the political nature and defensive strategies that characterize most work relationships. Resistance to change is therefore inevitable.

When organizational participants are asked at the completion of a critical phase of a change effort what aspect was the most difficult personally, they often mention "sharing honest feelings." What they mean is not only the ability to be authentic with one another, but the actual process of learning to express what they feel coherently. Many explain that it is not required of them. In fact, they point out that internal organizational politics promote insincerity and mistrust between supervisors and subordinates, and among peers. While they find their technical skills are adequate for accomplishing routine tasks and procedures, they seem to lack the linguistic and interpersonal skills, and the facilitative organizational culture, necessary for communicating emotions. Most comprehensive interventions focus on changing the organizational culture; few concentrate on enhancing language and communication skills. Finding and assessing an organization's identity require the effective communication of feelings about members' experience of and interaction with the organization and its leadership.

The ability to use language to communicate meaning and experience and the capacity to share a common understanding are acquired developmental skills. Though we are not born with this adeptness, the cognitive potential is present from infancy. Communication dexterity ripens in what H. S. Sullivan calls the *syntaxic mode of experience* (1953). The term *taxis* refers to the ability to arrange experience linguistically. *Syntaxic* refers to comprehensive ordering through language; specifically, to learning through language "to order experience in some manageable and mutually validatable fashion" (Levenson, 1983: 142).

Individual experience, particularly when filled with emotion, is hard to share: accessing and rearranging feelings linguistically in order to communicate that experience to others requires cognitive and dialectic proficiency. This means communicating with others in such a way that both the sender and receiver can explicitly confirm the meaning of the message and can thereby reach a mutual understanding that is publicly acknowledged.

The contribution of mastery in communications to organizational change may rest on the development of linguistic and interpersonal competence for sending and receiving affective messages. Communication of feelings rooted in, but not exclusive to, organizational experience presents the opportunity to alter activities and relationships that cause errors, distortions, demoralization, and ineffectiveness at work. The aptitude for transmitting affective messages within institutions and among participants is essential to organizational change and long-term effectiveness.

The organizational literature—psychoanalytic, cognitive, behavioral, or otherwise—deals very little with the linguistic and communication skills required in successful change efforts. Argyris' (1978) notions of double-loop learning and the good dialectic come closest, but they lack an explicit appreciation for the underlying developmental psychodynamics necessary for openness and the genuine exchange of feelings, thoughts, and ideas. Psychodynamic organizational interventions, such as that offered by Kets de Vries and Miller (1984), emphasize the importance of acknowledging transferences and countertransferences, and the therapeutic process of working through feelings about change, but they do not include a theory of the psychodynamics of linguistics and communication.

Neither the psychoanalytic nor the cognitive psychological literature on organization change and development has yet incorporated the role of linguistic and communicative maturity in realizing more sophisticated reasoning and processing of events. I attempt to do so by drawing primarily upon the interpersonal theory of Harry Stack Sullivan (1954) and the practical applications of that theory in the clinical writings of psychotherapists Leston Havens (1986) and Edgar Levenson (1983). While the concepts are new and, I admit, rather awkward, I ask the reader for his or her indulgence, because I believe learning new concepts is necessary to adapting alternative frameworks for more deeply understanding organizational change.

In Table 6.1, I show the connections that exist among psychological attributes of organizations, emotional and cognitive levels of communication, developmental phases of separation and individuation, unconscious basic assumption groups, transferences of emotion, and language use in the consultation process. My purpose is twofold: (1) to identify the links between communication skills and unconscious group dynamics in an organizational change effort and (2) to show how this knowledge can be applied in organizations so that participants can better confront their anxieties about relationships and enhance their adroitness in communications with others. While Table 6.1 presents a framework for thinking about these complex psychodynamics, it is intended to sensitize organizational consultants to the appropriate use of language at different stages of group development and at different levels of proficiency in communicating. My goal is not simply to help organizational members to talk consciously about their unconscious wishes. It is to help them recognize and act on certain unconscious wishes and experience safely the consequences, which they can then talk about.

First, language and communication in infancy and childhood are presented as the psychological foundation for language and communication in adult organizations; then the psychodynamics of communications, language, and group development in the practice of psychodynamic or-

Table 6.1
The Psychodynamics of Communication and Language in Organizational Change

Communication Skills	Basic Assumptions	Transferences	Language Use	Separation-Individuation Phase	Organizational Attributes
Prototaxic (1-5 months)	Dependency	Mirroring /Idealizing	Empathic	Symbiosis	Preorganizational (or mob)
Parataxic (5-9 months)	Fight/Flight	Persecutory	Interpersonal	Differentiation	Defensive Organization
Syntaxic (3 years)	Pairing	Twinship	Performative	Individuality	Resilient Organization

ganizational change and development are explored with a case illustration in Chapter 7.

LINGUISTIC EXPERIENCE AND COMMUNICATION: THE IMPACT OF INFANCY AND CHILDHOOD ON ADULT ORGANIZATIONS

Three modes of linguistic experience occur at different phases of development: prototaxic, parataxic, and syntaxic levels of cognition. "The difference in these modes lies in the extent and the character of the elaboration that one's contact with events has undergone" (Sullivan, 1953: 29). For Sullivan, maturity and stages of interpersonal development parallel linguistic and communicative mastery. One's ability to arrange (intersubjective) experience linguistically progresses with each phase of development from infancy through adulthood. Adeptness in ordering, comprehending, and communicating meaning is, for example, more evolved in normal children at three years of age than at one or two years of age. However, the individual growing up among parents and siblings he or she views as dangerous, unavailable, and anxiety-provoking may experience retardation in the development of communication skills.

Similarly, adults under pressure and feeling anxious may behave regressively at work, and such regressive action may produce immature communications reminiscent of conflicts that arose during stages of childhood separation and individuation. Regressive action and frustrated communication may further distort thinking and provoke defensive projections of internalized bad feelings among organizational members. These projections are characteristic of less advanced (prototaxic and parataxic) modes of psycholinguistic experience and prevail among adults in many organizations. The metaphor for such dysfunctions may be discovered in the vicissitudes of infancy and childhood. The following two discussions explain the metaphor and attributes of each.

The Prototaxic Mode (Preorganizational Identity)

In the prototaxic mode of experience, one's inner elaboration of events is preverbal, oriented around the body and sundry tensions—what Freud called unconscious and primary processes. Experience in the prototaxic mode occurs at the symbiotic (and attachment) phase of normal infancy, prior to self-awareness, where all that the infant knows are "momentary states." His or her field of observation is undifferentiated (Mahler, 1975). There exists little cognitive separation between self and other. "The infant vaguely feels or 'prehends' earlier and later states without realizing any serial connection between them. . . . His felt experience is all of a piece undifferentiated, without definite limits. It is as if his experience were 'cosmic' " (Sullivan, 1953: 28)—no limits, no boundaries, and no cognitive associations.

Anxiety originates in the parent-infant relationship. Anxiety in infancy is experienced as a threat unintentionally induced by the parent. The baby experiences the parent's anxiety through the medium of an "empathic linkage" (symbiosis). The infant does not comprehend the source of anxiety, which opposes the satisfaction of needs and is symbolized by the withdrawal of tenderness. Bowlby, for example, pinpoints "separation anxiety" as the first significant anxious response in the child to real or imagined loss of the mother (or parent) (Bowlby, 1973); Kernberg (1980) blames a lack of "object constancy," where parental caretaking in infancy is inconsistent, inadequate, or absent and, consequently, produces anxiety detrimental to ego integration. Winnicott faults the absence of "good enough" parenting and an insufficient "holding environment" for causing anxiety. All share the belief that anxiety stems from a significant interruption in, or absence of, adequate parent-infant bonding.

The prototaxic mode is preorganizational. It is more akin to a mob or crowd. There are no identifiable boundaries; one cannot distinguish between members and nonmembers—the equivalent of a symbiotic (mergerlike) relational state. Leadership is absent. Human relations are scattered and ill defined. Some organizations may have these attributes from time to time. When they are dominant, it can be said, the organization is in irreversible decay. For the present purposes, I use the prototaxic mode to describe the psychodynamics of human experience (linguistically, cognitively, emotionally, and relationally) prior to the birth of an organization—the mob. It can also describe the most severely regressed state of organizational life, the point at which organizational decay results in a broken system.

For example, one government agency had had such frequent leadership transitions that the division lacked a coherent policy commitment and direction. Managers had no sense of role boundaries and limits to their authority. Workers were unclear how to handle their caseloads. Applicants for assistance from the agency were often denied access. Services were nearly paralyzed, and no one had a clue what to do about their dilemma. It was as if the agency had become so disorganized and fragmented that nothing short of a rebirth of its authority structure and service procedures could render it functional.[2]

The prototaxic, undifferentiated experience occurs at approximately one to five months of age; the parataxic, differentiated experience, which we now turn to, occurs simultaneously with separation from the mother at approximately five to nine months of age. *Separation* is "the intrapsychic achievement of a sense of separateness from mother and, through that, from the world at large (Mahler et al., 1975: 8). The parataxic mode first appears in differentiation, the first subphase of separation-individuation (Mahler et al., 1975). The emerging cognitive ability to differentiate oneself from the other, and one object from the next, is then fundamental to the beginnings of language.

The Parataxic Mode (Defensive Organizational Identity)

As the baby matures, the lack of differentiated experience, characteristic of the prototaxic mode, is interrupted. In the parataxic mode of experience, what Freud called "preconscious" and "secondary processes," infants come to observe themselves in relation to others. Awareness of their actions increases. While crying, cooing, babbling, and the like, may evoke tenderness and nurturing responses from the parent, the infant is unable to connect fragments of experience in any logical or causal fashion.

They just happen together, or they do not, depending on circumstances. . . . The child cannot yet relate them to one another or make logical distinctions among them. . . . Since no connections or relations are established, there is no logical movement of "thought" from one idea to the next. The parataxic mode is not a step by step process. Experience is undergone as momentary, unconnected states of being. (Sullivan, 1953: 28n)

Differentiation is incomplete.

The cognitive potential for and beginnings of differentiation between self and other, however, cause the preverbal and later verbal (linguistic) tendency to categorize good and bad experiences. By late infancy, the child introjects symbols of "good me," "bad me," and "not me." These categorized introjects are the result of normal anxiety experienced in relation to the caretaking parent. In response to parental absence, withdrawal of tenderness, hostility, or ambivalence, children experience feelings of anxiety as a threat to personal security. In order to control anxiety, they contain (suppress) the threat by internalizing good and bad experiences and associate such feelings with their developing sense of self. Such interpersonal experiences and the manner in which they are perceived by children come to influence their self-image. Moreover, experiences of high-level anxiety produce dissociated or "not me" images that serve as a defense against feelings of self-disintegration.

In the parataxic (preconscious) mode of experience, where separation of self and other is initiated, distorted thinking prevails. However, differentiation, dissociated events and objects, necessarily produces selective thinking in early childhood, thinking which is often characterized by categories of opposites—white or black, good or bad, love or hate, all or nothing. Thus, childhood anxiety experienced in the prototaxic mode of attachment and the parataxic mode of separation-individuation may later distort adult communications. Rational thought and action often mask repressed experiences and unconscious memories. Consequently, the presence of parataxic distortions, or what is best defined as inadequate differentiation due to the onslaught of infantile anxiety, produces (emotional-cognitive) splitting and projections. This lack of integrated self-image influences the number and quality of cognitive defenses (preconscious and secondary processes) put into operation during adulthood. In organizations, members protect themselves against dangerous situations and perceptions by taking refuge in these primitive defensive actions.

Organizations dominated by parataxic modes of interpersonal experiences are defensive social systems, what I discussed at length in Chapter 2 as externalized self-systems. Relational separateness and distinctiveness are anxiety-provoking and foster envy among organizational members. Managerial control of subordinate behavior and interactions is of paramount concern. System boundaries are excessively rigid, poorly managed, and insufficiently open and inflexible. Managers are overprotective, mistrustful, and inaccessible. Authority relationships provoke subordinate anxiety and insecurity. Information is withheld. Power is concentrated at the top. Authority and responsibility are unbalanced and often ambiguous. Mistakes and errors are concealed. Conflicts are avoided at all costs and competition thwarts coordination of activities. Finally, actions are disconnected from their human origins and thus personal responsibility is absent.

Categories of parataxic distortions present in defensive organizations include transferences of emotion and defensive acts of splitting and projections, activated in response to the imagined danger of authority relationships. To accentuate the concept of "the imagined" is to acknowledge the critical associations among cognition, anxiety, and distorted communications. Self-deficits result not only from inadequate supervising (parenting) and authorizing (nurturing), but from the subordinate's (child's) inability to arrange experience linguistically. Disconnected experience, for example, promotes splitting and compartmentalization of people and things; connected and integrated experiences facilitate the repairing and mending of split images into whole objects (e.g., the breast versus the mother).

For example, the director of a public agency operating with limited resources is frustrated by the poor coordination of tasks across functional divisions within his department. His managers are in conflict and distrust one another. The more he tries to intervene and mediate between divisions, the more defensive and resistant his managers and staff become. A "we-they" attitude prevails in which divisional members view themselves as good and other divisions as bad. Work is accomplished but with great difficulty and minimal effectiveness and efficiency. The sharing of information and communication among divisions is poor.

Clarifying otherwise distorted communications in the workplace is a reparative activity, which if successful must involve the act of arranging experience linguistically and confronting anxiety about relationships. These cognitive-linguistic and interpersonal skills are categorized in what is called the *syntaxic mode of experience*.

The Syntaxic Mode (Resilient Organizational Identity)

On reaching maturity, Sullivan writes,

The child gradually learns the "consensually validated" meaning of language—in the widest sense of language. These meanings are acquired from group activities, interpersonal activities, social experience [and from contact with the physical world as meaningfully understood]. Consensually validated *symbol activity* involves an appeal to principles which are accepted as true by the *hearer*. And when this happens, the youngster has acquired or learned the syntaxic mode of experience. (1953: 28 n.9)

Sometime before adolescence the interpersonal desire for intimacy appears in the syntaxic mode of experience. Human relations are characterized, for example, by consensual validation of a friend's personal worth through intersubjective communication and mutual understanding. Preadolescence ushers in the capability of love. Signals of maturity surface as the child develops the ability to attend to the security needs of friends. Later in adolescence this capacity for intimacy expands into consensual validation with a member of the other sex at about the same moment (what Sullivan calls) the "lust dynamism" emerges as a significant motivating force.[3]

Experience in the syntaxic mode illustrates the maturity of cognitive skills, as well as the growing awareness in the youngster of his or her own as well as others' emotional needs. Genuine interpersonal intimacy requires minimum defensiveness and, therefore, minimal anxiety. Success in preadolescent development offers the good prospect that earlier disturbances with the self are reversible. Sullivan suggests, "Because one draws so close to another, because one is newly capable of seeing oneself through the other's eyes, the preadolescent phase of personality development is especially significant in correcting autistic, fantastic ideas about oneself or others" (248).

Preadolescent needs for intimacy serve twinship motives (discussed in previous chapters) through the medium of seeing oneself in resemblance to the other. This transference of emotions, along with the desire for intimacy, either validates one's sense of self (through this essential alikeness) or further distorts one's self image. A rudimentary identity is confirmed or questioned through syntaxic, consensually validating experience. Adolescence presents the emerging self with a crucial opportunity to establish self-identity through experiences of intimacy.

Actualization of the syntaxic mode of experience does not imply the disappearance of parataxic and prototaxic modes, or the lack of influence of unconscious and preconscious processes on consciousness. Parataxic distortions, characterized by defensive and selectively inattentive acts, are common safety measures of everyday life. People in complex social systems do not always comprehend the relationship of events. They "can grasp the issue of causality in the world only as it is told to [them]. To develop the syntaxic mode, [they] must order the world, put events in proper perspective" (Levenson, 1983: 40).

SUMMARY

The awareness of prototaxic, parataxic, or syntaxic modes of experience is helpful to organizational participants and their consultants. Emotional well-being, satisfaction, good communication, learning, and effectiveness among organizational members require consensual validation and collaboration. The act of learning to communicate negative feelings and overcome defensive barriers to correcting errors and solving problems is crucial to organizational change and development. In so doing, participants reinforce, if not acquire, syntaxic aptitude. In the psychodynamic approach to organizational change that I proffer, consultants and clients are required to develop and practice communication and interpersonal skills that enable them to confront their anxieties about relationships. The syntaxic mode of experience fosters a level of intimacy necessary to solving problems among organizational members.

The organizational equivalent of the syntaxic mode is the resilient organization that I discussed in the previous chapter on groups and will present in the following chapter of Part II. I, then, return to it in the concluding Chapter 11. In Part II I present five consultation cases in four chapters in which I try to give the reader a variety of illustrations of how these psychodynamic principles and ideas may be applied to organizations.

Next, in Chapter 7, I explore the defensive organization from the standpoint of communication and language in the parataxic mode of experience and discuss a transition to the resilient organization through the acquisition of communication and interpersonal skills in the syntaxic mode of experience.

NOTES

1. As I have noted elsewhere, projections are acts of rejection of negative feelings about oneself, such as anger and hostility, emotions that can be displaced onto others, enabling one to hold on to good feelings about oneself. This act, in effect, diminishes anxiety by externalizing bad feelings. In organizations, projections are common responses to critical incidents, whereby members act to blame and scapegoat one another but refuse to share responsibility as members of a cooperative enterprise. Organizational members tend to contain their problems in other individual members, work groups, and organizations, producing a handy vehicle for denial and defense against anxiety.

2. Many contemporary and future-oriented organizations are described as boundaryless. Diversification, mergers, cooperative arrangements between organizations, and the like, are fostering these seemingly boundaryless companies. Consequently, workers are faced with having to learn more psychologically sophisticated interpersonal and communicative skills. Thus, attending to the various modes of linguistic experience (prototaxic, parataxic, and syntaxic), I believe, becomes ever more essential.

3. The syntaxic mode of experience is present much earlier than Sullivan assumes, however. It appears somewhere in the third year of life, and simultaneously with the establishment of gender identity and individuality based on sufficient object constancy (Mahler et al., 1975).

II

PRACTICE

7

INTIMIDATION AND SHAME
ANXIETY AT WORK

THE CASE OF THE HUMAN SERVICES AGENCY

A human services agency requested my assistance in "team building." I was contacted by a training specialist, who said her superiors were interested in enhancing the "effectiveness" of agency caseworkers. She complained that they were "overwhelmed by information and excessive workloads" and went on to say that workers had "no focus or ideal." She also chafed at the fact that they felt degraded and ashamed about making mistakes of which their superiors might become aware. She pointed out that there had been many changes of leadership over the last nine years. In fact, there had been four directors in the last five years at the agency, and with each new director came some form of reorganization.

The agency had two working groups: fiscal and programs. At the time of my consultation, the Human Services Agency had lost another director. The new leader, Mr. Grant, presently served as the deputy director. His staff described him as competitive, vindictive, and perfectionistic. He would yell at his staff for making mistakes and communicate to his agency the expectation that their work performance be flawless. To his staff in public he would proclaim, "Our goal is to be perfect," yet mistakes were inevitable. For example, management routinely revised the staff's letters to their clients. Correspondence, when first composed, characteristically flowed two levels up the chain of command for Mr. Grant's approval. Rarely, if ever, was a letter adequately written the first time according to his standards, which became those of the agency. (Typically, the leader's ideal of perfection becomes the followers'.) He revised and returned each document to middle management. At that level, the supervisors would examine the letters bearing Mr. Grant's scribblings in red ink, become inflamed at the flawed performance of their subordinates, and with quiet disappointment or expressed scorn return them for corrections.

The staff felt intimidated and ashamed when they were presented with their inadequate efforts at correspondence, yet did not understand the nature of their mistakes. Their errors were not merely grammatical or semantic—rather, the most confusing corrections made were subtle shifts in language, the basis of which was political in nature. The deputy director, Mr. Grant, well versed in the politics of client agencies, made valid corrections based on his knowledge yet did not share with his staff the rationale that would allow them to minimize such mistakes. In fact, he further confused them with ambiguous statements, such as the following communication to several staff members, which took place in the agency offices: "Don't be too ambitious about regulating agencies at this time." The program technicians and professionals, fearful of making any mistakes and afraid to use their own judgment, interpreted his statement as follows: "No more evaluations of agency programs!" Why did they interpret it that way? Because that interpretation led them to the safest of all responses in a no-win situation, the path of least resistance. Mr. Grant first heard the interpretation in a session with me (the consultant) and his staff. He was angry and perplexed, not understanding how his staff could take "a suggestion for moderation," which is what he "intended to say," as a command for his staff to halt proactive regulation.

The situation perpetuated itself. Without specific directives and knowledge of relevant policies, it was impossible for the staff to act consistently and independently, and very difficult to make correct decisions about appropriate language and content. Their discretion was severely limited and, consequently, they felt disparaged—unable to master tasks for which they were held responsible. Moreover, the lack of adequate leadership provoked anxiety among the staff, which, in turn, encouraged projections of aggression, hostility, and suspicions of Mr. Grant and his management staff.

Analysis

The only certainties for the Human Services Agency were a heavy workload, a politically sensitive environment, and constant change (such as leadership transitions and associated reorganizations). The tumultuous environment produced instability, disorganization, and confusion among staff members. Each new director attempted to "get a handle" on the situation by structurally reorganizing (which often meant reinstituting hierarchical arrangements and dependencies) and further promoting the systemic suppression of negative feelings and the denial of problems among staff. The agency had a history of nonparticipative management in which professionally trained staff would carry significant responsibility and no authority. Inadequate bottom-up communication combined with ambiguous top-down information was characteristic.

The staff felt demoralized and worthless; they were incapable of correcting their own errors and denied the opportunity to air problems. Accordingly, they internalized degrading attributes and very low collective self-image, which led to the projection of undiscussed and suppressed bad feelings. As a result many of these hostile feelings were displaced onto management and staff in other units, as well as onto clients.

Anxiety distorted cognition and dialogue among staff, resulting in defensive actions. Fantasies, assumptions, and untested attributions ran wild. Misunderstandings dominated consensually validated discourse. *Parataxic* distortions (otherwise known as splitting) in which organizational members think and talk in either-or, black and white categories shaped their attempts at communicating with each other. A "we-they" attitude persisted: you were either outsider or insider. That being the case, people were stereotyped and placed into oversimplified categories. Prejudice and narrow-mindedness were typical. Why did relations and communications deteriorate to such a degree?

Mr. Grant managed by intimidation, unconsciously conveying his superiority and disrespect for his staff through his actions. He sincerely felt and rationalized that his staff "didn't need to know" his rationale for (political) decision making that forced them routinely to revise and correct their work. Thus, his staff, not knowing the reasons for his corrections of their work, felt incompetent. By withholding information that might clarify policy parameters and political implications for them, Mr. Grant unwittingly sabotaged their effectiveness. More importantly, he held them to an impossible set of standards: They had to perform perfectly; there could be no mistakes. Yet, correcting errors was central to their work.

Errors in a regulatory agency as political as Human Services was always problematic for a director, and sensitivity to the political implications of correspondence with clients was a prudent strategy. However, Mr. Grant showed excessive sensitivity that, combined with unattainable standards and withholding of information, merely stymied his staff.

As a young child Grant had had polio. He felt this experience had something to do with his perfectionistic expectations of himself and others. A punitive superego combined with an unattainable ego ideal produced low self-esteem and hostility toward others at work. Under stress, Mr. Grant would project his negative self-image onto his staff, viewing them as incompetent and inferior. His staff would unconsciously accept the projection and find themselves feeling intimidated, inept, and ashamed—which was how Mr. Grant really felt about himself.

Without going into a deep analysis of Mr. Grant's life history and unconscious motives, it seems clear in this case that the leader's personality in combination with the organizational culture and hierarchic design produced a double-bind for the agency staff. Recognition for a job well done was out of the question. It simply wouldn't happen. All of their correspondence had to be scrutinized and inevitably corrected. Hence, they were left feeling degraded and ashamed.

Intervention

To produce collaboration and problem solving a consultant must interrupt anxious relationships and attend to long-suppressed and denied feelings of anger and disappointment. For example, on numerous occasions such as that of Mr. Grant's ambiguous message, I used the opportunity to produce a syntaxic mode of experience in which the deputy director and his staff could reach mutual understanding and reconciliation. At the times the director was confronted, for instance, with how his ambiguous messages were interpreted by his staff, I encouraged participants to discuss how they felt about it openly. I asked the program staff, "How do you feel about the mixed messages?" After three or four weeks of work with them, some admitted feeling anger and resentment. I then inquired, "What effect did it have on your ability to do your job?" Some expressed a feeling of paralysis and lack of direction. After hearing this message repeated many times from his staff over many weeks, Mr. Grant, with my encouragement, began to explore with his staff why they felt as they did and what could be done about it. This was not to be treated as Mr. Grant's problem. It belonged to the work group, and they would have to share responsibility for solving it. This particular consultation seemed to me to illustrate more than most the role of language and communication as a central factor in organizational change efforts.

TRANSITION FROM DEFENSIVE TO RESILIENT ORGANIZATIONAL IDENTITY

It is essential that participants view the consultant as empathic, if they are to work through their differences and long suppressed feelings successfully. Moving the Human Services Agency from a parataxic (defensive) to a syntaxic mode of communication meant facilitating the production of an emotionally safe environment—what D. W. Winnicott calls a holding environment (1971). The construction of a safe environment resulted from the unacknowledged testing of the consultant by the clients, as they attempted to determine whether I could be trusted. In the Human Services Agency case the following incident occurred at the beginning of our relationship.

Top management called for a private briefing with me after the first group session. Two of the four managers were absent from that first consultative session. All four managers and Ms. Block, their training representative, were present at the private briefing. The two who had missed the first session, the deputy director, Mr. Grant, and his assistant, were anxious to hear firsthand exactly what had occurred. When asked, I redescribed the general purpose and objectives of that consultative session while not disclosing what was said by those who attended the first meeting. Mr. Grant and his assistant persisted in their demands that I disclose information about the first session. I refused, stating that "it would be inappropriate and harmful to the process." The briefing then concluded. The training representative contacted me several days after the briefing. She explained, "Mr. Grant and his assistant were not convinced they could trust you; they now feel more confident of your discretion." Subsequently, the weekly sessions continued with the deputy director and his assistant present much of the time.

From the outset I insisted that everyone, staff and management alike, be present at each session. This request created a membership that, with the exception of me, constituted the natural work group. Minimally, this means an adequate representation of all roles and positions of the work group. Maintaining a group composition identical to that of the work group allows for the reconstruction of situations and dynamics appearing in the workplace; the point, of course, is to allow us all to monitor changes in behavior and experiences from week to week, and to discuss these issues at weekly sessions. In the absence of the deputy director and his assistant, the unveiling of participant emotions occurred at the first three-hour session. Staff members felt "less inhibited" in communicating their anger, resentment, and disappointment about past and present agency leadership.

I felt very much like a container of the group's hostility toward Mr. Grant, the deputy director, and experienced the participants' sense of themselves as victims (Bion, 1970).

Eventually, trust and empathy between me and the group evolved into a holding environment in which I assumed the role of dependency leader (Bion, 1959). Of the dependent group, Bion writes:

> The basic assumption of this group culture seems to be that an external object exists whose function it is to provide security for the immature organism. This means that one person is always felt to be in a position to supply the needs of the group, and the rest in a position in which their needs are supplied. (1959: 74)

Empathy and a desire to help without humiliating or embarrassing others were repeatedly communicated. Assuming the role of dependency leader, I implicitly acknowledged the group's unconscious wish to be taken care of and their desire to be treated equally. This wish is often represented by a group's silence and passivity from the outset, where the group desires to be led by the consultant to a "solution" or "cure" for their problems. It is also common to groups that consider the consultant the "all-knowing" expert.

Technically speaking, the creation of a dependency leader is critical to establishing an atmosphere of trust and empathy and is essential to legitimize the expression of feelings in the group and thereby the development and testing of language and communication skills. Addressing the consultant's empathic role in the dependency group, Bion elaborates: "The problem of the leader seems always to be how to mobilize emotions associated with the basic assumptions without endangering the sophisticated structure that appears to secure for the individual his freedom to be an individual while remaining a member of the group" (1959: 78). Group interventions, successful or not, often begin with a basic assumption of dependency and then ideally at a later time abandon that dependency for relative independence and personal responsibility.

Shifts in Unconscious Group Assumptions and Language Use: The Intervention Strategy

In transition from defensive to resilient organization, members of the agency shifted unconscious basic assumptions from dependency to fight-flight to pairing.[1] Dependency allows the consultant to get inside the experience of group members and validate their emotions via empathic language (Havens, 1986). I expressed the way I experienced their relation-ship to me in statements such as: "I believe the group wishes to be taken care of," or "I feel the group wishes I alone could solve its problems," and "Is the group's dependency on me akin to its reliance on Mr. Grant?"[2]

"The conditions of empathy are the therapist's power to imagine the experience of the other and then to express it" (Havens, 1986: 24). In the Human Services Agency, this meant identifying with both the frustrations and degradations of staff and the disappointments of management. The ability to locate and acknowledge the feelings of both management and staff helped them to find each other. The group's dependency facilitated their looking to me as a role model for change. In expressing what each side hoped to achieve I became the group's ego ideal. This dependency was based on an idealizing transference in which the group eventually came to perceive me as the good parent (all-protecting, all-nurturing, all-encompassing, and always understanding).

While on the surface this transition would seem to be a negative development, it is a necessary stage in the group's striving to become a syntaxic (consciously reflective and resilient) organization. Initially they looked to the "gentle and sensitive" consultant to help them transmit feelings and emotions, not believing that it was possible for them to do this themselves.[3] Eventually, however, I abandoned a purely nurturing role and encouraged them to communicate emotional issues among them-selves.[4]

In so doing, I shifted from an empathic language to an interpersonal language, and as Havens (1986) points out: "The verbal instrument for the management of distance is interpersonal language" (83). Here I distanced myself from group members by asking them to examine their projections; for example, I suggested, "Let's take a look at what has happened, and how it has affected your performance." Acting as if they could project the circumstances and associated feelings "out there" on the wall, I asked them to join me in the exploration. Asking for confirmation or disconfirmation, I described my observations of management and staff interactions and suggested a possible connection to present circumstances. Since the legit-imacy of their projected feelings had already been established through empathy and dependency, it was now time to encourage externalization of their circumstances—to examine the problem holistically.

Altering my consulting role from caretaker to confrontational facilitator met some resistance, as did the concomitant requirement to work through participant feelings about this change. Some group members responded with anger and hostility at my attempt to externalize the problem so it could be examined at a distance from me and group members. It seemed insensitive and reminded them of management's style. They felt betrayed and unappreciated. "You're expecting too much of us," was a typical comment, as was "We thought you were on our side." I was then accused by the staff of taking management's side.

Their immediate reaction to my attempt at confrontation was fight-flight behavior, based on their narcissistic rage activated by my rejection of their wish to idealize me further and to feel comfortable in my presence. They felt assaulted and manipulated by my shift from warmth and empathy to coolness and distance and momentarily treated me as their enemy or scapegoat with whom they must fight or from whom they must flee. After the group members had expressed their anger, the succeeding anxiety over having done so caused them to become silent, to delay returning after the group's break, and, most commonly, to change the subject. The atmosphere in the room was tense and depressive, as if someone had died, and the group—as do most at this point—became paralyzed or "stuck."

At this point the group moved out of the fight-flight phase and into a depressive one. At the next work session I verbalized the group's sense of grief and then asked whether it might be a result of feeling bad about being angry with me. There was nervous laughter, and then one brave individual volunteered affirmation. "Yeah, I guess I did feel bad about it," he said. "I even thought about calling you at home, but I thought it might be inappropriate." And then others chimed in with similar feelings.

After this period of expressing guilt and loss of me in my caretaking role, I was exonerated.[5] Group members realized that my stepping back from the group was necessary for their own empowerment and future development. This fact was acknowledged in a group evaluation of my performance (which I insist upon, periodically, throughout the group intervention). They agreed my consultative actions consistently required them to take responsibility for their actions, which they appreciated in retrospect.

Next, I intervened to suggest there was more than enough blame to go around for the agency's problems, some of which were within their control and some not. I further submitted that if the group was ready to take responsibility for itself, and, therefore, the consequences of previously suppressed emotions and avoidance of conflict, then I felt they were prepared to identify issues and resolve problems that they had thus far denied. These were the first comments I offered that were clearly instructive—what Havens (1986) calls *performative language* (165). For example, I suggested, "It appears by now that the agency's problems are out in the open; let's identify them and begin discussing what needs to change."

My intent was to use my authority, as leader/consultant, to minimize self-effacing and self-punitive judgments and maximize their willingness to take action and change. This led them into a pairing mode (Bion, 1959). At first there were allegiances formed within the group, gradually leading to the coming together of the group as a whole. A sense of hope and a desire for association emerged. The anxiety about confronting each other and their problems, which in the past was consistently avoided, momentarily exaggerated the individual striving for organizational affiliation and role conformity born out of the defensive need for security and safety.

For example, managers would pair with managers, technicians with technicians, and the like. This initial pairing seemed to establish a suffi-cient degree of temporary security among members, enabling them to listen and acknowledge the perceptions, feelings, and experiences of members in related sectors of the agency. Polarization was absent. Typical comments were "I could never understand why you felt that way but now that I see things differently from your position, it makes sense!" The deputy director requested of his staff: "Let me know when directives are unclear or too limiting. I can't tell unless you say something!" As to his demands for flawless performance, he concluded, "I can't ask you to be perfect, but I do have problems with repeated mistakes." Whereas earlier staff would hear only that he demanded perfection, they were now willing to test his expressed acceptance of the inevitability of errors and the potential for learning inherent in their detection and correction (Argyris and Schon, 1978). Shared feelings of reparation (Klein and Riviere, 1964; Hirschhorn, 1988) resulted in a desire to "put the pieces together." Management and staff now saw the destructive consequences of ambiguity, mixed messages, suppression and withholding of information, and the like. They had accepted responsibility and were now committed to action.

SUMMARY

In this chapter I have offered a case illustration of how organizational change rests on the development of mature language, communication, and interpersonal skills from which members can affirm intersubjective expe-riences, perceptions, and feelings at work—establishing a positive and realistic awareness of organizational identity. As the consultant guides the client group through the various phases of dialectic and interpersonal development, she or he shifts into the language appropriate to each phase.

Language and communication proficiency are defined as the capacity to express feelings, the psycholinguistic origins of which are located in the nuances of separation and individuation phases of childhood development.

Dialectic dexterity may be learned; however, most organization cultures, their leaders and politics, suppress this form of learning. Such are the circumstances of many individuals in defensive organizations. People resist sharing their feelings because of system norms and values that govern their behavior, for example, to suppress negative feelings and promote so-called rationality, norms promoted by organizational leaders and managers. Institutional members may come to rely on defensive strategies, such as suppression, denial, splitting, and projections, which distort cognition and reflective thinking by selective inattention to anxiety-ridden activities and relationships. To interrupt such demoralizing and counterproductive circumstances, an awareness of the psychodynamics of communication and language in group process will prove useful to the consultant to organizational change.

In the case of the Human Services Agency, Mr. Grant unconsciously reinforced organizational defensive routines. However, I treated the organization as a total system and, therefore, did not blame Mr. Grant for the agency's paralysis. Instead, I engaged him and his staff in sharing responsibility and moving toward a solution collaboratively. The effectiveness of the consultation process seemed to rely on the ability of the agency workers to learn to communicate their feelings and confront their shame anxiety.

In the next chapter, I discuss another consultation with an organization coping with the stress and anxiety of leadership transition and workload expansion.

NOTES

1. *Dependency basic assumptions* refer to a group's unconscious wish to be taken care of by the perceived or desired leader. *Fight-flight basic assumptions* refer to a group's search for an enemy to whom it can direct its aggression, or an enemy from whom it can flee. *Pairing basic assumptions* refer to two or more subgroups of individuals to whom the group can look for a sense of hope for a better future, and through whom they can fantasize about the coming of a messiah. See Bion (1959) for greater detail and elaboration.

2. Eventually the focus must move to the group and its "real" leader, the deputy director.

3. One might argue that the organization is not providing an adequate holding environment for its members. That is, the organization is not an adequately playful and supportive culture. It's simply not good enough and therefore members are discouraged from intimacy and collaboration.

4. In other words, once I felt satisfied that organizational participants experienced their relationship with me as trusting and supportive, I could move ahead with the work of identifying and solving problems.

5. This partly involved my explaining what I was doing. I was still going to be supportive, but now it was time to get to work on some of the concrete problems before them.

8

A PUBLIC AGENCY COPES WITH EXPANSION AND TRANSITION

THE CASE OF THE DEPARTMENT OF PUBLIC WORKS

In this chapter, I tell the story of the Department of Public Works (DPW),[1] a state agency undergoing the stresses and strains of expansion. DPW illustrates the extent to which ritualistic organizational defenses, discussed in Chapter 2, dominate a professional bureaucracy attempting to contend with political change. Consultation was sought only months after Dan Mosley took office as director, and one year after voter passage of a $600 million bond issue. Having previously operated on a $5 million budget, the agency was faced with an enormous increase in projects. The new director wanted to help his agency better cope with the extraordinary changes, and he wanted, in particular, to solve existing personnel problems. Primarily, he was interested in the consultant's helping him to deal with the conflict between his two assistant directors, Jim Hall and Sam Green.

Mosley was chosen as director by the commissioner on the basis of his technical and administrative credentials, and his experience as an executive in the public sector, albeit at the local level. He was perceived by government executives as someone who could turn around a department such as Public Works, despite its legacy of poor performance and low productivity. He was uncomfortable with the status quo and believed that work in the public sector could be of "high quality, challenging, and fun." Mosley was an innovator, driven to redesigning and reinventing work procedures. He discovered early in his tenure as director, however, that the political nature of work in state government often constrains the highest of managerial ideals.

Mosley claimed to be a participative manager, an administrative style that contradicted the organization's nonparticipative culture. The agency had a history of top-down leadership characterized by unilateral decision making, tall hierarchy, and multilayered chain of command, demonstrated in the leadership style and personality of the previous director—a retired military officer.

Mosley was caught in a dilemma. His superiors expected him to improve the agency's public image—a role that required him to spend time outside the agency. His better judgment told him that he had to repair the conflict-ridden internal affairs of the agency, and so he hired a consultant.

However, Mosley seemed to enjoy the political side of his role as director more than the administrative side. He liked being at the center of attention—in the limelight of state politics. He was known to lament, however, the political interference of the legislature and public interest groups in the internal affairs of his organization. He complained about the imbalance of public expectations and the allocation of resources. "Legislators and the public demand too much for too little money," he would say.

Despite his reservations about the public sector and his frequent thoughts of working for a private business, Mosley was dedicated to public works and to improvement in the level of performance and satisfaction among DPW staff. During his frequent absences, he expected his assistant directors to take charge and help to improve the quality of service. This did not occur, and Mosley was angry and perplexed.

One of my first interventions with the agency required confronting Mosley about the consequences of his frequent external activities for the agency. I pointed out to him that while he was aware of the conflict between his two assistants, he appeared unwilling to take responsibility for his absences and might be perpetuating the turmoil. It was my observation that the degree of his time and energy spent on external matters, however justifiable, left his assistants feeling neglected and abandoned. Mosley had moved too quickly into the political arena and had, apparently, withdrawn from the agency's internal problems. I then asked whether he had hired me to take away his own responsibility for dealing with the two assistants. While I believed it within my role to help resolve the conflict, it was beyond my role to "assume any of the director's responsibilities!" It seemed crucial for the director to acknowledge the significance of this implicit role expectation he might have of me. After declaring his shock at my directness, Mosley considered the comments and, with some reluctance and chagrin, said he agreed with my observations. This exchange, which took place rather early in the consultation process, was an excellent opportunity for the director and me to clarify a central question of every consultation: Who is the client? At this time, I stated to the director, "The Department of Public Works is the client of the consultation—not any one individual member."[2]

The consultation began with several months of extensive interviewing at all levels of organizational operations. Personnel at every layer of the agency were consulted. Their ideas, feelings, and thoughts were then shared by the consultant with the executive group. After three months of weekly meetings of the consultant, his assistant, and an executive group of DPW, a planned change was under way. This plan attempted to respond to current problems and conflicts voiced by organizational members to the consultants. These executive group meetings were the beginning of collaboration and problem solving among managers accustomed to working independently.

Structural and procedural change seemed reasonable and inevitable to almost everyone under the circumstances; however, resistance and barriers to innovation persisted and were not discussed by the executive group. Conflict among the assistant directors and between them and the director made the transition problematic.

Initial Contact with Client

Before the new director took office and I was hired as a consultant, the organization was a typical professional bureaucracy. The chain of command included the previous director at the top, with the assistant director, Jim Hall, at the second level. At the next level were three assistant managers representing three professions: engineering, architecture, and construction. Below them was another layer of assistants superordinate to an interdisciplinary staff of technical managers.

The new director hired me to facilitate a change effort. I was selected on the basis of a referral by a colleague from another university where Mosley (the new director) had earned a graduate degree. As a result of collaborative efforts by me, executives, and management to improve communications and productivity, the agency was restructured. The first layer of assistant managers was taken out of the chain of command and reassigned elsewhere in the agency. Staff members were then reorganized into regional work groups, each group coordinated by a regional manager who reported to the assistant director of the technical section, Jim Hall. In addition, an assistant director of administration was hired at the time Mosley took over. Because of what amounted to about a threefold increase of employees, Hall gave up his additional responsibility for administration. Both assistant directors reported to the director.

Intrapersonal Conflict

Jim Hall was assistant director of the technical section. He had been with the organization more than twenty years and had watched several directors come and go. Hall was highly regarded by his subordinates, who viewed him as knowledgeable in the technical aspects of their work and admired him for his ability to survive the annual political battles between the agency's leadership and the legislature. But they also saw him as frustrating their abilities to complete work and as withholding information.

Hall had high standards of performance that no one in the agency could meet. These standards slowed the work and frustrated his subordinates. He was overworked and usually appeared physically and emotionally exhausted—some might say "burnt out." Work flow from subordinates was, in fact, consistently bottled up in Hall's office because of his meticulously detailed reviews of all contracts and change orders, and the near-absence of authority delegated to his professional subordinates.

On the one hand, the technical staff appreciated Hall's meticulous reviews of their work, which often caught serious errors in judgment. On the other, they felt intimidated and constrained by his superior standards and were frustrated that all decisions of any consequence had to flow up the chain of command to him, and sometimes to Mosley, before staff could take action.

Their relationship to Hall was filled with ambivalence. They simultaneously admired him and held him in contempt. One manager exclaimed, "Our work is mediocre; we're not given the chance to do better!" Responsibility in the technical core of the public agency was not adequately matched by appropriate authority (Baum, 1987).

Talented, skillful, and knowledgeable professionals, all experts in their respective fields and responsible for overseeing the design of costly and often highly political tasks, were ineffective. They had little authority to make decisions—decisions they were the best informed about and most qualified to make. For example, change orders required six signatures for approval. Authorization of superiors, and their superiors' superior, and ultimately Jim Hall (assistant director) and Dan Mosley (director) was routine procedure. Several members of the technical staff reported how they felt it necessary to include all of their superiors anytime they talked with Mosley or Hall.[3] Competent professionals felt incompetent, helpless, and powerless. Snug controls and little discretion prevailed.

When I first met Hall for an interview, I experienced him as withholding, tired, and distressed. He complained of "inadequate staff support" and said that his "project managers are doing too much clerical work!" He made it clear that he was not opposed to change, as he suggested others believed him to be. He seemed particularly annoyed that the new assistant director, Green, took Hall's personal secretary from him, and that now he was faced with having to replace her. Attempts to invite his assistance in solving organizational problems failed. He responded persistently with rationalizations such as "I don't have the time to devise a new system; we are overloaded as it is now!" and "Look at that pile of contracts on my desk to review" and "We may have some problems and I don't think we're perfect, but we are able to get projects finished. So why change anything?"

Hall expressed support for change, but in the same conversation expressed opposition to it. He claimed acceptance of imperfection in emphasizing success measured by completed projects. However, his control over authorizations and his scrutiny of staff requests signified the contrary. He further acted as if he were responsible for doing all the work, displaying an attitude of superiority consistent with his perfectionistic standards.

Hall might be viewed by some as a classic obsessive-compulsive. He was obsessional about standards and details, compulsive about control of subordinate behavior, and withholding. The division's tall hierarchy and policy of limited discretion and minimal delegated authority required compulsive behavior supportive of top-down control and rigid adherence to a multilayered chain of command. But the key to Hall's actions and the question of his potential for change and development lay not in an inflexible and rigid personality and concomitant organizational strategy and structure, but in his wounded self-esteem.[4]

Green arrived shortly after the new director, Mosley. He then became assistant director in charge of administration and facilities. These responsibilities had belonged to Hall. This fact and Green's taking Hall's secretary with the implicit endorsement of the new director hurt and angered Hall, who was not someone to express verbally his negative feelings and demand a reversal of action. In addition, the loss of his secretary also meant losing someone he depended upon for crucial administrative tasks and procedures. This negatively affected the performance of his section of project managers, an added blow to his feelings of self-competence and self-worth.

Perfectionism is a key attribute of narcissism (Rothstein, 1980). Organizational members like Hall cannot correct errors or solve problems because they cannot readily admit them. Admitting their errors would cause the presence of a conflicted self-image to surface: recognition of their limitations, therefore, would be anxiety-producing and might strip them of necessary defenses.

Hall sought perfection in an imperfect, constantly changing, stressful and political environment. His initial rationalizations and resistance to change stemmed from defenses against awareness of a conflicted self-image and anxiety over losing control. That is, to his subordinates he projected an image of superior standards and expertise. He was someone to go to for advice, someone who took responsibility for everyone, and someone who desired to see himself as perfect and ideal in the eyes of others. His actions, however, contradicted his true feelings. Hall's narcissistic and perfectionistic tendencies were a defense against deeper feelings of inadequacy and low self-worth, which surfaced in his relations with Mosley, his superior, whom he experienced as intimidating.

In conversations with me, Hall would express surprise and puzzlement at how dependent upon him staff were for his technical advice and counsel. He genuinely did not understand it. Hall was unaware of how his actions perpetuated their dependency. He was equally surprised at their frustration with him. He stated on numerous occasions that he was only trying to "help and protect them from making costly mistakes." I asked him whether he understood how his staff could hold him in high regard for his talents and skills, on the one hand, and despise him for interfering in their work, on the other. He did not know. I then inquired whether he thought he demanded their respect but, at the same time, felt undeserving of that respect. He was not sure. At another meeting, I asked whether he saw any inconsistencies in his actions that might reflect such an unconscious conflict. He did, and then went on to justify it, stating that he had to hold his staff accountable. "It was for their own good," he argued.

Like previous directors, Mosley depended on Hall to manage the internal organization so that he, as director, could devote his own time and energy to managing the organization's political environment. Unlike his predecessors, Mosley disapproved of Hall's leadership and was critical of the performance of Hall's section. Both Hall and Mosley, in other words, disapproved of each other's leadership styles and avoided confronting each other. The subject was taboo.

The entrance of Mosley as director and his demand for organizational change aggravated Hall's suppressed conflict. Hall's apparent inner conflict combined with his position of authority had affected his entire section, often nearly paralyzing subordinates.

Hall's perfectionistic and withholding style unwittingly produced a pattern of repressed rage, resentment, and mistrust among his subordinates. These internally suppressed emotions, however, preceded

Mosley's arrival as new director. These sentiments originated with the personality and authoritarian leadership of the agency's first director and were perpetuated by subsequent directors (Schein, 1985). Anxiety was then heightened by unprecedented organizational expansion and new leadership. Organizational members continued to suppress their anger. Defensive routines, mistrust, suspicion, low morale, and productivity persisted; their implications are discussed further in the section on group conflict. We turn now to the interpersonal conflict between Hall and Green.

INTERPERSONAL CONFLICT: HALL'S RELATIONSHIP WITH GREEN

Assuming Hall's role, the new assistant director of administration, Sam Green, reported directly to Mosley. Green and Hall had equal authority in the agency. Green arrived only months after the director, Mosley. Hall said he did not mind losing responsibility and control over the administrative operations of the agency. He did, however, resent losing staff, particularly his secretary, and its consequences for the performance in his section. Here as elsewhere, the director's actions contradicted his espoused participative style—the hiring of Green and authorizing of his taking Hall's secretary occurred with no consultation between Mosley and Hall. Hall's anger at Mosley for what he called "a poorly thought-out decision" (the establishment and structural positioning of Green's role) seemed displaced onto the new assistant director of administration, Sam Green. *Displacement* here is "the process by which the individual shifts interest from one object or an activity to another in such a way that the latter becomes an equivalent or substitute for the other" (Rycroft, 1968: 35).

How did I know Hall was doing so? In conversations with me, Hall consistently expressed disagreement with, and doubt about, the new director's decisions for reorganization of the agency but stated that he (Hall) would do whatever Mosley requested of him. Hall admitted to only philosophical disagreements with his new boss, no anger or resentment. On the surface, his actions showed no hostility toward the director—at least not directly. But with respect to Green, Hall communicated disrespect and distrust for him from the outset.

Green was hired to perform several varied functions that included managing the administrative section. Green's superiors, at the highest levels of government (Mosley's superiors), were responsible for his recruitment and selection. They were impressed and had great expectations of him.

Green had grand ideas he would share with Mosley, but he was unresponsive to his own staff, who complained to the consultant on numerous occasions how he ignored their requests. He would not listen to their complaints nor their ideas for improving staff performance, yet he expected to be treated with respect and admiration. Green claimed to be a "people manager" but in practice was not. He also referred to himself as "task oriented" yet had no interest in details. His staff was disappointed with him.

In the first of many interviews with me, Green said that he thought one of his primary objectives as an assistant director was to "change the public's attitudes toward the agency." This comment was followed by "the agency is viewed as uncooperative, and when I first arrived there was a morale problem." This seemed to be intended to suggest to me that Green had already accomplished a great deal, such as improving morale. Then, he exclaimed, "I heard about Hall before I took the job." When I asked what he meant, Green suggested that many of the problems of the department were due to Hall's poor attitude and antiquated management practices. Green concluded with the observation that there was "no cohesiveness in the power structure. It's a control issue between Hall and me; we're into this 'we-they' dynamic."

During a later interview, Green reported a recurrent dream in which he would find himself working late at night in his office. The empty office was disquieting and made him feel uneasy. As he sat behind his desk in the dark, his office door would suddenly fly open. Barely visible in the dim light would be Jim Hall, the sharp edge of a knife glimmering in his right hand. Green reported that he would then awake in an anxious sweat.

On the surface, the dream seemed to suggest that Green was sensitive to Hall's suppressed rage at Green's taking away his secretary and a great deal of power and authority in the agency. When I suggested this to Green, he had little difficulty accepting it. The level of anger made him anxious and he did not know what to do about it. After all, he had the blessings of the director, Mosley.

Green, in fact, did pose a threat to Hall's institutional status quo and was, therefore, an insult to Hall's status and position. Green's public criticism of the division at his arrival is best illustrated by his response to Hall's claim that he was understaffed and his people were overworked: "I can count on my two hands the number of managers who are not busy in this office!" While Green's assertion ultimately threatened Hall's ideal view of himself and his division, it provided Green an opportunity to make points with the director—whose admiration he sought and toward whom he felt angry for abandoning him.

In a session with both men, each admitted to feelings of disappointment and rage at the other. Both agreed their rage began in disappointment with Mosley for leaving them to work out their new roles and directives. Despite their anger at the director, his superior position and the organizational taboo against the expression of feelings meant they did not feel they could confront him. It is possible that Green's dream represented his own homicidal wish displaced onto Hall, but meant for Mosley.

Hall's and Green's defensive reactions were symptomatic of the organizational identity. Instead of directly communicating their frustrations with the director, they focused all their anger and resentment on each other and their respective units, displacing anger intended for Mosley. Hall became, in the view of Green, the major obstacle to the agency's progress in improving public image, productivity, and effectiveness. For Sam Green, Jim Hall carried the negative legacy of the agency's poor performance.

Conflict between Hall and Green influenced the entire organization. It promoted group conflict and exaggerated individual defensive tendencies and defensive routines common to professional bureaucracies (Jaques, 1955; Menzies, 1960; Argyris, 1985; Diamond, 1984; 1985; Diamond and Allcorn, 1985a). This perpetuated internal conflict and counterproductive competition between the units. Secrecy, mistrust, and withholding of information reinforced rigid boundaries between the units, rendering ineffective the coordination of tasks and communication on projects.

INJURED SELF-ESTEEM, AUTHORITY, AND ORGANIZATIONAL CONFLICT

To understand the antagonism fully, it is important to examine the initial conflict between Hall and Green, recognizing that displacement of bad feelings such as Green's and Hall's stems from mutually wounded self-esteem. Hall pursued an exaggerated ideal of perfection through detailed and superior performance, while Green pursued a fantasy of grandiosity and omnipotence through power seeking and communication of grand ideas. Both men, however, felt low self-esteem and an exaggerated need for approval in relation to the director. Neither Hall nor Green was willing to express negative feelings toward Mosley. He was in a superior position and they feared his retribution and rejection. His absence and resignation from the problem infuriated them. Both men were safe targets of aggression for each other. Ironically, they both felt undeserving of the admiration, loyalty, and love they apparently demanded of their respective staff. Both shared a reliance on hierarchy, in their mutual superordinate roles and for their self-esteem derived from organizational status and prestige. While their demands of subordinates signified "love and admire me," their deeper sentiment, expressed to me, was "I don't really deserve their [staff] respect."

Here was an instance of displacement. Hall displaced his bad feelings toward Mosley onto the image he held of Sam Green. Green and his assistant, Harold Freeman, became Hall's scapegoats for the agency's inefficiencies. In Hall's mind, it sometimes seemed that Green and Freeman were the only obstacles to the agency's operating at optimal efficiency. Hall's feelings toward Green and Freeman were shared by his staff, and they seemed to influence many of their subordinates to denigrate Green; his assistant, Freeman; and their section. As long as this continued Hall and Green could avoid confronting Mosley.

Subordinates identified with a common superior. Their affiliation as members in a group (unit or section) was then solidified by a common identification with their leader. Here the identity of a superior like Hall served the subordinates' common need to idealize a leader. As Freud (1921) suggests, the image of a leader in the minds of his followers replaces their ego ideals with that of the leader. In other words, the normal narcissism of subordinates may be transferred to and replaced by the image of a superior. In this instance, Hall's subordinates identified with his hatred of Green and his staff. This perpetuated conflict throughout the organization.

INTERGROUP CONFLICT

Staff was not immune to the Hall-Green conflict. Hall's immediate subordinates identified with his negative view of Green, Freeman, and their unit, while Green's section despised Hall and his unit. This view persisted despite the fact that both sections felt ambivalent toward their respective heads. People from each section complained that the other was uncooperative, was ineffective, and received special treatment from the director. Polarization of units of the agency and a "we-they" mentality continued.

During group sessions with staff members of opposing units and me, members acknowledged how their subordination and hostility toward each other diminished morale, perceived competence, and organizational effectiveness. More importantly, they saw how their interactions reflected the conflict between Hall and Green at the top. Beyond the initial blaming of the opposing unit, staff members recognized that as long as inordinate power and authority resided in Hall and Green, their interpersonal conflict would continue to be everyone's problem.

Thus, once with the help of the consultant these conflicted professional groups understood that their differences were primarily grounded in the conflict at the top, a structural and procedural solution to the problem of conflict at their level of technical operations, such as reducing hierarchy and delegating authority, could be of some value. That is, structural and procedural changes, including delegation of authority and responsibility, could be useful once they understood their role in perpetuating the central conflict between Hall and Green.

The power and authority necessary to implement work were concentrated in the director, his embattled assistant directors, and their assistants. Before the intervention at the intergroup level, people at the technical core felt the conflict passively; they were victims of conflict at the top. Regardless of their professional knowledge and expertise, they felt powerless to reverse the effects of interpersonal conflict—they were spectators rather than key players. Their inaction appeared to condone the conflict, and their displaced emotions onto the perceived enemy unit tended to confuse matters further. In not publicizing their feelings at the time of the initial expansion and change, and in not demanding some role in redesigning their future, they had colluded in organizational camouflage. The combination of project expansion, antiquated bureaucratic strategy and structure, and executive conflict fueled the diminishing effectiveness and potential paralysis.

The two sections polarized. Emotional and cognitive splitting of group images in which each group viewed the other as all-bad and themselves as all-good occurred. These distorted perceptions and concomitant actions, I would conjecture, were due to the emotional need of people in both sections to project hostile feelings somewhere acceptable: outside the unit and away from management. Melanie Klein et al. (1964) pointed out that through the act of *projective identification*, one's bad feelings may become tolerable when viewed as belonging to another person or object such as members of the other divisional unit in the case of the agency.

The consequences of unresolved conflict at the group and organizational levels are similar to those at the intra- and interpersonal levels. Displacement, splitting, projective identification, and projective aggression; acceptance and rejection of images of oneself and others; contradictions in what people say and do; and defensive strategies and routines are commonplace. Conflict is eventually suppressed, forgotten, or denied, persisting as an unconsciously sustained structure and operating at multiple levels of organizational experience—resulting in an unstable organizational identity. When suppressed and denied, conflict becomes unconscious and constitutes a latent social structure.

If the initial conflict is experienced passively, then any effort at conflict resolution must first reverse the passive experience and empower organizational participants to solve their own problems and change themselves. Organizational defensiveness disguised as diplomacy, consciously and unconsciously intended to prevent conflict, must give way to greater constructive confrontation and conflict resolution. These are the primary tasks of the psychoanalytic organizational consultant in his or her work with the client system.

INTERGROUP INTERVENTIONS

In group sessions focused on interpersonal and intergroup conflict, staff members eventually understood the effects of the Hall and Green conflict on their own interactions. This realization did not occur without significant resistance and hesitation among group members. Not until it was clear to them that it was safe to think critically and reflectively were they able to explore the reasons for their mistrust and disrespect for each other. Eventually, they came to understand that in identifying with their respective assistant director and his antagonisms they had previously made no effort to test their assumptions and attributions about the other unit and its leadership. They asked no questions and requested no information. They had operated on the basis of fantasy and imagination.

In intergroup sessions, I encouraged them to question their private assumptions of each other's role and to share information about their respective units. I expressed my bewilderment at the suspicion and disrespect they shared for the other group. For example, I said, "Help me understand why you mistrust one another." At first they denied any lack of trust. Then I said, "We know of numerous incidents of information withholding and suspicious motives between the groups. The problem is not an absence of concrete examples or proof of conflict. Help me better appreciate the difficulty you have in discussing it with each other." Directing their attention to their resistance, the struggle in confronting the problem and each other, enabled them to start talking. It eased them through their anxieties about sharing negative feelings and taking responsibility for themselves.

Professional staff members of both sections then acknowledged their perpetuation of and responsibility for the intergroup warfare. Consequently, the technical staff understood better the political and legal requirements of budgetary requests from administration, and administration better understood the time constraints, project subtlety, and workload burden of the technical section. Rather than suspecting that the other group was vindictive and projecting blame, the unit could now work out a mutual solution to budget requests and other organizational problems previously exaggerated by displaced emotions and perceptions. Structural change by itself, absent of the psychological insights and shifts in work relations among group members, would not have lifted this organization out of its dilemma.

ASSESSMENT OF THE CONSULTATION

By requesting a consultation, Mosley had exposed the organization and himself to the reflexive inquiry necessary for critical appraisal. His professional staff had operated under conditions of virtually no authority but considerable responsibility. This imbalance produced great frustration. Prior to the consultation they felt powerless and helpless to do anything. The imbalance was only partly rectified through structural and procedural reorganization. It was more deeply and fundamentally corrected by working through feelings of loss about change, collaborative problem setting, problem solving, and intergroup conflict resolution sessions. Consequently, conflict at the top was more visible and resolution more likely.

After three months of planned change sessions between the two consultants and the division's executive group, and nine months after the initial interviews, the agency's director, Dan Mosley, requested that his staff begin delegating authority. This organizational change moved considerably greater authority to key staff members, those responsible for projects. The evolving strategy for change met with great resistance from Hall and his staff, who relinquished significant power and authority, status, and prestige. The change, however, freed Hall from detailed control of day-to-day operations and allowed him to devote his talents and skills to advising managers on request and to expensive and highly sensitive political projects. Hall no longer had the next to last word on all projects. But he was now in a position to manage the technical core effectively.

The director also shifted Green away from his supervisory role in administration, replacing him with Freeman so that he could devote more of his time to his other two roles. He expressed his concealed grief about losing some control by communicating relief and appreciation to some while acting arrogant and vindictive toward others. He resigned a short time later. The technical staff was delegated the authority necessary to utilize its competencies more effectively, and all layers of hierarchy between them and Hall were eliminated, so that the primary responsibility of the organization was revitalized and subsequently improved.

Among project managers and their staff, the change was empowering. It renewed the professional staff members' sense of competence and, at the same time, uncovered the previously ill-conceived organizational strategy and structure. It replaced the passive experience of the technical staff with greater mastery over their work. While the conflict between Hall and Green remained until Green's departure, it represented a less substantial barrier to comprehensive organizational change and development. Unfortunately Freeman, Green's replacement for administration, carried much of the persistent conflict with Hall into his new position. Because of Freeman's strong identification with Green, he took over not only Green's position but his ongoing conflict with Hall. But now the organizational core, project management, was functioning effectively, and the Hall-Green (and now Freeman) conflict was out in the open. They no longer could conceal conflict behind organizational symptoms. Conflict at the top had to be confronted.

Further interventions with both men revealed persistent resistance to change rooted in an organizational arrangement that no longer supported their mutually narcissistic requirements. The unresolved conflict between Hall and Green remained, and so did the question of whether or not they were capable of change and resolution. After Green's departure, Hall and Freeman were able to work through some of the residual conflict.

Intergroup sessions, involving management from both sections, were directed at facilitating problem solving and conflict resolution. Hall and Freeman were useful in getting their staff to acknowledge conflicts and take responsibility for themselves. Using the intergroup sessions as an opportunity to explore and observe the psychodynamic interactions between the two work units, projects and administration, proved most helpful in resolving conflict through reversal of passive experience.

Within eighteen months of the initial consultation, Hall showed some indications of change. He started to attend problem-solving sessions involving staff from different units and divisions and in his role facilitated more integrative thinking and constructive confrontation on unsolved problems. As I continued to act as a consultant on the process and took a less directive role, both Hall and Freeman seemed to become more helpful in conflict resolution sessions with staff. Consequently, these developments enabled Mosley to focus better on the external relationships of DPW.

As a consequence of consultation, individual personalities *were not* changed; organizational arrangements and ways of interacting, thinking, and feeling among participants about conflict were altered. Members saw conflict more as an opportunity for learning and problem solving than as something to be avoided at all costs.

POSTCONSULTATION: THREE YEARS LATER

Nearly three years after the initial contact, Hall resigned. Although he showed some evidence of change and adaptation to a more participative and collaborative system, he was never comfortable and enthusiastic about it. Despite the successful change effort, one cannot help but think that fundamentally the personalities of leaders and executives in organizations must match shifting organizational cultures, and when they do not, one or the other must go.

On the other hand, Mosley's external stance may be viewed as a way to get rid of history (Hall) and poorly managed internal (low-status and boring) concerns and to provide a buffer zone for negative affect (between Hall and Green and their staff) while he (Mosley) looks good dealing with exciting, high-status political outside groups. Even with consultation he remains "good" while the changes he "wants" lead to a better functioning organization, at the cost of Green's and Hall's resignations.

PSYCHODYNAMIC VIEWS OF CONFLICT IN ORGANIZATIONAL CONSULTING

Both normative and structural interpretations of conflict are valuable. Certain organizational norms and structures foster conflict while simultaneously encouraging the avoidance and denial of those very conflicts. Nevertheless, conflict is also a highly subjective, personal experience. Individuals take conflicting feelings with them into the workplace, where they are often acted upon in relationships between and among members. Conflictual relationships are promoted by hierarchical organizational design and competitive values that are reproduced by individuals. Resource scarcity, superior-subordinate relationships, and environmental stress do instigate conflicts in organizations. The nature of and willingness or unwillingness to resolve these conflicts, however, are ultimately determined by the intra- and interpersonal dynamics of key organizational members. Not excluding structural and normative variables, my approach insists on the willingness of individuals to take personal responsibility for their actions, and thereby take responsibility for their role in producing or perpetuating (and not resolving) conflict whether perceived as stemming from the public realm or the private self.

Individuals are ultimately the most important factors in understanding, interpreting, and resolving conflicts in organizations. Strictly structural explanations for conflict in organizations obviate personal responsibility for participants' actions (actions that perpetuate such structures). Individuals come to blame the system and, consequently, are disconnected from their actions.

Strictly normative explanations for conflict, on the other hand, overlook the unconscious intentions underlying organizational strategies and structural characteristics that affect actions and outcome. Individuals may refuse to explore the original intent of strategies, an activity which would require examining the purpose of and motivation for designing procedures in a specific manner. One's personal values as well as organizational norms affect the nature of one's relationships, and one's approach to conflict is, therefore, significantly influenced by past experience with others within and outside the organization. Values, whether promoted by the organizational hierarchy or not, are personally generated. They are an essential part of the personality. Behind organizational strategy and structure lie unconscious human aims rooted in earlier intrapersonal and interpersonal conflict of key personnel.

How individuals perceive and cope with conflict is related to past experience, present self-image, and circumstances. This combination of variables affects their willingness (or unwillingness) to deal with others and resolve conflict and affects their ability (or inability) to learn from problem solving and conflict resolution.

PSYCHOANALYTIC BASES OF CONFLICT DEFINED

Conflict is defined here as opposing aims and motives, what psychoanalyst Roy Schafer (1983) calls "paradoxical actions." It is a complex action. The person experiences himself or herself as contradictory or paradoxical (92). Some analysts might describe this as feeling "split" or "fragmented"; nonanalysts might say they feel torn or pulled apart. A person in conflict experiences feelings in opposition simultaneously, such as love and hate, pleasure and pain, good and bad, admiration and contempt.

People in conflict generally feel anxious. They may perceive a situation as dangerous but not understand why. This, in effect, produces a lack of cohesiveness, continuity, and self-integration. For G. S. Klein, "The component tendencies of a conflict are embodied as an unconsciously sustained structure (unconscious fantasy) which may be repetitively enacted throughout life" (1976: 185). This psychic structure is the result of repression and is the essence of self-image. Many psychoanalysts would view this conception of conflict as a neurotic, though not uncommon, compulsion to repeat—in psychoanalytic terms, *repetition compulsion*—or simply another way of describing defensive actions repeatedly enacted to minimize the anxiety about confrontation or personal fallibility.

This unconsciously sustained defensive structure comprises internalized interpersonal relationships that influence our image of social organizations and the reasons and motives underlying our often paradoxical actions within organizations. These are the conflicts we carry with us into the organization and the conflicts we reenact in the facilitative culture of the organization. Such reenactments occur at the intrapsychic, interpersonal, and group levels of organizational activity and are triggered by circumstances within and outside the organization and its membership.

G. S. Klein notes that in psychoanalytic theory, conflicts or "experienced incompatibilities are not necessarily negative influences, but may engineer change and development" (185). He correctly argues that "psychoanalytic understanding lies precisely in the 'recognition of themes' which we have never completely lived down, nor successfully outlived" (185). The presence of conflict in organizations, once acknowledged and claimed, represents potential for learning and problem solving essential to growth. Conflict is viewed as a potentially positive force in an organization, one that represents the essence of renewal.

THE CONSULTANT'S ROLE

Conflict occurred at the intrapersonal, interpersonal, and group levels of organization. Group conflict resulted from intrapersonal and interpersonal conflict and was acted out primarily between two organizational leaders and their respective sections. The advantage of a psychoanalytic approach to conflict resolution and change in organizations lies in the attempt to elicit an organizational participant's eventual awareness of his or her ambiguous performance by acknowledging conflict, and in what G. S. Klein calls the "active reversal of passive experience," or the intent to "turn a blow passively experienced into an experience of environmental mastery" (207).

In helping to resolve conflict, organizational consultants can assume a therapeutic role by enabling people who are otherwise paralyzed under particular circumstances to act. Whenever possible, this is facilitated by (1) reinforcing talents and skills of organizational members (Kohut, 1977; 1984) to enhance their self-integrity, which is under attack; and (2) collaborating with organizational participants in acquiring insight into the reasons for present conflicts.

Organizational members in conflict often feel powerless to do anything about the conflict and, therefore, experience themselves as victims. Competence motivation is, therefore, an important aspect of the relationship of interventionist and client. Clients must pay attention to proven talents and skills, in addition to conflict. For example, one frustrated manager, knowing he could do better work but feeling constrained by his superiors' demands for control and accountability, exclaimed: "I'm not in a position to do anything about it. I'm stuck between a rock and a hard place. I just pretend it's the best I can do!" This man's predicament was in part brought about by an imbalance between his responsibilities and inadequate authority, exasperated by interpersonal conflict at the top (Baum, 1987). By surfacing the underlying organizational conflict causing his predicament and inviting his participation in finding a solution to the problem, the consultant helped him eventually renew his self-respect and confidence. When I requested his assistance in turning things around, he brought his previously denied talents and skills to bear on the problem; consequently, he soon felt empowered to do something about his immediate predicament.

Genuine self-esteem of organizational participants is not derived from power located in hierarchy, but in recognition and activation of self-competence. Organizational members' tendencies to blame structural and normative constraints for their problems without also acknowledging how their actions, thoughts, and feelings reinforce and perpetuate such limits are counterproductive and, ultimately, ineffective. This is an example of resolving conflict with the active reversal of passive experience—clients' abilities to change and resolve conflicts are restored where previously they felt helpless, powerless, and incompetent to do so. Ultimately, the key to change lies in the client's willingness to take personal responsibility for his or her actions.

As Chris Argyris (1970) suggests, ultimately consultants must have more confidence in their clients' abilities than they often have themselves. In my experience, the key to competence motivation for change and resolution of conflict primarily lies in the transmission of (what Kohut calls) empathy and introspection between consultant and client. This means the consultant has to develop "the capacity to think and feel [oneself] into the inner life of another person," and to "experience what another person experiences, though usually, and appropriately, to an attenuated degree" (Kohut, 1984: 82).

In the organizational consultation this does not mean exploring childhood traumata but, more importantly, identifying and appreciating the affective quality of the client's experience of present and ongoing conflicts in the organization. The consultant's ability to identify a client's unique experience of conflict by redescribing (accurately interpreting) that experience, assuming (without judging) its early developmental origins and role in organizing self-image and ego integrity, communicates respect for the client's individuality (often absent in the organization) and facilitates collaboration between client and interventionist that is necessary to resolving conflicts.

In organizational life, conflicted managers can affect their staff, staff relationships with other units, and, consequently, an entire organization. Conflicts in organizations are often repressed and unconsciously sustained in a latent social structure; denied and unresolved, they drain psychic and physical energy from staff who invest in "managing" around them. A psychoanalytic comprehension of conflict adds interpretive depth and dimension to analysis of behavior and change in organizations and, in the practice of intervention, can empower organizational participants to resolve conflicts and promote change. It is essential to promoting truly "reflective practitioners" (Schon, 1984) and, thereby, transcending the perpetuation of technocrats.

EMPOWERING THE CLIENT: ORGANIZATIONAL CONFLICT RESOLUTION

Psychoanalyst James S. Grotstein writes: "Ultimately, psychic conflict is not only the conflict over the fantasied or actual use or misuse of one's experience of will, but also the existential conflict between having a will and being helpless" (Goldberg, 1983: 182). In organizational life, conflict is experienced as alien and disconnected from personal actions. Threatening and dangerous perceptions of conflict are denied, screened off, and put out of consciousness. A wall of psychological defensive solutions structures behavior and interactions so that experience of conflict and associated anxiety are circumvented.

For example, Green, his assistant, and his staff were consistently bypassing Hall's office to request budget data from Hall's staff. In order to evade Hall's compulsive scrutiny and suspicions of Green and his staff, Green's section covertly removed Hall from the process and maneuvered around him. Whether or not this defensive strategy was reasonable given past experience with Hall, it was not a solution to, but rather a symptom of, the conflict among Hall, Green, and their respective staffs. The withholding of information only served to provoke anger in Hall and his staff toward Green's section. This, in turn, perpetuated the antagonism between the two units. Green and his staff had unwittingly constructed a social system of defense against anxiety of open conflict (Diamond, 1984; 1985a; Jaques, 1955; Menzies, 1960) and a psychological obstacle to collaboration and problem solving (Baum, 1987).

Feeling helpless to do or say anything about the conflict between Hall and Green, agency members constructed a set of strategies for preventing open conflict. Hall and Green displaced bad feelings for Mosley onto each other; their respective staff displaced bad feelings for Hall and Green onto the other unit. These defensive routines were eventually taken for granted and unconscious.

Both Hall and Green viewed themselves as victims. Hall experienced himself as a victim of leadership transitions, politics, superior knowledge and expertise, authority and responsibility, and organizational history. Green experienced himself as a victim of Hall's legacy and the division's poor reputation, the incompetence around him, and those who did not recognize his superiority and greatness. Neither was willing to take responsibility for his actions. Hall's and Green's narcissistic characteristics may signify early emotional deprivation, and one might conjecture both had experienced psychological trauma early in life, at a time when they were powerless.

SUMMARY

Individuals act defensively in organizations. They do so to rid themselves of anxiety and deny the presence of conflict. Conflicts in organizations are defined as paradoxical actions that manifest themselves in unconsciously sustained and repetitively enacted social and psychological structures. For example, organizational members often ask themselves, paradoxically, Why do problems recur? Why don't they just go away? People in large organizations may acknowledge their problems, whether personal or organizational, but do not take the time or make the collaborative effort necessary to understand why their problems persist.

Groups and organizations tend to make people feel detached from their own actions, and, consequently, unwilling to take responsibility. What is overlooked in the assumed rationality of organizational life is that intrapersonal conflicts, stemming from early childhood and then repeated throughout development into adulthood, affect present perceptions and actions at work. In fact, critical organizational events renew defensive strategies among members that in the past proved successful in minimizing their anxieties. In the organization, psychological defenses are shared by members and eventually taken for granted and unconscious. The ways in which individuals deny and avoid conflict in organizations are suppressed and momentarily removed from their awareness.

Conflicts occur at different levels of experience: within individuals, between people, and within and among groups. What begins as an inner conflict, within one person, can jump to the interpersonal level and then to the group level of organization. It does not occur randomly and without reason. It is, in part, a tangible representation of a person's (or group's) unconscious needs and expectations being played out in contradictory actions. But conflict need not remain under wraps and unresolved.

If organizational members are encouraged to uncover and reflect on the reasons for their ambiguous performances, they will better understand how their needs for affection, aggression, and self-esteem influence their interactions at work. Moreover, conflict may be produced by unreal and superhuman expectations and fantasies. When the importance of unconscious expectations is understood by organizational members, they can begin to discuss which needs can be satisfied and which cannot in the reality of the workplace. This was one of my objectives as the interventionist in the case example to follow.

The identity of an organization arises from the interactions of many individuals who all have their own needs and expectations, who all have their fantasies regarding work relationships, and who all have and create conflict. Within a hierarchy, the predominant structure of contemporary organizations, it is inevitably the conflicts of those at the top which have the most impact. If the conflicted individual is a key member who plays out his or her disappointment and frustrations with another top executive— as in the case example to follow—the entire organization suffers.

The task of the organizational consultant is to find the connection between puzzling acts and the client's unconscious needs and expectations. Conflicted actions, inconsistent and contradictory behavior, in the workplace are viewed as the outcome of personal and situational factors. Personal factors include individual personality; situational factors take account of organizational, political, and environmental variables. Regardless of whether paradoxical actions are conscious or unconscious in nature, individuals are treated by the interventionist as responsible agents. Unconscious reasons and motives, for example, are viewed as actions themselves (Schafer, 1983).

This so-called analytic attitude of the consultant (1983), along with the opportunity for planned change implicit in the intervention itself, assists the client organization in reversing unresolved conflict by insisting on their participation in the change effort. Despite the fact that many clients assume the consultant's role is to solve their problems, he or she is there to enable organizational members to solve their own problems. This must be communicated at the outset.

Interpersonal experiences are subjectively organized and come to form an individual's personal history. That history comprises internalized images of oneself and others and is not without conflict. It may, in fact, become the source of conflicting aims and motives that shape self-image and human actions. Self-image, in turn, influences relationships, both present and future, by affecting the expectations and needs formed with regard to them. If such expectations and needs are derived from intrapersonal conflict, then present interpersonal relationships may be misrepresented and emotionally overcharged. The manager's need for self-esteem, derived from the respect and admiration of others, may overshadow task accomplishment. Organizational consultation may become necessary to sweep away the cobwebs of the past, allowing current interactions to be viewed more clearly and helping individuals to interpret present conflict as the mutual responsibility of all organizational participants.

The next chapter illustrates the impact of conflict avoidance on managerial roles and presents a more detailed example of consultation with an organization.

NOTES

1. The names of the agency and its participants are changed to preserve anonymity.

2. While my relationship with Mosley, who hired me, was central to the consultation, it is important to establish that all behavior and relationships are to be looked at in the context of the system or organizational culture. Thus, although Mosley may have been my client in one sense, he was in fact only a part of the client system of DPW.

3. This illustrates the manifestation of ritualistic organizational defenses discussed in Chapter 2. Similar observations of social defenses are discussed by Argyris (1985), Menzies (1960), Jaques (1955), and others.

4. Again, note how this exemplifies the externalized self-system portrayed in ritualistic organizational defenses, described in Chapter 2.

9

THE IMPACT OF CONFLICT AVOIDANCE
ON ORGANIZATIONAL IDENTITY

The story of the Department of Community Development, Regulation and Commerce (DCDRC)[1], a midwestern state agency, is one of a medium-sized bureaucracy undergoing the aftershocks of several policy shifts and reorganizations. The case of DCDRC shows the effects of conflict avoidance on organizational identity.

The presentation of this case is organized as follows. After a discussion of the method used in the study, I describe the organization's structure, divisional missions, and environment. Next, I discuss the events of a partial intervention and diagnosis, which entail the consultants' observation of a central problematic theme: management based on conflict avoidance. This theme, I will show, emerges from numerous symptoms, such as confused power and authority relations, frustrated dependency needs, role ambiguity, and diffuse authority and accountability. Next, the consultants' diagnosis is proffered, and the organizational members' response to the intervention is detailed. Then, an analysis of the case dynamics clarifies themes that contribute to the literature on organizational identity, and on organizational change and development. Let's begin by looking at the issue of method.

METHOD

The method for collecting and organizing data in the DCDRC case draws from many valuable sources. First, I relied on Harry Levinson's

An earlier version of this chapter was written in collaboration with Guy B. Adams, who assisted me in the consultation.

Organizational Diagnosis (1972: 55–65). Levinson provides a case study outline that I have found helpful. In a very abbreviated form, it suggests gathering and arranging data in the following manner:

1. GENETIC DATA
   A. Identifying Information
   B. Historical Data
2. DESCRIPTION AND ANALYSIS OF CURRENT ORGANIZATION AS A WHOLE
   A. Structural Data
   B. Process Data
3. INTERPRETIVE DATA
   A. Current Organizational Functioning
   B. Attitudes and Relationships
4. ANALYSES AND CONCLUSIONS
   A. Organizational Integrative Patterns
   B. Summary and Recommendations

Levinson's approach is particularly useful in maintaining a perspective on the total system and in distinguishing between factual and interpretive data.

Second, I referred to *The Neurotic Organization* by Kets de Vries and Miller (1984: 169–75), which describes "four steps in intervention." It suggests, first, making a simple listing of the primary symptoms and problems; second, making conjectures about the syndrome, working backward from symptoms to discover the underlying roots of the problem; and third, generating a set of alternative solutions and choosing the one that best seems to address the roots of the syndrome. Appraisal of the desirability of the different solutions should include a variety of criteria: completeness, side effects, economy, depth of solutions, timeliness, and political feasibility. Finally, the fourth step entails developing a plan of implementation. Kets de Vries and Miller's strategy underscores the deeper relationships between presenting symptoms and the social-psychological foundation of many problems in organizations. They stress the effect of personality on organizational culture, and the fact that many problems cannot be dealt with by "superimposing 'rational' techniques on the organization" (Kets de Vries and Miller, 1984: 175). In other words, they do not assume that people are always rational, and so it follows that the method of intervention should not rely solely upon "rational solutions."

The intervention strategy for DCDRC, which is described in detail in the case study to follow, is quite similar to that found in Larry Hirschhorn's *The Workplace Within* (1988). In his appendix "Consulting as a Method of Research," Hirschhorn presents a three-step process: First, interview organization members whose roles and interests are centrally connected to the presenting problem that leads executives to ask for help; second, write what practitioners at the Tavistock Institute call the "working note," a hypothesis based on the data of the interviews and presenting a theory of the client's presenting problems. The third step is to meet with the participants to discuss the note, review its implications, and develop a general plan for the consultation (Hirschhorn, 1988: 243–44).

Finally, in *The Invisible Bureaucracy*, Howell Baum (1987: 171) concludes with "guidelines for intervention" that accent the complexity of organizational consultation:

Each situation to be changed may be regarded as a combination of actions or influences in four domains. The first involves individual thinking, feeling, and action. The second involves interpersonal relationships. The third involves the organizational social structure, either formal structures or consistent, organization-wide patterns of interaction. The fourth domain involves societal structures and cultural norms that influence the structure of social institutions, patterns of personal interaction, or individual thinking and feeling.

The method of data collection, intervention, analysis, and strategies for change attempts to consider these four domains.

Put simply, the method of consultation and intervention includes the collection of factual data: case notes beginning with the initial contact and including individual interviews at all levels of the organization, observations of operations, group sessions for feedback and validation or disconfirmation of data collected and hypotheses generated by the consultants, group sessions for problem identification and solution, and planning for future change and development. My approach integrates the thinking and practices put forth by Levinson, Kets de Vries and Miller, Hirschhorn, and Baum and adds the notion of *organizational identity* as the focal point for assembling metapatterns of interaction and transference dynamics between superordinates and subordinates, which, taken together, constitute an organizational theme distinguishing one case study from another.

An important question asked by the psychoanalytically informed reader at this point would be, How did the consultants deal with transference and countertransference between themselves and their clients? After the interviews and each of the group sessions, we would meet to discuss our feelings, thoughts, observations, and concerns. The purpose of these meetings was to create a reflective dialogue that would enable us to debrief one another, reexamine our intervention strategy, and generate hypotheses about the psychodynamic issues in DCDRC. Our consulting roles were defined for the clients at the outset and one of us was designated as the lead consultant. This clarification of roles and the regular debriefing enabled us to deal with emotional issues produced by the consultant-client exchange.

As I explained in great detail in Chapter 4, organizational identity is a window into the intersubjective structure of organizational life. It is a theory of organizational meaning, which is based upon the assumption that the most critical unit of analysis for understanding behavior in organizations and for helping them to change is interpersonal, self, and other relationships. On the basis of the clinical findings of psychoanalytic object relations theory and self psychology, capturing the essence of organizational identity requires an analysis of transference and countertransference dynamics among key organizational members and an estimation of the organizational metapatterns at work. In DCDRC, we found the central metapattern of conflict avoidance throughout the system and discovered that a persecutory transference[2] between the director and his deputy was mirrored among middle managers. The combination of the conflict avoidance metapattern and the persecutory transference resulted in an organizational culture dominated by fight-flight basic assumptions—producing the collective search for an enemy to fight, blame, or flee. In addition to these dynamics, we found an organization split between two politically diverse missions—community development and economic development. These diverse missions represented opposing ideologies and exaggerated the organizational members' regressive tendencies under stress. Consequently, psychological splitting and projective identification led to polarized thinking and tension between community development staff and business development staff. These are the central theoretical issues detailed in the case study to follow.

DCDRC

The Department of Community Development, Regulation and Commerce (DCDRC) is a state agency, which comprises fourteen divisions engaged in disparate and, in some instances, unrelated tasks and missions.

In the 1980s, DCDRC became the state's lead agency for economic development; previously its emphasis was on community development. Through a major reorganization in the mid-1980s, a central part of DCDRC's mission in this midwestern state became creating jobs and attracting capital investment, that is, economic development. Within this diverse and fragmented agency, a structural unit known as Economic Development Programs was formed in an attempt to give organizational coherence to the state's economic development policy. This unit was the focus of intervention.

As described here, Economic Development Programs has had considerable success in its various programs. At the same time, DCDRC is one of a minority of state economic development agencies in the United States currently operating without a strategic plan (Grady, 1989). Compared to other states' economic development agencies, DCDRC would not be among the highest ranking in terms of overall effectiveness measures (Grady, 1989). Organizationally, Economic Development Programs was certainly able to function from day to day before the intervention. At the same time, there was sufficient dysfunction systemically, as well as sufficient discomfort psychodynamically, to induce the executive team to approach the authors for assistance.

Economic Development Programs consists of four offices, Business Development, Current Business, Community Programs, and Research, each headed by an office manager. Also included is a small component of Job Training, which focuses on customized training packages in support of economic development efforts. Together these programs employ well over 100 people in the state capital. During 1989, Economic Development Programs recorded more than $1 billion in new investment for new and expanding plants, factories, warehouses, distribution centers, major office operations, and related commercial facilities in the state. This new investment was expected to create some 20,000 new jobs in the state. In order to describe the roles of DCDRC participants, we briefly describe each of the Economic Development Programs offices.

Business Development

Business Development, which seeks to attract new foreign and domestic enterprise to the state, worked with some 250 prospective new companies that were considering locating in the state during a recent year. This office directly assisted in the location of thirty-eight new companies and the resulting creation of approximately 3,400 jobs.

Current Business

Current Business encourages and assists new and expanding in-state companies to retain or create new jobs. This office provides services in the areas of business start-up, licensing, financing, procurement, and research and development. Current Business handled about 3,100 business inquiries during 1989 and actively worked with some 225 companies on potential expansion projects.

Community Programs

Community Programs offers assistance and support for community development projects that enhance the quality of life and economic growth potential in communities and neighborhoods in the state. In a recent year, the Community Development Block Grant program awarded over $23.8 million in grants, loans, and loan guarantees to seventy-four cities and counties for public infrastructure improvements, neighborhood and downtown revitalization, economic development, and emergency projects. The Neighborhood Assistance Program also approved $8.75 million in tax credits for business contributions totaling $16 million to more than 300 approved neighborhood assistance projects. These projects included drug and alcohol abuse counseling, youth and senior citizen centers, family housing programs, and many other community services.

Research

The Research office compiles extensive social and economic data on communities in the state and prepares custom presentations tailored to the specific needs of companies considering locating in state. Job Training often works closely with Research on job training aspects of these presentations. Research is also responsible for administering business financing programs, which helped provide about $67.9 million in financing in a recent year for new business locations and expansions.

The Political Environment

DCDRC as a whole is a highly political organization comprising conflicting subcultures. Its political nature, in terms of competing interests, is especially evident within Economic Development Programs. Business Development and Current Business are market-oriented in their values and actions. Community Programs and Job Training are much more oriented to serving disadvantaged individuals and communities throughout the state. Reflected in these different orientations in part are conservative versus liberal ideologies. Research is service-oriented, but more responsive to Business Development and Current Business. This may in part be due to shared ideology. In the political climate at that time, however, the power and influence of Business Development and Current Business on human and technological resources within DCDRC were substantial.

Charles Wright, the director of DCDRC, is committed to developing and retaining business and finding export markets for state products. The offices most aligned with this direction—a gubernatorial policy commitment—experience the highest level of integration and identity within Economic Development Programs. They are also somewhat more sensitive and adaptable to external political pressures on decision making. DCDRC is seen by some as the governor's favored agency, a circumstance which guarantees strong and continuous legislative scrutiny, since the legislature is controlled by the opposite political party. The more politically visible and economically beneficial projects involve the director's time and energy—and sometimes the governor's time as well.

Wright is viewed most favorably by the national business section of Business Development, while others in Current Business and even within the international section of Business Development are less enthusiastic about his performance. Many feel they do not get enough of his time and attention. In contrast to Business Development and Current Business, Community Programs does not have favored status in the department, and many Community Program managers feel they are scapegoated and victimized by the executive group and other office managers. They refer to themselves as the "orphans," as community development is no longer as important a function of DCDRC as it was during the 1960s and 1970s. Community Programs operates defensively in that they protect themselves from the intrusion of other offices and the executive group. Its management attempts to isolate itself and feels engulfed by being part of Economic Development Programs. Members of Community Programs feel abandoned and rejected by what they perceive as an uncaring department.

INITIAL CONTACT

Background

In the spring of 1990, the state legislature mandated that all state agencies develop strategic plans by January 1991. This request was partly a response to an ongoing fiscal crunch. The four-member executive group of DCDRC decided that their agency had organizational problems that had to be addressed before strategic planning could proceed. It was agreed that Joseph Martin, the director of administration, would initiate discussion with the consultants, one of whom was known to have extensive organizational consulting experience with state government.

Joseph Martin then phoned me to discuss the idea of DCDRC's contracting for consulting services. The discussion included mention of the mandated strategic planning and the perception among leadership that the agency was not ready to enter into strategic planning until it was able to deal with internal organizational problems. This was the presenting problem for the consultation, which was repeated in the initial session but altered as consultants and clients entered the process of consultation. Also discussed in this phone conversation were a brief orientation to our consulting methods, the setting of a tentative time frame of three months for the consultation, and details about contractual arrangements. It was agreed that a meeting would be held with the four-member executive group of DCDRC to discuss these issues in greater depth.

Initial Meeting

At an initial meeting between the executive group and the consultants, the four top managers had difficulty describing the nature of the problems in Economic Development Programs, the part of DCDRC that was to be the focus of the consultation. Besides Wright, the agency director, and Martin, the director of administration, the executive group included James Gooden, deputy director for Economic Development Programs, and Rick Harvey, deputy director for the remaining divisions of DCDRC. This first meeting of consultants and clients was quite rushed and characterized by some anxiety. It took place during lunchtime at a DCDRC conference room in the state capitol. In their initial attempts to describe this polyglot agency and its rather intricate organization chart (See Figure 9.1), one of the executives made a comment which was to be repeated many times. Describing one of the fourteen divisions that appeared unrelated to the others in terms of task and mission, he referred to it as "something else that doesn't belong here"—a characterization that expresses the conflicted identity of DCDRC well. The initial meeting closed with the agreement that at the next meeting of the consultants and the executive group, an intervention plan for organizational diagnosis would be presented by us. We left knowing we still needed explicit commitment from the executive group to the objectives of the organizational intervention.

Figure 9.1
Department of Community Development, Regulation, and Commerce

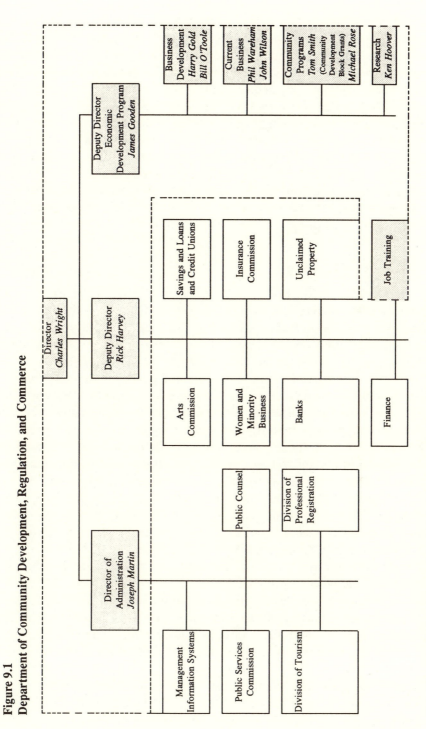

Dotted line represents boundary around that section of the organization that was the focus of consultation.

The presenting problem was slightly elaborated during this session. The executive group amplified the rather vague "organizational problems" by talking about reorganization, about other possible structural solutions, and about ways to increase accountability for Economic Development Programs (EDP) staff. Describing both problems and solutions in such formalistic terms was consistent with both the transference dynamics and the metapattern of conflict avoidance characteristic of this organization's conflicted identity. In a process consultation such as this, one of the chief aims is to move from a presenting problem consistent with the organization's symptoms to the underlying problems, which members of the organization always have some difficulty facing directly (as staff often called them, "the things we don't talk about").

The Second Session

The half-day agenda of the second meeting with the executive group, set by the consultants, included the following: (1) to clarify the contractual agreement and expectations; (2) to generate data on actual operations, on authority relations, and on actual linkages among offices; (3) to clarify roles of executive group members; (4) to request documents—factual data such as procedures, historical data, annual reports, job descriptions, personnel statistics, and budgets; (5) to obtain the director's commitment and agreement to communicate to staff the purpose of the consultation and to stress confidentiality; and (6) to request outside information to give the consultants a better understanding of how the organization fits with the external environment. We then presented an intervention plan, which was discussed and agreed upon by the executive group (see Appendix 1).

The focus of the meeting now turned to the agency's problems. After considerable discussion that was characterized by a lack of clarity similar to that of the first meeting, I referred to an apparent ambiguity of authority and responsibility throughout EDP. This remark triggered a strong, though initially anxious, response, and the executive group began to talk more directly about problems in DCDRC.

During this session, it became clear that the roles of the four offices of Economic Development Programs, as well as the small section of Job Training involved with EDP, were conflicted and riddled with problems. Business Development was perceived as having the status of the premier program; it was viewed as glamorous by staff in the other offices. Consequently, Business Development staff drew envy from many other EDP staff members. One of the executives described Community Programs as trying to isolate themselves. And, indeed, the entire seventh floor that housed the four EDP offices was described as a "zoo." Later events would confirm and elaborate on these conflicted role relationships.

These initial descriptions by the executive group prompted us to request that the executives engage serially in a description of their own roles. It became clear at this point that two of the three deputies, Rick Harvey and Joseph Martin, had only peripheral relevance to the operations and problems of Economic Development Programs. The remaining two, Charles Wright, the agency's director, and James Gooden, the deputy director for Economic Development Programs, on the other hand, were central. The director demonstrated a clear managerial identity in his self-description of his role; however, because of his involvement in Business Development projects in the field, he was often absent from the office. This left Gooden, the EDP deputy director, in charge; Gooden described his role as a "liaison, coordinator, troubleshooter, and handholder." The pattern of management based on flight from conflict and responsibility began to emerge.

Individual Interviews

The next stage of the consultation involved individual interviews (see Levinson, 1972) with thirty staff members from all EDP units, including the director, Wright, and deputy director, Gooden. After an explanation that the interview was a component of data collection for organizational diagnosis and a reassurance that answers would be treated as confidential, the following questions were asked:[3]

1. How long have you been in the agency?
2. What is your position and role in the agency?
3. Who are you accountable to?
4. What are your perceptions of leadership in the agency?
5. What are the objectives of your office?
6. Do you know what the other Economic Development Programs offices do, and how are you dependent upon them (which ones, in particular)?
7. What problems or issues do you see that make it difficult for you to do your job?
8. What are your career ambitions?
9. If the organization were a person, how would you describe it?
10. What is the overall Economic Development mission?
11. What else might you add that you think would be of help?

OVERVIEW

These interviews confirmed the prevalence of problems of unclear authority and responsibility, conflict avoidance, and ambiguous roles throughout Economic Development Programs. From one interview to the next, people agreed and offered examples suggesting that questions of authority and responsibility, conflict avoidance, and role definition were of considerable proportions. Interviews thus confirmed conflict avoidance as a central metapattern in the agency and the common perception of management based on a fight-flight mentality (although interviewees of course did not use this terminology).

It was readily apparent to us that most interviewees took to the meeting their own prepared agendas, a manifestation of widespread anxiety within the organization. Some had lists of issues they wished us to address, while others seemed eager to break into the interview schedule with particular points of individual concern, which was permitted. From the interviews, it appeared that most EDP personnel had some broad version of an Economic Development mission that was shared across the agency, and that most employees were customer-oriented in their attitudes and approach to their work responsibilities. Indeed, it should be emphasized that DCDRC staff were *normal* state employees—that is, by far the majority of them were dedicated, well-intentioned, competent workers with some sense of public mission. However, as members of an organization with a conflicted identity and a predominantly fight-flight managerial subculture, most workers found their behavior structured into less than optimal patterns of performance.

The lack of role clarity between and among workers was of central significance and turned out to be a critical issue for the operations of EDP. Moreover, given the confusion about authority and responsibility among staff and the tendency to avoid efforts at clarification (management based on fight-flight basic assumptions), there seemed to be little in the way of limits on individual interpretations of roles. In fact, roles were defined, if at all, idiosyncratically by organizational members. Consequently, interpersonal relationships became aggressive and coercive: control-oriented and manipulative behavior, often taking the form of projective identification,[4] emerged as a modus operandi.

Some interviewees claimed that DCDRC and Economic Development Programs management operated in a "fluid and open" manner, giving this a positive connotation. But at the same time, they expressed feelings of resentment of what they described as a "lack of management" and "unclear expectations" with little or no evaluative feedback, both of which clearly echo the theme of management based on fight-flight basic assumptions. The interviews confirmed that while Charles Wright was perceived as a strong leader of the department and Economic Development Programs in particular, it was also observed that he was absent much of the time. When he was available, those with Business Development projects—especially those attempting to locate new enterprise in the state—had primary access to him, and many others expressed resentment at that fact.

The interviews supported the fact that James Gooden was not operating fully in his role as deputy director in Wright's absence. Many described him as "indecisive" in all areas of EDP with the exception of issues in Community Programs and Community Development Block Grants—reflecting his own background in community development, his previous organizational home.

In sum, the interviews confirmed numerous problem areas the executive group had reported, including a perceived lack of direction from the top, competition and envy between offices and among individuals, and inadequate cooperation and poor coordination among offices. We then generated a list of issues for the executive group to confirm or reject (see Appendix 2).

FEEDBACK AND VALIDATION OF PROBLEMS

In our third session with the executive group, the four members validated the list issues (Appendix 2) for their department and agreed that they should be addressed by the consultation process. In this meeting, discussion of the interview schedule occurred first; this was safe ground to begin the dialogue and move toward a more frank conversation about problem areas. Although there were moments of collective anxiety and defensiveness among the executives, the group did not evade any of the issues surfaced by the consultants. To their credit, they were able to acknowledge "conflict avoidance" as a pervasive issue in the department and in their own actions. In addition, they agreed that the four EDP office managers did not, in fact, perform management functions adequately.

Interviews with the director, Wright, and the deputy director, Gooden, indicated that organizational problems were mirrored in—and perhaps inspired by—the dynamics between them. While their own working relationship appeared harmonious—and indeed was described as such by each—significant differences were present, and these reverberated throughout the agency. The organization's conflicted identity, signified by the competing ideologies of economic development and community development, was clearly embodied in the differences between the director and his deputy. Deputy Director Gooden's values and role identity still belonged to community development programs. Director Wright, on the other hand, was a political appointee under a conservative governor—a careerist who knew that moving the state ahead in economic development was both good for his political career and consistent with his political views.

Gooden, a career civil servant with a master's degree in public administration, began his public service in community development. He talked with some ambivalence about the transition that became apparent in the 1980s when the emphasis on community development diminished and economic development emerged as a state and federal priority. As he says, "There has always been a split between Community Programs and Economic Development." Gooden described his working relationship with Wright in positive terms, indicating they had discussed written role descriptions on several occasions; he clarified this by stating that the intent of such an exercise was "more for others than for us." In discussing "the things we don't deal with," Gooden acknowledged that the four office managers did not really manage: they gave little or no direction to their staff.

Wright, an attorney active in conservative party politics since his law school days, was the governor's chief aide in the first of two successful election campaigns. The post as DCDRC director was the one he wanted in the new administration, and he described his own style as "hands-on and aggressive." Wright is described by department staff, and certainly appeared to us, as a competent, caring manager, faulted only for his frequent absences, although these are an integral and appropriate part of his role. Asked about the role of Gooden, the deputy director, Wright said it was "probably never clearly enough defined to staff." Asked about his deputy's decision making, he noted that Gooden "passed most decisions up." Gooden himself said, to the contrary, that he made most decisions on Community Programs, while he passed up most decisions related to Business Development and more broadly to economic development.

LARGE-GROUP SESSION

The next phase of the consultation was an all-day large-group session with all EDP staff who had been interviewed but without the executive group. The purposes of this session were to present the problems and issues which had emerged in the interviews and been confirmed by the executive group and to seek the staff's confirmation or rejection of them. This setting also had the intended effect of reproducing the workplace and its dynamics in a compressed format and offered a kind of "publicity" across the four offices that is rarely available in the normal run of organizational events.

Naturally enough, the initial period was characterized by a certain amount of anxiety and some avoidance of issues. There was a pronounced, but expected tendency in the group to "locate" the problems up the hierarchy—that is, within the absent executive group. Gradually the group acknowledged, more and more openly, the prevalence of conflict avoidance in the agency. In a telling slip, as the discussion grew more open, one of the senior managers in Business Development, Bill O'Toole, stated, "The duty of top management is to avoid."

The second half of the morning was devoted to two small-group breakout sessions designed to facilitate movement through the rather long list of issues and problems (Appendix 2). After lunch, each of the small groups gave a presentation of their discussion and conclusions, sparking further review of the issues. In exploring competition and envy between the offices, it was asserted by several participants that one cannot pass bad news up the chain of command. This was followed by the observation that there are "good-bad guys and bad-bad guys," meaning that top management is receptive to the mistakes of some, but not of others. In general, the group confirmed all of the identified issues, with minor amendments to a few (items 9 to 12 in Appendix 2). Of greater significance, they heard others' characterizations of the problems; this served to confirm the shared nature of most of the issues and had the effect of bringing EDP staff together in significant ways. For example, the Community Programs staffers described themselves as "orphans," and others described them as "trying to isolate themselves." In this session, staffers from other EDP offices made genuine and repeated attempts to integrate Community Programs into the overall mission of the agency by making statements such as "Communities *are* the product we are selling." These statements had considerable positive impact on Community Programs staff.

Large-group events such as this one, because people are together in a group which rarely assembles in the normal course of work and because their collective feet are held to the fire in discussing problems, become significant events in the life of an organization. One vivid moment during this session occurred during the afternoon. The agency's mission was the topic of discussion, and there was a general hubbub, when someone said loudly enough for the group to hear, "Are we the Department of CDRC, are we Economic Development Programs, or are we Community Programs—what are we?" This statement, made in a tremulous voice, was an expression on behalf of the group of the agency's conflicted identity and the widespread anxiety it generated.

SECOND LARGE-GROUP SESSION

Some ten days later, another all-day large-group session was held, this time with the EDP managers and the executive group—eighteen people in all. This session would come to be known later as "the day from hell." It began with coffee and rolls, and a great deal of nervous humor about conflict avoidance, which was particularly evident among the executive group. Much more than during the previous session, this group proved very difficult to keep on track; most of the discussion skirted and obfuscated the issues, with a great deal of time spent on unrelated and trivial topics—all characteristic of a fight-flight mentality. The investment in the group's collusion to avoid unspeakable topics—"the things we don't talk about," such as the four office managers' not performing management functions—was considerable. Once again, small-group breakout sessions were held, and both groups failed to make much progress in discussing the identified issues, which had already been confirmed by all of the people present, but in different formats.

In the afternoon session, a role clarification exercise was undertaken. All members of the group stated what their perception of their own role was, and others in the group were free to raise questions and engage in discussion. It was of more than symbolic significance that James Gooden, the EDP deputy director, led off, characterizing his role once more as "adviser, troubleshooter, coordinator, somewhat as a decision maker." In the ensuing discussion, Gooden stated that the office managers reported to Charles Wright, and Wright stated that they reported to Gooden. The consultants suggested that the office managers state whom they thought they reported to. The Business Development manager, Harry Gold, stated that he reported 85 percent of the time to Wright. The Community Programs manager, Tom Smith, initially said Wright, but then said, "I don't know." The Research manager, Ken Hoover, said Wright, but that he also dealt with Gooden. This forty-five-minute discussion of one key manager's role provided stark and vivid confirmation of the degree of role confusion and ambiguity in the upper managerial echelons of the agency, stemming from the effects of fight-flight assumptions on managerial role behavior.

Later, the Community Programs manager, Tom Smith, described his role as that of a "utility infielder" and went on to note, "It fills my day." The manager of Business Development, Harry Gold, then described his role as being "hands on" for international business development, which he then described as being on the road a great deal—mirroring the absence of the agency director. The manager of the Research section, Ken Hoover, gave a reasonably clear role description, which was nonetheless not heavily managerial. Within the Research office, however, many of the ill effects of a lack of management were not felt, most likely because staff in this office have much more independent roles themselves. The last person to offer his role description was Phil Wareham, the manager of Current Business, whose remarks over the course of the afternoon had taken on an increasingly plaintive, even whiny tone. Wareham offered a long, meandering account of his duties and closed by stating, "I have no problem with administrative responsibility"—an assertion negated by his previous remarks. This account, by perhaps the weakest of the office managers, was the painful punctuation mark of a long and difficult afternoon, which made clearly apparent the role confusion, both in the executive pair and at the level of the office managers. People went away discouraged.

FINAL SESSION

Two days later, the consultants held a final session with the executive group in which we offered them an assessment (see Appendix 3).

This last session with the director and his three deputy directors began with a reference to "depression" from the preceding day-long session. All of them felt discouraged with what seemed like a lack of progress; they had hoped for more attention to developing solutions. They acknowledged and voiced their frustration but then went on to do good work during this session. They recognized the ambiguous role definitions at the executive level and were willing to meet the problem of minimal management at the office manager level head-on. They made decisions at this session, independent of any advice from the consultants, to terminate one office manager, demote a second, and issue clear expectations for increased managerial behavior of a third.

Five days later, the agency director issued a memorandum to the office managers that (1) asked what additional authority each of them needed, (2) established an Education Committee to review training activities and performance evaluation, (3) named a Strategic Planning Steering Committee, and (4) requested their review of earlier documents pertaining to EDP mission and objectives.

The responses of three of the office managers to the "authority question" memorandum from the director mirrored their statements in the group sessions and demonstrated their attachments to past practices associated with conflict avoidance and management based on fight-flight assumptions. Wareham, the manager of Current Business, sent a five-page highly bureaucratic memo that clarified very little. The manager of Community

Programs, Smith, sent a short memo that concluded with the following: "The bottom line is that there is much uncertainty about who has the authority to do what. Uncertainty breeds anxiety." Gold, the manager of Business Development, stated in his response, "I guess basically I have no problem with the authority that I think that I have."

Several weeks later, the personnel actions were taken, and much more decisive managerial behavior by the director and, more significantly, the deputy director began to emerge. Subsequent communications with DCDRC indicated a good start on objective setting as a prelude to strategic planning. The identified problems were beginning to be addressed.

ANALYSIS OF THE CASE

An entrenched pattern of ambiguous role definitions and unclear authority and responsibility among organizational members was found to be perpetuated by basic assumptions of fight-flight[5] and a central metapattern of conflict avoidance[6] evident at the top, but pervading the entire organization. The form of case presentation in this chapter represents an effort to document the process of intervention strategy and organizational diagnosis. It is also a description of the behavioral and organizational effects of members' anxieties with regard to dealing with conflict. Finally, it is an illustration of the value of the concept of organizational identity[7] to understanding organizational dynamics.

The leadership of DCDRC did not offer explicit direction in the form of performance expectations, role definitions, and task assignments for management. This oversight, more deeply signifying psychological resistance, created an organizational void in which authority and responsibility were unclear among middle management and the executives themselves. From a more clinical perspective, the absence of role boundaries triggered splitting and projections[8] of aggression in the form of interpersonal and interdivisional hostilities, turf battles, envy, and other regressive psychodynamics among DCDRC members. Rather than engage in intimacy and confront emotionally loaded organizational problems, managers avoided responsibility. Furthermore, the director began to travel the state more often than necessary, while the deputy director depersonalized his relations with his managers. Consequently, he (deputy director) was then only called upon to interpret personnel policy and budgetary guidelines. These organizational dynamics permitted an escape for the director, his deputy, and management from a threatening world of face-to-face interactions and interpersonal conflict. The director was not only in flight from internal organizational conflicts but from assigning authority to his deputy director.

Consequently, the deputy director was abandoning the opportunity to solve internal personnel and management problems and to take charge of the agency in the director's absence.

Put simply, DCDRC leadership was in flight from its managerial responsibility, provided little direction, and permitted ambiguous role boundaries among its members. We (consultants) experienced the four members of the executive group as detached and isolated from the internal organizational dynamics. Task and managerial boundaries were, for the most part, undefined. Consequently, middle managers and staff were suspicious of one another and tended to experience conflict over issues of authority, responsibility, and power. Not surprisingly, this produced a fight-flight mentality among members, in which primitive defensive routines took hold.

In an organization of fourteen divisions with disparate and unrelated tasks, one expects to find managerial problems. Add to that a strong policy shift within the last decade—the move away from community development and toward an emphasis on economic development—as well as a reorganization that produced the new unit of Economic Development Programs, which included Business Development, Current Business, Community Programs, Research, and Job Training, and you have the ingredients for role ambiguities and difficulties in task coordination. The intervention and consultation helped better define roles and clarify authority and responsibility among organizational levels and staff. DCDRC leadership and management were in essence trapped by a central metapattern that affected the nature of human relationships throughout the agency—avoid interpersonal conflict at all costs. This did not mean that conflict did not exist. It meant that the presence of conflict and problems in the organization was routinely denied—management based on fight-flight assumption.

For example, DCDRC was a highly political organization comprising competing subcultures within Economic Development Programs. Organizational members referred to the staff of Business Development and Current Business as the "80s MBA types," while they called the staff of Community Programs and Job Training the "60s hippies." This not only acknowledged some real differences in style and appearance but also signified their ideological differences (conservatives versus liberals) and the degree of self-righteous attitudes on both sides. The DCDRC director was committed to the advancement of economic development programs in the state, and most people in the organization recognized the reality of the new policy commitment. However, there had been little effort to redefine and explicitly link the activities of community development and those of economic development. This required public acknowledgment of the policy shift and its implications for the four EDP offices. Conflict avoidance made dealing with such issues almost unthinkable.

As noted, Community Programs staff viewed themselves as the orphans of Economic Development Programs. This produced feelings of mistrust and defensiveness between the two subcultures within the agency. Some Community Programs staff, and here we would include the deputy director, James Gooden, mourned the loss of their former status in the organization. Lacking the opportunity, prior to the consultation, to deal with their feelings of loss, they remained stuck in a state of anger and anxiety—caused by their experience of abandonment and rejection. Unwilling to contain the negative feelings, Community Programs staff displaced their aggression onto Business Development and Current Business staff, and onto the deputy director, Gooden, who they felt betrayed them. In the second large-group session, Tom Smith, Community Programs manager, betrayed Gooden by his initial assertion that he reported to Wright rather than to Gooden, when the opposite was in fact true.[9] Coordination of tasks and necessary information sharing between the offices suffered as a result.

These historical, political, organizational, and cultural dynamics are the context within which Economic Development officials carried out task responsibilities and contributed to the agency's mission in state government. However, different people deal with such stressful circumstances dissimilarly. Patterns of organizational identity, the unconscious dimension of organizational culture, can be identified by examining managerial role performance in depth. For the consultants, the DCDRC mystery could be deciphered by exploring the tangle of role relationships that tied together key organizational participants.

As noted earlier, the director, Wright, had a clear sense of mission for Economic Development Programs. He was at best ambivalent about Community Programs and Community Development Block Grants. He appeared in favor of Community Programs' role as long as it supported the mission of Economic Development. Wright symbolized the entrepreneurial character common to a new breed of public officials in the field of economic development. This character type was prominent among Business Development managers and staff, and to a lesser extent, Current Business as well. Not surprisingly, Business Development exhausted the director's time and was the unit most strongly identified with him. The director's attention to national and international business development frequently kept him away from his office. When in his office, Wright functioned as a leader and directed the agency.

In responding to our questions as to who was in charge in his absence, the director told us that he believed he had delegated authority and responsibility for the operation of EDP to his deputy director, Gooden. Gooden did not see it that way. He was indecisive in all EDP areas, with the exception of issues in Community Programs.

We concluded that a tacit agreement existed between Wright and Gooden. This covert, private, and unacknowledged agreement enabled Gooden to respond to issues and problems of Community Programs but not to those of Business Development. Gooden's considerable anxiety about Business Development programs and his conflicted feelings about leaving the fold of Community Programs were diminished by the unspoken agreement. Since Wright's career depended upon the success of business development, we believe he experienced less anxiety knowing that Gooden would not interfere with these "pet" programs. Of course, this covert pact produced ambiguity and the sense that no one was in charge when the director was out of town, which (as we have established) was much of the time.

Gooden felt ambivalent about the Economic Development mission and the director's priority but had not told him so. Gooden was not quite adjusted to his relatively new role as deputy director of Economic Development Programs. His focus and identity remained with Community Programs, even though his organizational position had not been there in nearly a decade. His authority and responsibility were unclear to him, as they were to the office managers, who operated quite independently. Gooden described himself in his role as deputy director as a "liaison, coordinator, troubleshooter, and handholder"—not nouns describing a leader, but a mediator at best. As noted, Gooden resigned himself to answering questions on personnel and policy, making few decisions, and giving little direction. His fight-flight response rested unconsciously with what we perceived as his passive-aggressive position. In not taking control during the director's absence, he knew at some level that his entire organization would suffer. In particular, it was evident from his actions that deterioration of Business Development and Current Business was guaranteed by his lack of involvement and oversight.

Gooden's perception of his role had significant implications for management throughout Economic Development Programs. In fact, we found that office managers were doing little or no management of their staff, although, as mentioned, this caused relatively few problems in Research. Accountability for performance was largely absent, authority and responsibility were unclear, and the rationales for the construction of roles were individually and unconsciously based, rather than organizationally prescribed. People defined their own roles in a manner disconnected from the requirements of overall system management and the effective coordination of tasks and information. In some instances, we observed *role enlargement* in which individuals hierarchically located below the office manager level filled the void as a result of a lack of direction and inadequate task initiation at the top and middle by assuming the role, or parts of the role, for themselves in an unauthorized and compensatory fashion. Such unilateral role enlargement produced a great deal of confusion among staff members.

Indeed, the conflicted loyalties of the director and deputy director further perpetuated the avoidance of conflict, particularly in the area of personnel problems. Wright, for instance, was publicly defensive of the poor management of Business Development, and Gooden did not confront the incompetence of management in Community Programs. Both were invested in camouflage behavior ("the things we don't talk about") and in denial of problems in their pet units. Moreover, both Wright and Gooden unconsciously colluded to ignore perhaps their most serious management problem in Current Business.

The current Business manager, Phil Wareham, resented being transferred several years ago from Business Development to a less prestigious section. Wright and Gooden admitted that this move was an effort to avoid confronting Wareham's poor performance. Wareham was known to ignore his staff—another version of fight-flight. He frequently took actions that were directly opposite his staff's requests. Wareham was susceptible to temper tantrums and preferred to be left alone. His staff was angry at the lack of recognition and opportunity for feedback, but, more importantly, they felt shamed by the fact that leadership refused to deal with their incompetent and unresponsive manager. John Wilson, a junior manager on the Current Business staff, took it upon himself to assist others in the office. He had constructed an expanded role for himself that assumed many of the managerial responsibilities Wareham abdicated. Of course, this led to role confusion for other staff members, who were unaware of the presence of covert roles, constructed to compensate for managerial abdication.

Wareham's hostility extended beyond his own office. It influenced his office's relations with Business Development in particular. The Business Development managers, Harry Gold and Bill O'Toole, were in regular conflict with Wareham and Current Business—conflict that remained unaddressed and therefore unresolved. Gold and O'Toole were also engaged in their own role confusion and ambiguity. Gold was absent much of the time, and O'Toole assumed managerial responsibility, but only in some areas—breeding considerable confusion among Business Development staff as to who was in charge of what areas. Neither office seemed willing to take the initiative to settle jurisdictional disputes between them. This resulted in a lack of coordination between the offices. For example, it was unclear at what time responsibility for business development projects was to be transferred from Business Development to Current Business (e.g., at the time when a newly located factory opens). While there were documents that clarified this procedural question, defensive routines of conflict avoidance among management encouraged them to resist facing these problems.

Community Programs manager Tom Smith also did not manage his office. He referred to himself as the "utility infielder." His ambivalence toward the authority and responsibility of management was quite similar to that of the deputy director, Gooden. Not surprisingly, the deputy director evaded managing the apparent incompetence of Smith. Most of the Community Programs staff felt that Smith ought not to be in his position, an attitude not dissimilar to that of the Current Business staff about their ostensible head. Community Programs staff were resentful and alienated from Economic Development Programs and DCDRC. Michael Rose, in charge of Community Development Block Grants, the next level manager in Community Programs, behaved in a paranoid manner and controlled the flow of information from his staff to the office manager, Smith, and the deputy director, Gooden. Rose frequently warned them not to talk to anyone but him, saying: "They don't care about us. They just don't understand what we're about. Stay away from Smith and Gooden." Community Programs did not coordinate its responsibilities with either Business Development or Current Business. This lack of communication had negative results, for instance, failure to prepare communities to attract new businesses.

Gold, Wareham, and Smith mirrored the ambiguous and conflicting role relations between Gooden and Wright based on fight-flight assumptions. Before the consultation they had no incentive to identify and correct these problems. There were no apparent role boundaries or clarifications of authority and responsibility among management. Role analysis in this situation became a critical intervention strategy. It enabled members of the organization to admit publicly the role confusions and ambiguities, and to acknowledge the metapattern of avoiding conflict. Publicizing and taking individual responsibility for this in a group setting empowered them to commit themselves to solving their problems with our assistance, a process that they have now initiated.

The role analysis session left the EDP managers and DCDRC executives feeling depressed—a sentiment expressed and validated by the executives in the final session. From a clinical perspective, we concluded that this depressive position was a consequence of their experience in beginning to confront, not as yet having worked through, painful and longstanding problems in their organization. On the basis of an application of object relations theory, we believed that this depressive position[10] represented progress beyond the earlier schizoid position[11] of organizational members—what Melanie Klein would describe as a reparative process had begun.[12] We (the consultants) suggested to the executive group that this depressed state signified their (organizational participants') acceptance of the problems identified during the process consultation and their commitment, however reluctant they might understandably feel at present, to resolve conflicts and move ahead.

SUMMARY

Organizational identity is a schema for interpreting the unconscious life of organizations. It requires the consultant (action researcher) to pay special attention to repetitive relational patterns along vertical and horizontal axes. Thus, the appearance of a central metapattern of conflict avoidance in the case of DCDRC was of special interest to the consultants and only perpetuated the conflicted organizational image held by members. Recent policy shifts and reorganizations created a stressful and uncertain climate for organizational members as well. Members shared an unconscious fight-flight assumption that tended to internalize the conflict within the organization and added to the polarization between offices within Economic Development Programs.

Organizational identity rests with the analysis of transference dynamics between superordinates and subordinates, which assists consultants and researchers (like us) in making sense of nonrational behavior in organizations so that we can assist clients with insight, development, and change. In the case of DCDRC, the subject of persecutory transference was Gooden, the deputy director, who fled from the responsibilities of leadership. The consultants believed that unconsciously, he felt persecuted and treated unfairly by Wright, the new director. As noted, Gooden identified with the values and mission of community programs, the previous goal of DCDRC. Now, as deputy director, Gooden felt conflicted, angry, and guilty that he could not commit himself to the new DCDRC mission of economic development as symbolized by Wright and the conservative governor and his administration. This persecutory transference at the top affected all of Economic Development Programs. Wright's absence only exaggerated these feelings in Gooden, and Gooden took flight from his anxiety by withdrawing and refusing to take charge. Gooden's flight was then experienced by middle managers as a passive-aggressive attack, and they responded by ignoring their managerial responsibilities, a response which took its toll on the staff. Abdication of leadership at the top led to fight-flight behavior among middle managers, and between them and their respective staff.

Process consultation took the form of making the organizational members identify common problems and take steps to solve those problems so that they could then develop a strategic plan for Economic Development Programs. However, in order to do so, the consultants had to unmask the source of resistance to insight and change—or the partly tacit metapatterns of interpersonal relationships that perpetuated and reinforced the problems in the first place. The concept of organizational identity assisted us in doing so by analyzing the unconscious and repetitive dimensions of key relationships, such as the persecutory transference between Wright and Gooden, and between Gooden and the middle managers.

Organizational conversions, whether produced by leadership changes or policy shifts, are fundamentally emotional events. Nevertheless, typical philosophies and practices of organizational leaders and managers ignore this fact. In the next chapter, I address this issue with two brief cases from my consulting work that show the organizational and psychological effects of leadership transition and the psychodynamics of (what is called) object loss in coping with change.

NOTES

1. The names of the agency and its members have been disguised to preserve anonymity.

2. The subject of the persecutory transference is Gooden, the deputy director, who removes himself from the responsibilities of leadership. Unconsciously, Gooden feels persecuted or treated unfairly by Wright, the new director. Gooden identifies with community development and the prior mission of DCDRC; now as deputy director of the entire agency, he feels conflicted, angry, and guilty that he has not as yet accepted the new mission of economic and business development symbolized by Wright and the new state administration. This persecutory transference at the top affects the entire Economic Development Programs group.

3. See Levinson (1972), for the interview schedule that we found most helpful in formulating our own.

4. Segal (1964) states that through the act of projective identification, one's bad feelings may become tolerable when viewed as belonging to another person or object such as members of another division or group. The unconscious intent of this manner of projection is either to experience one's feelings vicariously through another, hence the notion of identification, or to control and coerce the other by attributing one's feelings to

him or her. Placing one's negative feelings elsewhere, externally, makes them easier to handle. In addition, it can mean influencing the other to act in a way that meets the subject's unconscious demands.

5. The concept of a basic assumption of fight-flight comes from Bion's (1959) *Experiences in Groups*, in which he identifies the unconscious components of work groups. This component signifies that group members come together with the assumption that they are there to acknowledge the enemy whom they must fight or, in this study, from whom they must flee.

6. *Metapatterns* are defined as repeating, partly tacit sequences in relationships (Ingersoll and Adams, 1992). In organizations, they serve to organize members' patterns of interaction; they operate beneath the surface and have a kind of contagious quality, reverberating through all levels of the organization.

7. *Organizational identity* is the totality of repetitive patterns of individual behavior and interpersonal relationships that, when taken together, constitute the unacknowledged meaning of organizational life. Organizational identity accords a prominent position to the analysis of transference between superordinates and subordinates, and among organizational members themselves, as a method of interpreting unconscious organizational dynamics (Diamond, 1988).

8. *Projection* involves rejecting part of oneself, typically a negative image or experience, by placing it in someone else and then attributing it to him or her (Moore and Fine, 1990).

9. This metapattern of betrayal and counterbetrayal bears a close resemblance to the pattern of scapegoating discussed in Eagle and Newton (1981).

10. The depressive position is a psychological space for integrating split-off part-objects and making them whole again. It is a time of sadness in that there appear to be a recognition of and ability to tolerate contradictory, good and bad, love and hate, feelings. The depressive position represents a positive developmental shift away from paranoid and schizoid thinking.

11. The schizoid position is characterized by a profound sense of helplessness and hopelessness. The depriving experiences with others have produced a fear of and antipathy toward life so intense and pervasive that this central portion of the ego has renounced all others, external and internal, real and imaginary; it has withdrawn into an isolated, objectless state. In this flight from life, Guntrip suggests, the regressed ego seeks to return to the prenatal security of the womb, to await a rebirth into a more hospitable environment. Thus regression involves a flight and a longing for renewal (Greenberg and Mitchell, 1983: 211).

12. The reparative process is central to the depressive position in which the individual or group moves from the fragmented view of self and others toward the integrated and holistic acknowledgment of good and evil in everyone.

APPENDIX 1

1. *Initial Meeting with Executive Group.* Meet with Executive Director, the two Deputy Directors, and the Director of Administration, who compose the Executive Group in DCDRC. Discuss initial perceptions of problems, clarify objectives and expectations for the consultation, and outline the intervention plan and procedures.

2. *Session with Executive Group* (Half-day). Finalize intervention plan and procedures. Request and collect factual, historical, and interpretive data from the director and his deputies on the Department of Community Development, Regulation and Commerce.

3. *Individual Interviews of Senior Managers and Staff* (Two full days). Request and collect data from a total of 30 management and staff members through structured interviews of about an hour each. Begin to identify organizational themes and problems that are shared by the majority of interviewees.

4. *Session with Executive Group* (Half-day). Provide general feedback on themes and problems discovered in the interviews, and confirm or disconfirm their validity.

5. *Session with Senior Managers and Staff Group* (Full day with 28 staff). Provide general feedback on themes and problems discovered in the interviews and confirmed by executives, and confirm or disconfirm their validity. Large and small group work sessions aimed primarily at problem identification and clarification.

6. *Session with Executive Group and Senior Managers* (Full day with 18 staff). Provide general feedback on themes and problems discovered in the interviews, confirmed by executives, senior managers, and staff, and, once again, confirm or disconfirm their validity. Incorporate a role clarification exercise to surface ambiguities and inconsistencies. Begin to identify possible solutions for problem areas.

7. *Session with Executive Group* (Half-day). Overview of identified problem areas. Development of directions for solutions to these problem areas. Assess what has been accomplished and evaluate the consultation.

APPENDIX 2

1. Conflict avoidance.

2. Ambiguity of authority and responsibility among management at the top and the middle of Economic Development Programs.

3. Interdivisional conflict among Business Development, Current Business, and Community Programs (how people deal with aggression, dependency, affection, and ambitions).

4. Lack of adequate departmentwide planning and direction.

5. Absence of the director and unclear delegation of authority to deputies.

6. The extent to which people construct their own role definitions and the consequences of that for the chain of command.

7. Competency of office managers and project managers, and the inadequacy of performance evaluations and public expectations.

8. The degree to which politics drives the department and how to balance administrative and political demands adequately.

9. To what extent is Economic Development Programs dependent upon Community Programs funding, and what are the consequences of that?

10. Consideration of Economic Development Programs physical space.

11. Why the recent reorganization?

12. Why the consultation at this time?

13. The challenge of managing an organization with a conflicted identity that must adapt to diverse cultures.

Items 9 and 10 were subsequently dismissed as significant problems, and items 11 and 12 faded in importance over time. All other items were confirmed as problems repeatedly—in this session and those which followed.

APPENDIX 3

CONFLICT AVOIDANCE

Conflict avoidance is a thematic problem that pervades nearly all of the problem areas discussed below. The consultation has been an initial step in confronting conflicts and in building new daily habits of action that will minimize conflict avoidance in the future.

Confirmed Problem Areas with Suggested Solutions

1. Ambiguity of authority and responsibility among management at the top and the middle of Economic Development Programs (inaccessibility of the director and unclear delegation of authority to deputies) is pervasive.

   Guiding question: To what extent do directors/managers need authority that they do not have, in order to perform their responsibilities?

   • What responsibilities of the Director should be delegated?

   • Clarify and communicate the roles and responsibilities of the Director and Deputy Director for Economic Development Programs.

   • Clarify and communicate roles for managers, including Deputy Directors and Office Managers.

2. Interdivisional conflict among Business Development, Current Business, and Community Programs (issues of aggression, affection, submission and dominance, dependency, and ambition).

   • Managers from Business Development and Current Business should meet and develop joint policy recommendations on issues in conflict.

   • Offices should define their respective roles and what recognition they need within the Economic Development Programs.

   • Further development of shared identity and mission in Economic Development Programs should mitigate these conflicts.

3. Relative absence of management at office level (Director and Deputy Director for Economic Development Programs frequent engagement in compensating activities; the extent to which people construct their own role definitions and the consequences of that for the chain of command; ambiguous roles of office managers and managers of programs and projects; and the inadequacy of performance evaluations and unclear role expectations).

- Clarify and assess
- Accountability based on role definitions

4. The degree to which politics drives the department and how to balance administrative and political demands adequately.

   - If decision is "political," it needs to be explained to those involved.
   - Professional identities of personnel should not be compromised by political decisions.
   - Top management should clarify and communicate some guidelines on political issues (e.g., legislators' announcements of project awards, prior notice of negative decisions).

5. Lack of adequate departmentwide planning and direction; the challenge of managing an organization with a conflicted identity that must adapt to diverse cultures; Economic Development Programs vs. Department of CDRC; question of division status for Economic Development within the department.

   - Recommend using a *participative* planning exercise (strategic plan, if possible; alternatively, a day-long mission-definition retreat) to clarify and develop shared identity and mission for Economic Development (must include a clear and valued role for community programs, and community aspects of other Economic Development offices).

PROBLEM SOLVING AND PLANNING NEXT STEPS

Activities which assume the mitigation of conflict avoidance practices and habits (clear role definitions, delegation of adequate authority, more open and direct communication; timely confrontation of interpersonal and organizational problems and issues).

1. Identity and mission building activities (Retreat and/or strategic plan).
2. Performance evaluation procedures to enable management to confront and solve personnel problems on an ongoing basis.
3. Training of management in performance evaluation; management training for newly selected managers; training across offices as well as within offices (to promote linkages and shared understandings across offices of Economic Development Programs).
4. Develop activities that promote informal linkages between and among offices.

10

EXAMPLES OF LEADERSHIP
TRANSITION AND OBJECT LOSS

In Chapter 4, I stated that *organizational identity* is the unconscious dimension of organizational culture or that which denotes the unacknowledged meaning of organizational life. Then, in Chapter 5, I claimed that organizational identity represents the means by which work groups orient themselves toward the organization and from which individuals acquire their own sense of security and identity as members. Earlier, in Chapter 2, I observed that organizational identity often comprises ritualistic organizational defenses produced by (what I call) *the externalized self-system*, or what Shapiro and Carr (1991) call "the organization in the mind." Thus, I have gone as far as to suggest that organizational behavior is often the manifestation of collective compromise formations. Moreover, I have conjectured that the beginnings of organizational identity are grounded in the infant's first comprehension of herself or himself as separate from others, a realization that results in normal feelings of ambivalence and separation anxiety—a developmental period between ages two and three in which the ego defenses (of the self-system) are integrated into the personality. This developmental understanding of the emergence of the sense of self is a tenet of contemporary psychoanalytic thought. This principle is pivotal to my interpretation of the two cases presented in this chapter.[1] Childhood mastery of separation and individuation hinges on the quality of object constancy, which is crucial to good enough parenting. Let me begin by explaining the notion of object constancy.

The names of the agencies and their members are disguised to preserve anonymity.

Psychoanalytic ego psychologists and object relations theorists claim that the unfolding of a core identity is grounded in the infant's experience of *object constancy*. Hamilton (1990) writes: "Object constancy means the ability to hold a steady image of the object, especially the mother, whether she is present or absent, gratifying or depriving" (Hamilton 1990: 53). He continues to say that

> the achievement of individuality usually goes hand-in-hand with the ability to form a more or less constant image of the object. Self-constancy begins to coalesce. This increasingly secure sense of self allows for more purposeful activity. Because the child knows who he is and what he wants, even when mildly frustrated, he can now persist with tasks. (Hamilton 1990: 55)

By internalizing the nurturing and reliable parent (mother), the child is able to secure a sense of identity (a cognitive sense of self) that may withstand fluctuations in the external world. In the words of Erik Erikson (1964): "Identity connotes resiliency of maintaining essential patterns in the process of change. It takes a well-established identity to tolerate radical change" (95–96). This fact, I believe, is not altered by adulthood and, thus, is an unconscious psychological consideration of organizational participants.

Individual emotional ties with organizations and leaders are a normal outcome of institutional membership. Where there is a history of bad organizational leadership in particular, transitions at the top can exaggerate separation anxieties and defensiveness among middle managers and their staff. Regular leadership transitions often detach members from their organizational anchors and render organizational schemas obsolete and safe navigation uncertain. Workers may feel adrift and anxious.

The two brief case examples presented in this chapter illustrate how leadership transitions can disorient members and unravel their organizational identities. In these instances, the absence of object constancy due to leadership transitions and the unfinished business of dealing with feelings about previous leaders provoke object loss in organizational members. In other words, leadership transitions destabilize organizational identities, shatter object constancy, and trigger deeper feelings of object loss. Anxieties are momentarily awakened and defenses weakened.

Under these circumstances, consultants may find participants who experience a lack of meaning and purpose in their work—a sense of hopelessness. In addition to the actual loss of a leader and her or his executive team, organizational members know that leadership transitions often mean a change in policy direction and reorganization. Greater uncertainty at work produces anxieties that distort self and other boundaries, which are typically regulated through defined roles and tasks. This critical event in the history of an organization often has a damaging impact on employee morale and motivation. Thus, it needs to be more deeply understood to prevent dysfunctional consequences.

The extent to which the experience of object loss and separation anxiety makes transition and renewal problems ultimately depends upon the persistence of good and bad feelings about previous leaders and the associated positive or negative impact of that collective experience upon organizational culture and organizational identity—the magnitude of institutional object constancy. Nevertheless, leadership transitions provoke object loss and the need to mourn old leaders and their organizational images in order to accept new ones. Though such transformations are often welcomed by participants, the need for a cognitive and emotional process of abandoning old structures, procedures, and relationships remains. Finally, there are often emotional issues of disappointment among organizational members that aggravate feelings of object loss during transitions, for example, among those members who apply for executive appointments and subsequently are turned down.

The following two cases illustrate the personal and organizational effects of leadership transitions, and the complexities of these incidents when they are experienced by members as a form of object loss.

THE STORY OF THE DIVISION OF MEDICAID DISBURSEMENTS

Introduction

The Division of Medicaid Disbursements (DMD), a medium-sized bureaucratic state agency, is responsible for approximately $850 million in medical services to more than 328,000 people. DMD provides many services through the Medicaid program: inpatient and outpatient hospital services; nursing home care; physician services; laboratory and x-ray; home health care; audiology, dental, optometric, and podiatry services; ambulance services; adult day health care; personal care services; nurse-midwife services; hospice services; case management for pregnant women and children; durable medical equipment, and orthotic and prosthetic devices; and ambulatory surgical centers.

Initial Contact

Sally Reynolds, DMD's director, and her assistant, Bill Haskins, contacted the author to help improve communication and coordination of tasks between them and the five deputies and among the deputies. The explicit goal of the consultation was to enhance the effectiveness of the executive team. The team of five deputies included Alice Welch, head of the office of Compensations; Patricia Small, head of the office of Administration; Zelda Baker, head of the office of Practices and Procedures; Melvin Connally, head of the office of Systems Management; and John Kellner, head of the office of Judicial Assistance. "We simply don't talk," stated the director and her assistant in portraying the most immediate problem of DMD.

Case Presentation

The DMD director, Sally Reynolds, took over the agency four months before the consultation. She telephoned the consultant and asked to schedule a meeting in her office to discuss the possibility of a "short-term" contract to help her improve communications with her executive team. Appointed by the director of the Department of Human Services, Reynolds catapulted into the director's position from the lower ranks of the department director's office. She admitted that her adjustment to the new position was "challenging." Frank Thomas, who had been interim director for four months, according to her executive staff, was inaccessible. Reynolds described DMD as "directionless" at the time she accepted her new role. The agency had 150 employees and was considered by Reynolds and her assistant, Haskins, to be understaffed. Haskins thought a crucial issue for DMD staff was the question, Who's in charge? Reynolds and Haskins characterized the agency's political dilemma in the following manner: the public and their legislators complained about the high costs of medical services and the recipients griped that there were too few services. The agency had an understaffed "complaint hotline," they said with much trepidation, which was located in the office of Systems Management. DMD, Reynolds told the consultant, "is engaged in crisis management." As she put it, "We're in a reactive mode most of the time around here!"

Like Reynolds, the previous director, Louise Snell, bypassed middle management in her rise from the lower managerial ranks to take over as director of the agency. Deputy directors and staff reported "a lack of confidence" in Snell's leadership. They resented her getting the appointment over them. They felt she was not qualified and, lacking seniority in

DMD, did not deserve promotion to director. They also felt this way about Reynolds. Zelda Baker and Melvin Connally had applied for the position of agency director. As a consequence, Reynolds reported "bad feelings" against her.

Nursing Home Administration Problem

In particular Zelda Baker reported to the consultant that Snell was "not competent and knowledgeable enough to be director of the agency." Resistance to her leadership encouraged Snell to leave DMD; she was reassigned to a new position as assistant to the director of Human Services. However, according to DMD executives, Snell continued to make internal decisions for the agency. For example, Reynolds claimed: "Compensation of nursing homes is our biggest problem. Authority for reimbursement policy rests outside the agency with Snell, the previous director, not with Alice Welch, who carries the responsibility." The consultant encouraged Reynolds to meet regularly with Snell and the department director to untangle the knot of ambiguity; in that way Reynolds could better manage the programs within her leadership domain. "This meant," the consultant suggested, "that Snell would have to begin letting go of her previous role in DMD, and the department director, Jack Smith, had to encourage the separation." Initiating and supporting a grieving process might enable Snell to experience the loss associated with change and further allow her to move ahead. Partially because of the institutional proximity and authority of her new position, Snell's behavior signified some difficulties in dealing with the loss and separation associated with her previous role as director. The consultant felt that if the new director, Reynolds, genuinely appreciated the emotional side of the transition, she could work more effectively and openly with Snell and the department director, Jack Smith. At the same time, this strategy would enlist Snell's assistance in clarifying authority and responsibility for compensation of nursing homes, in particular, and attaining the department director's commitment for the new director of DMD and her deputies. At the next meeting of the consultant, the director, and her assistant, nearly one month later, Reynolds reported progress, saying that Snell "was interfering less and less frequently."

Systems Management Problem

Reynolds also mentioned difficulties with the head of the Systems Management office, Melvin Connally. She stated that he was unavailable and, unlike her other deputies, did not consult her. She found him detached and unapproachable. When the consultant asked whether she had scheduled any meetings with him, she replied that he "had cancelled on at least three occasions." The consultant then suggested that she insist that he not cancel the next meeting and asked whether she had inquired why he had cancelled the other meetings. She had not. The consultant reiterated the need for her to reschedule and insist on his keeping the appointment. She did. At the next meeting she stated that they were now communicating and developing a better working relationship.

Conflict Between the Practices and Procedures and Systems Management Offices

Nearly one month later the consultant met with the director and her assistant. At that time Reynolds and Haskins noted the hostility between the office of Practices and Procedures (P&P) and the office of Systems Management. People in Practices and Procedures "get private offices and special status and prestige," they announced. "P&P get travel budgets that others don't," and they do not "have to listen to the public's condemnations," since complaints are handled by the office of Systems Management. "Are the other offices envious of Practices and Procedures?" the consultant asked. "Absolutely," they said. According to Reynolds and Haskins, the discord among the offices is more often verbalized among staff below the deputy level.

In another meeting with Reynolds and Haskins, preceding the executive group session, the consultant asked them: "On the basis of your observations, then, do you think the office of Practices and Procedures draws excessive hostility from the other offices?" They did. The consultant then asked how they would describe the individual deputies the executive team comprised. To paraphrase, they described Alice Welch, head of the office of Compensation, as an "outstanding performer and legal expert. She sticks to legal guidelines and strict interpretation of rules and regulations." They described Pat Small, head of the office of Administration, as "fragile, highly sensitive, and a poor performer." Zelda Baker, head of the office of Practices and Procedures, was the oldest and most experienced deputy, at age fifty-four, and was involved in politics throughout the state. Reynolds and Haskins called her "manipulative and controlling," a "strong personality." According to Reynolds, "She never forgets and is viewed as a real power source in the division. Trained as a professional nurse, she is extremely knowledgeable—a tremendous asset to the division. She watches out for her staff and effectively represents their interests." Reynolds and Haskins admitted relying on Baker for her policy and medical expertise. "Baker is looked up to by the other deputies," they added. Melvin Connally, head of the office of Systems Management, they depicted as a "detached expert. He's a good performer but not a team player like the other deputy directors." Finally, John Kellner, head of the office of Judicial Assistance, was described as Reynolds' "protector," someone ready to come to her legal defense whenever necessary.

After this session with Reynolds and Haskins and just before escorting the consultant out of her office, Reynolds showed the consultant Baker's office. Baker was out of town at the time, and it appeared that Reynolds thought that the author might learn something of value by seeing Baker's room. At first glance, the consultant thought it was a comfortable and relatively spacious office with nice furnishings. But that was not the point. Reynolds explained that Baker, before Reynolds became director, simply moved into the office without permission. Reynolds made it clear to the consultant, rather than to Baker, that this office was intended for the DMD director.

As in her conflicts with the previous director, Snell, and the deputy director, Connally, Reynolds had not as yet confronted issues with Baker. She needed the support and encouragement of the consultant to do so. The consultant's challenge was to help her resolve these problems in a manner that surfaced individual responsibilities and improved communications and coordination among the executive team—setting the stage for organizational change. To do so, without appearing to protect Reynolds because of her fear of Baker, would be tricky.

Group Session with the Executive Team

Reynolds and Haskins wanted to identify their agency's problems in coordinating tasks between and among the offices of DMD. Examples of problem areas, they noted, were regulatory processes and psychiatric hospitals. A full-day executive group session with the following structure was then scheduled:

   I. Discussion of effective work groups

  II. Identification of problems and resistance in working as an executive team for DMD

 III. Consensus on DMD problems and problem areas between and among units

 IV. Solutions and action plan for solving problems

This session was tape-recorded by the consultant. With the exception of Baker, everyone arrived on time. The session began with a discussion of effective and ineffective work groups. The consultant used this strategy as a technique for getting participants to start talking at a more abstract, theoretical level, which tended to minimize anxiety. This made it easier for them, somewhat later, to deal with more emotionally loaded issues. Later that morning, for instance, the consultant asked the group to share concrete examples of ineffectiveness from their experience in DMD. This engaged the group in surfacing conflict and beginning to identify common problems.

Baker arrived more than one hour late and during the initial discussion of ineffective work groups. The interaction seemed to change abruptly. Baker instantly overran the discussion and started lecturing the consultant and others on incompetent work relations and what DMD staff needed to do better. She prefaced all this, looking directly at the consultant, by stating that she believed in the importance of the intervention. This deflected attention away from Baker and her office and redirected concern to the executive team and their relations with the department head's staff. Although this conversation was productive in that it concentrated on the previous director's interference in DMD affairs, it also diverted group sentiments from Baker and issues internal to DMD. The group appeared not to resist Baker's domination of their momentum and purposeful direction.

The consultant intervened after fifteen minutes and asked: "What happened after Ms. Baker entered the room? Did anyone notice any change in the group's behavior? And, if so, is this indicative of what happens back at the office?" This produced much anxiety and a long period of silence. The silence was then broken by Baker, who returned the group, momentarily, to an abstract and theoretical discussion of teamwork. This angered Reynolds, who interrupted Baker and suggested that the group was "repeating what the consultant had intimated." She further proclaimed: "This occurs in our weekly staff meetings as well. We don't talk to each other; we don't listen," she announced.

Analysis

Sally Reynolds, the new director, and her assistant, Bill Haskins, were quite dependent on Zelda Baker, the deputy director of Practices and Procedures. They admired and respected her, and simultaneously, they were intimidated and frustrated by her. Baker controlled the knowledge and information that Reynolds and Haskins needed to run the agency effectively. If they were to be successful, they had to work well with her. Baker knew she was competent and influential and demanded that others, particularly members of the executive team, hold her in high esteem and treat her appropriately. She was also convinced that she, rather than Reynolds, was best qualified to direct the agency. Baker had not respected Snell, the previous director, and did not respect Reynolds. She perceived few, if any, boundaries limiting her role in the agency.

In contrast to the others, Baker and her staff traveled and had the best offices in DMD. The deputy directors and their staff envied Baker and P&P, thus producing negative feelings among them. Baker claimed to be a team player but the evidence was contradictory. Baker had political clout in the state and this concerned the others. She controlled and dominated the executive group, and she was capable of redirecting the group's attention in a way that made her look good and others look bad. She forced Snell, the previous director, to request a transfer, and her low opinion of Snell's leadership skills convinced others of the previous director's incompetence. Baker perceived herself as a very important person, and others reinforced that perception.

Publicly, staff spoke very "highly" of Baker, but, in private discussions, they expressed resentment of the special treatment of her staff. Like Snell, Reynolds and Haskins were infuriated by her. By not confronting her, however, they indulged her grandiosity. In fact, Baker unconsciously required the others to *mirror* her expansive self-image, and Reynolds and her executive group granted her wish to be *idealized*. The consultant's initial objective was somehow to deflate the mirroring-idealizing transference of the deputy director, Baker; the director, Reynolds; and the executive group. This could be accomplished by working through the suppressed anger, fear, and resentment toward Baker among the other deputy directors, the assistant to the director, and the director herself.

As long as the Reynolds and Baker transference persisted, the other deputy directors experienced ambiguity about Reynolds' position of authority and continued to aggrandize and simultaneously despise Baker. In addition, they continued to envy her office's benefits and special recognition and felt dissatisfied with the inadequate acknowledgment they and their staff received. Coordination of tasks and information sharing suffered. Services deteriorated. In a more rational frame of mind, DMD executives appreciated the difference between P&P and their units. They knew that the successful mission of P&P required travel, for example, and that of their own sections did not. However, as long as their need to idealize some member of the DMD group was directed at Baker, the division lacked credible leadership in the office of director. Bad feelings were suppressed behind the idealization, leaving the deputy directors, Reynolds and Has-kins, feeling conflicted. The consultant knew this from hearing the con-tradictory feelings vocalized by the executive group toward Baker and her staff, but only in her absence and in private and confidential interviews. Otherwise, they consistently expressed admiration of her.

Only four months on the job, Reynolds was reluctant to use her formal authority and deal with her problems with Baker directly. Unconsciously, she knew what she was up against—an executive staff, which included her, that idealized one of the deputy directors. Reynolds had avoided confronting two of her deputy directors, Baker and Connally, and the previous director, Snell. With the consultant's encouragement she spoke with Connally and Snell, and that proved helpful. However, not until the executive group session was she able to direct her action, in some fashion, to Baker.

If Reynolds did not work through her contradictory feelings of admira-tion and hostility for Baker, she might never acquire an authoritative role as DMD director. To assert her leadership, she had to clarify with Baker the role of director vis-à-vis the role of deputy director and what her expectations of Baker were. In so doing, Reynolds knew that she might disappoint Baker or risk attack through dismissal of her management abilities, and this anticipation made her anxious.

However, the group session offered her an opportunity to confront her staff and allow them to confront her. This represented a positive step in transforming power to the new director and improving the working relationships among her staff. To gain the respect of her staff, a director must be willing to evaluate their behavior and to encourage them to evaluate her actions as well. Mutual respect could only be established by defusing the perception of Baker's omnipotence among the executive group. The risks included Baker's becoming defensive and making change and problem solving more difficult. However, this was already the case, and the defensive and resistant behavior did not stem from Baker alone: It was systemic. Mistrust, withholding of information, and polarization among offices within DMD were prevalent.

To some extent, the executive group colluded in scapegoating Baker for their problems of poor coordination and faulty communications. They had also displaced anger away from Reynolds, who some felt did not deserve the promotion to director. Baker's competence aside, her grandiosity and intimidation were partly the result of the group's indulgence—their mir-roring her need for idealization. Though these narcissistic proclivities may reside in Baker, as they do in everyone, the group and organizational context either encourages or discourages these tendencies. In DMD, they were unwittingly promoted by weak leadership, scarce resources, and a difficult mission that would always meet with public dissatisfaction. *Projecting bad feelings* onto Baker and her office enabled all the others to shun personal responsibility for DMD's organizational problems and their genuine feelings.

CONCLUSIONS

Organizational change often requires altering members' roles and this entails (what psychoanalysts call) object loss. *Object loss* involves grieving for a part of oneself (what Kohut [1977] calls the selfobject), the internalized object relationship. Tasks and roles in organizations are internalized by members and eventually constitute their personal organizational (professional, vocational, role) identities.

What did the key players in DMD need to relinquish so that they could change their organizational dynamics? Snell, the previous director, had to work through her feelings of failure and disappointment associated with Baker, the deputy director of P&P. Baker represented Snell's idealized object. In taking her new role as assistant to the department director and reestablishing appropriate and functional role boundaries, Snell had to experience the feelings of object loss associated with separation and development. Reynolds, the new director, had to surrender her dependency need and her idealization of Baker. Like Snell, Reynolds fit into the mirroring-idealizing transference with Baker. However, the intervention produced an opportunity for her to remove herself from the dysfunctional bond. Perhaps this mirroring-idealizing transference was an entrenched metapattern; the new director faced a covert attempt to organize her behavior into the metapattern, to which she was to some extent susceptible. In fact, the consultant's role was to help her find her way out.

Baker, the deputy director of P&P, represented (what Bion called) the *basic assumption leader* of DMD. She had to relinquish her extraordinary need for control and the idealization of others. She had to become an equal partner of the executive team. However, Baker would always carry the considerable power and authority of her knowledge, expertise, and competence.

In addition to demystifying Baker, the other deputy directors had to deal with their feelings of rejection in not being appointed agency director. After these feelings of grief were resolved, they could see Reynolds as a whole person and better assess her abilities as their new director.

One year after the consultation, Baker remained with the agency and Reynolds was in charge. Of course, Reynolds still relied upon Baker, but she had firmly established herself as director of the agency. This enhanced role clarity and coordination of tasks among the executive staff and their offices.

Leader transitions engage primitive feelings, particularly those associated with object loss and separation anxiety. In this case and in the one to follow, organizational members experienced the psychological regression associated with shifting organizational identities. In both instances, the analysis of transference between leaders and followers was central to the consultant's ability to help the client system through the transition and loss and to assist in the reestablishment of a stable organizational identity.

THE STORY OF THE DEPARTMENT OF HUMAN SERVICES

Introduction

Created in 1974, the Department of Human Services consists of five government agencies which previously conducted social programs under separate administrations. Since the consolidation, the department comprises the following agencies: the Division of Family Assistance, the Division of Medicaid Disbursements, the Division of Child Protection, the Division of Elderly Assistance, and the Division of Juvenile Services.

The repositioning of these offices within a single, umbrella departmental structure signified an effort to create a coordinated approach to the delivery of human services to state residents. Formal authority and responsibility for the five agencies belongs to the director of the department, who is appointed by the governor with senate approval, and who, in turn, selects the five division directors. The Department of Human Services has approximately 7,000 civil service employees. In addition to the five program agencies, there are four support divisions: Facilities, Data Processing, Legal Assistance, and Finance.

Initial Contact

The assistant to the director of DHS, Beth Adler, telephoned the author to set up a meeting with the director, Jack Smith. At this meeting, the director and his assistant noted that their administration had been in place for one year and they felt it was time to establish a departmentwide mission statement. However, in order to do that, they thought it would be helpful to improve the coordination of tasks and communication among the five agencies. The list of departmental problems included "inadequate sharing of resources, poor communication between agencies, and a general lack of vertical and horizontal information-sharing." A tight budget, they added, would limit the amount of time and money allocated to the consultation.

The consultant suggested the following structure for diagnosis and intervention: First, the consultant needed to interview all of the executives for their observations and thoughts about the sorts of departmental problems that might block their ability to reach consensus on, and commit themselves to, a departmental mission statement. Second, the consultant had to meet with interdivisional groups of seven to eleven managers per group for one-day group sessions. These group sessions, five in all, would bring together staff and management from each of the divisions to focus on identifying problems of a departmental, as opposed to a divisional, nature. This would give division officials a rare opportunity to talk to each other and engage in departmental information sharing and problem solving. The consultant would then collect qualitative data from these sessions and report to the director and his assistant. The data would then be shared with everyone involved, and an opportunity for written feedback and correction of errors would be presented. Next, a retreat would be organized in which the five groups would have an opportunity to agree on the problems identified and to propose solutions; then divisional groups would meet to do the same. The goal of this one-and-one-half day retreat would be to reach departmentwide consensus on problems and what to do about them. As a consequence of this intervention strategy and consultation process, the divisions would find themselves working in a more collaborative mode, learning about one another as real human beings through direct interpersonal contact and dialogue. Minimizing the physical and psychological distance between them would help transcend interdivisional boundaries; this, in turn, would assist interdivisional problem solving and development of a departmentwide mission statement that adequately reflected their diverse responsibilities and interdependencies.

Executive and Managerial Group Sessions

Jack Smith, the director of DHS for one year, was viewed more favorably by his staff than his last several predecessors. Unlike previous DHS directors, Smith, formerly head of one of the support divisions, was hired from the inside. This fact seemed to matter to almost everyone. As one high-level manager put it, "Jack has background with the department, and that makes a difference!" "Jack can be trusted," said many of the division directors and their assistants. "He's one of us." In fact, small-group (interdivisional) participants expressed support and confidence in their new director. Many wished they had more of the director's time and requested a return to regularly scheduled executive meetings to improve the flow of information throughout the department.

After the second group session and into the retreat, it became strikingly clear that DHS management and their staff had suppressed anger and resentment toward two previous directors. This came as a surprise to the new director and his assistant. How did this manifest itself? Consistently in the group sessions and later at the retreat, participants mentioned incidents, most often humiliating interactions with the previous department director, Mark Holmes.

For example, many stories were told of his verbal abuse of staff members, calling them "stupid" and "incompetent" in front of others, shouting at them and divisional directors in public. He was known to punish his managers by taking staff away from their agencies, often for what he perceived as their disloyalty and insubordination. One of the most common stories was that of Holmes' dispensing of departmental lapel pins. In giving the pins to his most deferential and admiring followers, Holmes provoked resentment and envy among DHS employees and throughout DHS divisions. Ironically, recipients of the "eagle pins" were required by the director to wear them at all times; however, they admitted to wearing the pins only around the director.

The DHS Retreat

The one-and-one-half day retreat was designed as follows:

1. Interdivisional groups met in one large space with their director and the consultants. The format and objectives were presented by the consultant.

2. Interdivisional groups met to develop and confirm a list of problem areas to address. On a flip chart each group identified the most pressing problems. The consultant visited and facilitated the work of each group, while the director sat in as an observer. This event lasted the entire first morning.

3. After lunch on the first day, the interdivisional groups met with the consultant and the director in the large space. They presented their views on the major problems of DHS that needed to be addressed in the coming year and suggested strategies for solving them.

4. Divisional groups and one departmental (central office) group, which included the director, were established. The same task, to identify problems and propose solutions, was assigned. The consultant met with and facilitated each of the groups.

5. On the second day, the divisional and central office groups presented their lists of problems and solutions in the large space.

6. After a break, the group as a whole discussed the overall list of problems and solutions generated, and where to go from there. Responsibility for creating a synthesized list was then delegated and a deadline was set. This list would then be sent around to all participants for feedback and corrections. A final document with delegated responsibilities and deadlines would be prepared and signed by participants.

Analysis

Polarized relations between program divisions and support divisions surfaced. Program divisions complained that support divisions were too preoccupied with control and, consequently, were unresponsive to the needs of the programs. Support divisions, on the other hand, felt programs were withholding of information, uncooperative, and ungrateful and tended to pin the blame for problems on them. Support divisions voiced feeling victimized by the program divisions. One head of a support division put it this way: "Programs go around with the attitude, What have you done for me lately?" The sharing of information and acknowledgment of problem areas in the interdivisional group sessions tended to minimize some of the blaming and encouraged greater cooperation. Valid information and role clarification among divisional members helped as well. However, there seemed to be a great deal of frustration and anger among the participants. This was particularly evident in the cynicism of those who had been around for many years and worked under prior DHS administrations.

As noted, much sharing of a historical nature occurred, especially stories of previous directors. The effect of storytelling in the group sessions, the consultant observed, was to provoke a rather dramatic shift in group dynamics. Starting from a typically withholding and uncertain position, people would then look at one another, make eye contact, shake their heads affirmatively, and, finally, talk directly to each other instead of through the consultant. The author saw this as a symbol of psychological merger between group members based upon a shared emotional experience and identity. He also saw this as a shift away from a *dependency basic assumption* and toward what Bion (1959) called the *fight-flight basic assumption*, in which participants located an enemy, in this case someone outside the group boundary. The identification of an enemy, embodied in the memory of a past director, had the effect of pulling them together as a group engaged in a common emotional task—the work of seeking retribution by murdering, working through and letting go of, past leaders. However, the emotional work of DHS with their prior leaders was unfinished. The suppression of aggression was evidenced in comments, signifying *psychological splitting*, of retreat participants in the large-group meeting. For example, with the support and validation of his colleagues' nodding affirmatively, one member stated, "Under Holmes and Polk we got *bad projects*, but since Smith became director we get only *good projects*."

Although they were physically gone, the two prior leaders were present in the minds of DHS employees. Moving ahead and accepting a new leadership philosophy and practice meant renewing trust and self-respect through someone with whom they could identify. Jack Smith seemed to be that person. With past directors, DHS employees operated on the basis of a *persecutory transference* in which the outside world, the political and legislative arena, and the inside world, their intimidating and abusive director, were hostile and disrespectful. These bad feelings only enhanced the level of vicious competitiveness and mistrust they reported as occurring throughout the department. Many times, the participants referred to themselves as "survivors" of an unappreciative and often hostile public and victims of sadistic leaders. Though they were relieved to see both prior directors go, it seemed as if they had never expressed their angry feelings and had not mourned the loss of these "intimidating" and "hurtful" men.

Mourning the loss of someone loved and cared for seems understandable, but grieving for someone despised is unimaginable to many. *Projection*—the psychological tendency to reject bad feelings and place them outside oneself and to act as if they belong to someone or something else—makes grieving hard to do. With each group session and during the retreat itself, participants criticized and told painful stories about the previous two directors. "They were buddies of the governor," some said. "They lacked leadership skills, and they misunderstood the program divisions," others proclaimed. "Polk was corrupt and Holmes treated people badly," they agreed. Finally, and most pointedly for the consultant, "Jack Smith inherits the baggage of Holmes and Polk," several suggested. DHS members, the consultant felt, had to confront and let go of these negative feelings from the past, which affected their relations with one another and with the new director. They had to undo the persecutory transference that left them cynical and with little hope of positive change.

Conclusions

In the DHS case, persecutory transference between the staff and the previous director affected group and interpersonal relations (what I call organizational identity) one year after Holmes' departure. Group relations between program and support divisions were polarized through psychological splitting and projective identification. Little hope or optimism prevailed; cynicism was the predominant attitude among DHS staff. As evidenced in the interdivisional group sessions and the retreat, getting the participants to work through their anger at previous leaders, particularly Holmes, was critical to their developing the ability to collaborate and solve problems. Mourning the loss of a despised leader was essential to their constructing more realistic (and less pessimistic) perceptions of themselves as an agency, and to repairing emotional injuries (the splits and part-objects) that influenced their view of the current leadership.

SUMMARY

Both cases exemplify leadership transition as object loss and try to show the negative consequences for organizational identity. The psychodynamics of object constancy are shown to play a potentially positive role in assisting organizational members through the transition and reorganization. Paying attention to transference dynamics between leaders and followers is viewed as helpful to consultants and clients. Letting go of the old ways and taking on the new require a working through of feelings that enable organizational members to learn and develop task effectiveness. These processes are discussed further in the final chapter.

In Chapter 11, I conclude with some thoughts on the psychodynamics of organizational leadership and change—reflecting on the political theories of Thomas Hobbes and Jean-Jacques Rousseau as metaphors for the unconscious life of organizations. While I conclude that the persistently darker side of organizational life is best described as Hobbesian—an institutional Leviathan reacting to human nature as "nasty, brutish, and short," I view optimistically the processes of leadership and organizational change required in moving organizations successfully away from the Hobbesian Leviathans of defensive organizations and toward Rousseauian communities of resilient associations, companies, and governing agencies.

NOTE

1. See Margaret Mahler, Fred Pine, and Anni Bergman (1975); John Bowlby's three volumes on attachment, separation, and loss (1973; 1980; 1982); and D. W. Winnicott's writings on the "good enough" mother (1965; 1971), among other works.

III

CONCLUSIONS

11

THE PSYCHODYNAMICS OF
ORGANIZATIONAL CHANGE:

Renewal by Way of
Political and Psychoanalytic Metaphors

Through metaphor, we can describe various perspectives of organizational life (Morgan, 1986). The use of metaphor, I believe, deepens our understanding of organizational experience by clarifying the *observer's schema*—his or her way of arranging and making sense of the data (or nonsense) of organizations. Richard Sennett (1981) in his book *Authority* says that metaphor "creates a meaning greater than the sum of its parts, because the parts interact. The terms of a metaphor have meaning in relation to each other which they do not have apart. The whole creates the special meaning for the parts" (78).

Metaphors are valid techniques for conveying the meaning and telling the story of organizational life (Hummel, 1991; White, 1986). In one session with a group of architects and engineers, I asked them to draw their views of the organization now and in the future. These drawings told the story by way of metaphor of their organizational experience that, I believe, would not have surfaced, otherwise. One group, for instance, drew a picture of a covered wagon to represent the present and a rocket ship to symbolize the future. Another group drew a picture of an army tank for the present and a supersonic jet for the future; another group drew an elephant and a leopard. Consequently, these drawings elicited a dialogue among them that led to the detection of shared problems and, in some cases, inventive solutions to such problems. The drawings were organizational metaphors, which told a story, signifying their experience as workers—the meaning of which had to be elicited by the consultant.

In *Private Terror/Public Life*, the political theorist James M. Glass writes: "Storytelling provides a unique perspective in the social sciences; it delineates meaning and content through its power as symbolization and lived experience. It relies on metaphor as commentary on patterns of mind and desire" (14). To access latent meaning and a deeper understanding of the experience of organizational members, and the impact of that experience on actions, metaphor can be a powerful tool for reconstructing the intersubjective world of organizational life—the organizational identity. In his article on "Organization And Explanation" Sederberg (1984) states:

Metaphors pepper political discourse. Leaders prowl as lions and foxes; political machines manufacture electoral support; actors play roles in political dramas; and the state dominates the social world like a leviathan. We systematize our metaphors and label them models, maps, and simulations. It appears that we can no more escape meta-phorical characterizations of the world than we can dispense with language itself in explanation. Metaphor helps us economize our explanations. (167)

In the *Administrative State*, Dwight Waldo (1984) declares that admin-istrative thought is a branch of political theory. I agree, and in that spirit in this final chapter, I use some of the more familiar ideas of the political philosophers Thomas Hobbes and Jean-Jacques Rousseau as metaphors of two diverse organizational experiences. Reflecting on ten years of consult-ing to primarily American public organizations,[1] I find that one useful way to think of organizational responses to inherently unstable and continu-ously changing environments is a dynamic continuum bounded at opposite ends by political metaphors: At one extreme is the Hobbesian *leviathan*, a totalitarian fortress (Jacobson, 1978; Diamond, 1984; Schwartz, 1990) and at the other limit is Rousseau's *general will*, a collaborative and therapeutic community (Glass, 1976; 1989). Few organizations fit cleanly at either boundary, and most belong somewhere between these two ideal types. Most public agencies and businesses, however, tend to rest nearer the Hobbesian border.

Why are so many organizations more suitably characterized by the Hobbesian world than the Rousseauian? Because public and private orga-nizations operate under conditions of constant change and uncertainty—igniting the Hobbesian fear of the unknown (Blits, 1989). Regular change, minimal control, and uncertainty make public and private organizations stressful—evoking what I call *conflicted organizational identities*. Often characterized by a leadership void, these organizations seem directionless.

For example, I consulted with a company, previously owned by a well-known American corporation, that was purchased by a German conglomerate nearly seven years before the consultation began.[2] Midwestern employees of the company—a fulfillment center for businesses within this international corporation—had never truly accepted and never fully identified with the German corporation as their new employer. They felt no affiliation with the "foreign" organization. Moreover, the terminal illness of the company's president and changes in business strategies further complicated the matter.

On the surface, the fulfillment center's workers lacked an organizational identity because of the change in ownership, to which they had never adjusted. However, at a deeper level, the workers were on the verge of losing a beloved patriarch who had been with many of them for twenty and thirty years. To understand thoroughly the meaning of change for this organization required an identification via empathy not only with the loss of the company's ownership but more significantly with the potential loss of the company president. With no plans for a successor and their fate decided by faceless and distant executives, workers were anxious. Unable to grieve the premature loss of their beloved leader, they were not ready to assume a new identity—let alone changes in business strategies and corporate culture. Costly mistakes and a depressive climate persisted. Uncertainty and change produced defensive and demoralizing work patterns among the fulfillment center employees and with the parent company and its businesses. The most strikingly meaningful, and in this case the most painful, relationships in organizations are often those between leaders and followers.

It is my observation that *the capability of any public agency and business to withstand the storms of political and economic pressure and change stems from the psychodynamic character of organizational leader-follower relations.* Moreover, I think the personal, political, and ethical integrity of public administrators and business managers ultimately stands and falls on the degree of organizational resilience of each institution. Finally, that resilience, I observe, depends upon the effective leadership of change.

In this final chapter, I again assert the value of transference dynamics between leaders and followers for grasping more profoundly the intersubjective structure of organizational experience—the organizational identity. I begin with a discussion of conflicted organizational identities and then examine a variety of psychodynamic leader-follower relationships found among people in organizations with unstable identities. These leader-follower relationships typify the unconscious dimension of emotional expectations and desires that all of us have in relationships of all kinds. In organizations, these unconscious motives frequently produce compulsive and regressive actions between and among members that are often mal-adaptive and unproductive—characteristic of the Hobbesian fortress. The degree to which an organization can effectively respond to a continuously changing climate (political and economic environment), I believe, ulti-mately depends on the personality of its leaders and the concomitant relationships among top managers. Next, I look at the effective leadership of change—two requisite leadership components for dealing with change are discussed: collaborative and therapeutic—characteristic of the Rousseauian community. Finally, I present the concept of organizational resilience and conclude with a brief deliberation on the role of the psycho-analytic organizational theorist as consultant.

CONFLICTED ORGANIZATIONAL IDENTITIES

A *resilient* self (and organizational) identity exists where there are conscious points of reference and commonality that can withstand tumul-tuous periods of uncertainty and change. A well-established self-identity is steady in the face of change: that is, the individual self maintains essential patterns in the process of change due to its construction around common human values (Erikson, 1964). This is also true of humanly produced and perpetuated organizations.

Employing Hobbesian and Rousseauian political theories as metaphors, I suggest a schema for thinking about organizational experience. This conceptual framework may be described as a continuum: At one extreme is the Hobbesian fortress—embracing few human values beyond control and resistance and therefore no sustainable identity; at the other boundary is the Rousseauian community—resolute in adhering to the values of participation and empathy combined with internal changes, which result from transformations in the environment. The conflicted identity of the Hobbesian organization is primarily defensive, while the integrated iden-tity of the Rousseauian organization is fundamentally resilient. As noted, most organizations move dynamically between two political metaphors—the *totalitarian* leviathan on one border and the *democratic* general will at the other.

What I call *conflicted organizational identities* are most commonly found within rapidly transforming organizations, such as the fulfillment center, in which workers feel powerless. They seem to lack clearly defined and publicly shared objectives and mission, and are conflicted as a consequence of constant change forced upon individual leaders and their defensive organizational cultures. In fact, conflicted organizational identities result from the lack of planned change.

Anxieties about losing control as a result of change renders learning and responsiveness among key organizational leaders and followers unlikely. The Hobbesian fear of uncertainty and violent metaphorical death characterizes the unconscious life of many defensive organizations—consider the fulfillment center that faced the inevitable death of a leader and the omnipresent engulfment by a "foreign" giant organization. Similar terror and existential anxiety rest at the unconscious center of defensive organizational cultures that operate in changing and unstable task environments.

These feelings of anxiety and disorientation among workers are understandable, even among more typical organizations. Leaders come and go, policies change, projects are prematurely terminated, budgets are revised and constrained, legislators and chief executives scapegoat the bureaucracy or the "system," larger companies purchase smaller companies, corporate strategies are altered, new technologies are introduced, and so on. Nevertheless, reorganization and downsizing persist as popular managerial strategies for coping with change.

Maintaining personal integration and group and organizational continuity and sense of purpose amid this tumult, however, requires quite a balancing act—it necessitates a conscious awareness of group, interpersonal, and individual techniques for coping with change and the associated negative feelings. This awareness is often unavailable. Despite their cognizance of change, individuals often go about their work in the spirit of "business as usual." They have not incorporated the present nor rejected the past; they have little vision of the future. They are living as if nothing different is happening (Diamond, 1985a; Schwartz, 1990).

Organizational leaders are especially affected by change. They have a critical role in effectively managing institutional boundaries or the lack of such boundaries—the so-called interface between the organization and its task environment. During critical incidents the emotional well-being and integrity of leader-follower relationships are decisive factors in organizational responsiveness. When organizational members are unaware of the character of leader-follower relations, their response to change becomes automatic and unconscious. They lack the opportunity for critical thinking, reflection, and readjustment to the demands of the situation. Unless managers are prepared to make structural, policy, and, particularly, personnel changes, pointing out the unconscious dimensions of relationships within the organization is useless. In other words, organizational leaders must be prepared to confront painful relational conflicts and emotions tied to organizational membership that are unaddressed; again consider the two cases presented in Chapter 10. Confrontation of previously taboo issues and problems must take place.

In my experience, members are frequently willing to change the character of their professional relationships after they have identified the dysfunctional nature of those relationships, usually with the help of a consultant. They are particularly prone to do so when they are in emotional pain and distress—but not without some resistance to insight that can be found in the exploration of the psychodynamics of leader-follower relations. Personality may be an insurmountable barrier to change. In spite of this, I am continually surprised at the capacity for collective change in the manners of interacting and communicating. In this regard, we revisit briefly the varied relational patterns between leaders and followers that affect organizational responses to change.

THE PSYCHODYNAMICS OF LEADER-FOLLOWER RELATIONS

Organizational hierarchies provide the structural context for superordinate-subordinate role relationships. However, the distinctive quality of any particular set of role relationships is ultimately determined by individual personalities and the nature of their *internal object relations*.[3] Beyond the impact of rational organizational designs, norms, and strategies on organizational behavior, the unconscious expectations and desires of organizational members, individually and collectively, affect organizational responses to stress and change. Applying a psychodynamic framework, I submit that workers' predominant *unconscious relational needs* encompass the following three sets of desires: (1) recognition and approval, (2) membership and affiliation, and (3) sympathy, compassion, and retribution. As you may note with category (3), these unconscious requirements are not always compatible. Moreover, regardless of whether these desires are realized or frustrated at work, they influence, significantly, an individual's ability to cope with change and thus shape performance and morale.

Despite similarities in structure, goals, task environment, professional training of members, social class, and culture, organizational identities differ. Often overlooked, organizational distinctions are determined primarily by the character of relational patterns of superordinates and subordinates and their effect on organizational work bonds. Superordinate-subordinate dynamics produce subcultures within organizations that govern vertical and horizontal interactions between and among individuals and groups. In some organizations the pattern of leadership-followership may be consistent throughout, while in others the style of authority relations differs among the layers of hierarchy and between departments and among permanent subgroups. Often, this deviation is dependent upon the degree of autonomy and independence among the people and their units. Yet, in the last analysis, behavior in organizations is determined by shared emotions, transference dynamics between leaders and their staff. To put it simply, *transference* here signifies the subject's perceptions, experiences, and interpretations of interpersonal relationships at work— what I call *work bonds*.[4] Regardless of whether real or fantasy-based, these feelings about significant relationships at work influence performance and mutual expectations.

All of us need recognition and approval at work. Some need more of it than others. When an exaggerated and compulsive desire for recognition and approval is combined with a hierarchy, dominant-submissive human relations are likely (Denhardt, 1987). In her book *The Bonds of Love*, social theorist Jessica Benjamin describes the consequences of this Hegelian master-slave relationship, which she calls "the dialectic of control" (1988: 53):

> If I completely control the other, then the other ceases to exist, and if the other completely controls me, then I cease to exist. A condition of our own independent existence is recognizing the other. True independence means sustaining the essential tension of these contradictory impulses; that is, both asserting the self and recognizing the other. Domination is the consequence of refusing this condition.

Benjamin's "dialectic of control" may be extended to its ultimate psychological conclusion in Hobbes' *Leviathan*, where his fears of human aggression and uncertainty are projected in the image of an "artificial man" with whom the citizenry can identify and whom they can obey. In the example of the company presented earlier, workers expressed the anxiety of metaphorical death and felt completely controlled by a new company with a new strategy that no longer recognized their needs in the manner their dying patriarch had.

In *Group Psychology and the Analysis of the Ego*, Freud (1921) explains the formation of a group mind, which occurs through a process of identification in which individual followers replace their ego ideal with that of their leader. For Freud, group membership requires a sacrifice of individually directed ambitions and ideals—a forfeiture of certain essential liberties and freedoms of the self. Similarly for Hobbes, citizenship requires a sacrifice of liberties to a sovereign. In chapter 14, Hobbes (190) writes: "For as long as every man holdeth this Right of doing any thing he liketh; so long are all men in the condition of Warre." He later (191) continues, "Right is layd aside, either by simply Renouncing it; or by Transferring it to another." Finally (191) he claims, "The way by which a man either simply Renounceth, or Transferreth his Right, is a Declaration, or Signification, by some voluntary and sufficient signe, or signes, that he doth so Renounce, or Tranferre; or hath so Renounced, or Transferred the same, to him that accepteth it." As in Freud's leadership premise, Hobbes postulates governance as an individual transfer of liberty.

In chapter 17 of *Leviathan*, Hobbes (223) writes "of the causes, generation, and definition of a common-wealth":

> And Covenants, without the Sword, are but Words, and of no strength to secure a man at all. Therefore notwithstanding the Lawes of Nature . . . if there be no Power erected, or not great enough for our security; every man will and may lawfully rely on his own strength and art, for caution against all other men.

There is no doubt, in Hobbes, that terror and coercion are necessary functions of government. The Common-wealth must contain the state of human nature and humans' proclivity for envy and hatred of other humans. However, Hobbes did not understand that the containment of the state of nature in the "artificial man," the *Leviathan*, has psychological ramifications for the unconscious life of institutions.

In contrast to Hobbes, Rousseau (1762: 190) writes:

> I maintain, therefore, that sovereignty, being no more than the exercise of the general will, can never be alienated, and that the sovereign, who is a collective being only, can be represented by no one but himself. Power can be transmitted, but not will.

In Rousseau's *The Social Contract*, freedom and liberty always belong to the people and may be ensured by the sovereign through the general will and consensus. For Rousseau, organizational hierarchy (in the manner it typically operates) would reflect a failure of governance because it perpetuates inequalities and individual privilege at a high cost to what he calls "the bond of society"—"that identity of interests which all feel who compose it." For Rousseau, in contrast to Hobbes and Freud, the organization is only as good as the degree to which it serves the general will. In Rousseau, therefore, the collective takes precedence over narcissistic individualism and is held together by the sovereign's ability to reflect in his actions the collective interests adequately.

By *narcissistic individualism*, I refer to that primitive psychological state in which psychological boundaries between oneself and others are distorted and, at the extreme, potentially absent. Narcissism represents a self-aggrandizement and an expansive proclivity that require others' idealization and admiration. Some degree of narcissism, however, is appropriate and necessary to positive self-esteem. In this more positive form, individual narcissism does not cloud over the limits and normal boundaries of self-other relations.

Each of the following superordinate-subordinate relationships (Kohut, 1984; Mitchell: 1986) represents a version of the intersubjective structure of conflicted organizational identities. I need to point out, however, that while the following transference categories emphasize the negative side, each exists in positive and productive work bonds as well. It is a matter of degree, and for our purposes, I choose to focus on the negative side of transference dynamics at work. Why? Because as a consultant most often dealing with crises and conflicts in organizations, I am obligated to address these problems if the client system is to progress and prosper.

THE HEART OF ORGANIZATIONAL IDENTITY: TRANSFERENCE DYNAMICS AT WORK

The Mirroring Relationship: Recognition and Approval

The mirroring relationship consists of a leader (superordinate) who requires adoring and admiring followers, and followers (subordinates) who wish to be led by someone they can idealize. In psychodynamic terms, this phenomenon occurs by *projective identification*: fantasies in which the subject inserts (projects) his or her self—in whole or in part—into the other in order to harm, possess, or control the other (Laplanche and Pontalis, 1973: 356). In the mirroring relationship, followers reject that part of themselves we call their ego ideals, meaning the ideal images they hold of themselves, for that of the leader. The leader then introjects the followers' idealization of him or her, which then momentarily satisfies the desire for recognition and approval. The transference and countertransference are then complete. The leader, consequently, feels heroic, grandiose, and omnipotent, and this attitude exaggerates the superior-inferior character of their relationship and further inflates his or her (the leader's) narcissistic tendencies.

The unconscious basic assumption behind the mirroring and idealizing leader-follower dyad is dependency.[5] In the mirroring relationship, the followers come to the relationship seeking a protector or caretaker—much like the role of the good parent for the child. The followers (subordinates) are driven by a desire to avoid anxiety and uncertainty; feeling out of control, they seek haven in the fantasy of attachment to an all-powerful leader. As Jessica Benjamin suggests, "The wish to restore early omnipotence, or to realize the fantasy of control, never ceases to motivate the individual" (54).

The mirroring relationship may be a solution to the anxiety felt by both parties to the relationship, but it only reinforces the tendency of hierarchical relationships to produce closed systems that are unresponsive to environmental, organizational, political, and technological changes. Securing the character of the leader-follower relationship takes priority; information and feedback are often ignored. Systemic defenses produced by leader-follower relations censor data that conflict with predominant ideologies. Collective suppression reigns and reality testing becomes problematic.[6] Thus, organizational learning in the form of conflict resolution, problem solving, and correction of errors becomes unlikely.

People engaged in the mirroring relationship cannot cope well with change. They are too emotionally invested in hierarchic and authoritarian forms of interaction at work. This tends to promote overdependencies on authorities and experts and thereby reinforces top-down or one-way information flow in the organization. From a psychodynamic perspective, this is designed, moreover, to reinforce defensively a shared fantasy between a superior, perceived as savior, and subordinate, viewed as saved, at a high cost to organizational functioning and general well-being.

The Alterego Relationship: Membership and Affiliation

Many people enter organizations seeking friendship and collegiality. They desire membership in an institution of like-minded men and women. They expect to find leaders they can relate to and identify with—leaders who share their ambitions, ideals, talents, and skills. In the alterego relationship, followers are in search of leaders who are essentially like them—people who share their interests and values. However, the desire to experience what Heinz Kohut called an "alter-ego replica of the self" (1984: 70) in the other should be viewed with some suspicion. Granted, we all need to experience alikeness through affiliation, but the tendency to establish adult relationships based on the absence of differences is troublesome.

People enter a relationship desiring to merge with like-minded others and as a consequence of that merger experience a sense of themselves in others. In contrast to those in the mirroring relationship, organizational members of this group are more hopeful, for instance, that conditions will improve with the next fiscal year, with a change of administration, and the like. They often look to the not-too-distant future as a solution to present-day problems. Their hopefulness and optimism are derived from the symbolic meaning of the merger, which signifies procreation and regeneration. The alterego relationship may be perceived as an act of reproduction. Similar to the mirroring relationship, it too signifies an unconscious desire to return to the original narcissistic position, destroying differentiation and autonomy. Management of psychological boundaries becomes onerous.

The only distinction, other than their relative positions of authority, between superordinate and subordinate is that the leader is ideally someone with more professional experience and knowledge—an older, wiser, more "developed" version of the subordinate. On the positive side, leaders often assume a mentoring role with followers, which is constructive and contributes favorably to organizational development. For example, a manager may unconsciously wish to take care of a member of his staff so that he, the manager, may, in so doing, heal himself. There is nothing necessarily harmful in nurturing others and thereby indirectly repairing oneself. However, the alterego relationship may perpetuate homogeneity—an unhealthy parallelism among organizational members. Like-minded people, for instance, may be unwittingly recruited and selected into an organization's ranks over time. Consequently, a situation may emerge in which Janis' (1982) classic "group think" is an organizational reality.

Emphasis on organizational and interpersonal attributes of uniformity and similarity will, of course, limit the ability to process conflicting and contradictory information. Under stressful circumstances, organizational members may tend to bond with those with whom they share the most, thus producing organizational subcultures with rigid and impenetrable boundaries. Such interpersonal unions may exaggerate loyalties and parochialisms among members of the same vocations, professions, functions, or status in the organization. These groups and subcultures are characteristic of defensive organizations, Hobbesian fortresses, that foster structural, procedural, and interpersonal resistance to change.

The Persecutory Relationship: Compassion, Sympathy, and Retribution

Many organizations operate in hostile environments that generate feelings of persecution among members, regardless of whether these sentiments predate organizational membership. Their feelings of persecution become entangled by difficulties when the leader has paranoid proclivities.

The leader is then merged with the followers, who collectively feel abused and victimized by the public. In such cases, followers empower their leader by projecting into him or her the intensity of their persecutory feelings. Regardless of whether the leader is paranoid at the outset, he or she is compelled, in these instances, to carry the bad feelings of the people.

The persecutory relationship is characterized by scapegoating rituals whereby aggressive group members are in continual search of an appropriate target and home base for their bad feelings. Instances of conflicted organizational identity, such as this, are all too frequent in public sector institutions; the political nature of the environment, to some degree, guarantees some evocation of persecutory feelings. Where such feelings do not lead to projected aggression, a collective depression may result. In fact, it could be argued that the persecutory relationship is a defense against depressivity (or aggression turned inward), and that the depressive organization is one in which its members are unconsciously struggling with their feelings of persecution. The company described earlier exhibited many of these persecutory attributes.

Many people, on the other hand, enter an organization feeling victimized and angry as a result of previous work and childhood experiences. While, on the one hand, these individuals want compassion and sympathy, they desire on the other to control and hurt some individual or group they can blame for their misfortunes and bad feelings. The victimized, like the abused, become the victimizers—the aggressors.

Identification with the aggressor is a defensive response against persecutory anxiety, which operates on the psychological principles of what psychoanalysts call *projective identification*. The victim suppresses the bad image of the original aggressor and then copes with the bad (hostile and angry) feelings toward the aggressor in a way that sustains (rather than terminates) the fantasized relationship. The victim incorporates the original persecutory relationship, which then becomes an unconscious relational pattern of organized self-experience. Hence, this internal image unconsciously affects the character of future relationships at work.

Facing Organizational "Irrationality"

Unstable organizational identities, stemming from mirroring, alterego, and persecutory leader-follower relationships, are defensive reactions to constantly changing and stressful organizational environments. They are deeply intra- and interpersonal experiences of organizational and political climates, which, if they are to be fully appreciated, require the business manager and public administrator to reflect and take action beyond the superficial level of rational models of strategic management and the like. These psychodynamic categories help to explain the meaning behind seemingly irrational, tacit, and unconscious organizational actions. They enable us to breathe life back into the organizational member by recognizing his or her interior world of self-objects and experiences. In so doing, the study of human relations is returned to the reality of its intersubjective nature.

Discovery of conflicted organizational identity, located in the unconscious patterns of leader-follower relationships, can give coherence and continuity to an organizational member's awareness. Here rests the potential for authentic and lasting structural and relational transformation. In Kohut's (1977: 1984) self psychology, this refers to a developing core self—in which the self is better able to balance internal desires and external demands through empathy, introspection, and acceptance of intersubjectivity.

Organizational renewal must be rooted in a collective awareness of conflicted organizational identity. Observations and extensive one-on-one interviews between a consultant and clients often turn up prototypical relationships that are based upon practitioners' descriptions that fit the mirroring, alterego, and persecutory typology. Group sessions with a consultant may help superordinates and subordinates to share mutual (typology-like) experiences to see how they have contributed to perpetuating the organizational patterns of interpersonal relationships and their associated dilemmas.

Eventually, the capability of any organization to cope with external and internal pressures and constant change is dependent upon effective leadership and organizational resilience.

Collaborative Leadership of Change

Dealing effectively with change in organizations requires a mix of collaborative and therapeutic leadership styles. Borrowing on the metaphors of political theory, this could mean replacing the Hobbesian organizational culture of contained fear and aggression with the Rousseauian organizational culture of commitment to participation in problem solving and policy direction—a willingness to work through rather than control responses to changing environments. I use *leadership of change* rather than the more commonly used *management of change* because the two represent different approaches to and assumptions about handling change in organizations. Management of change is an impersonal process of controlling and directing people. This is commonly a top-down, one-way relationship. Although this approach has merit in some situations, I submit that it suppresses emotional and cognitive feedback and obstructs participation, fueling frustration and resentment. Moreover, it perpetuates the typical organizational norm of denying and ignoring negative feelings and assuming rationality.

One cannot solve problems or adapt to change effectively if negative feelings are not shared. The process of error detection and correction depends upon a collective willingness to admit to incompetencies and imperfections. Mirroring, alterego, and persecutory relations of superordinates and subordinates guard against such reflective practices by taking organizational members in flight from their actual circumstances—promoting inauthenticity and *false self* participation. The narcissistic nature of these interpersonal relationships (camouflage, face-saving, diplomacy) further complicates learning.[7]

In contrast to managers of change, collaborative leaders of change engage in an *interpersonal* process of task coordination and decision making by consensus. Collaborative leaders of change provide the system-wide and managerial rationale for change and then consult their staff on appropriate strategic responses. They act bilaterally, not unilaterally. They do not attempt to coerce by fiat members and their subunits and divisions into action. They use change as an opportunity for organizational learning and what might be called a rapprochement of members to the organization. Members explore the individual effects of change upon their roles and publicly discuss their systemic implications.

The collaborative leadership of change requires a willingness to experiment with different ideas and feelings, a team player mentality, a sharing of tasks between and among members, and a view of confronting conflict as an opportunity for learning and enhancing effectiveness (Argyris, 1970). However, such transformations of attitude and action do not come easily. To the observer of interpersonal behavior in organizations, human proclivities for control over oneself, others, and the environment seem intrinsic. Hobbes certainly thought so. Of course, resistance is inevitable (Diamond, 1986). The leader-follower mirroring, alterego, and persecutory relationships are rigid defenses, *leviathanlike fortresses*, that thrive in many organizations and perpetuate unstable organizational identities.

Collaborative leadership of change is necessary but not sufficient. It represents a reframing of how we think about work and relationships in organizations, but it does not confront the emotional resistance and processes inherent to personal change, such as separation anxiety and emotional loss. These suppressed emotions fragment and distort thinking and reality testing. To transcend the human tendency to manage change through psychological defenses that contain the emotions associated with uncertainty, we alter technical rational methods of organization management and become more reflective.[8] This cognitive and emotional role transition for leaders allows grieving and the experiencing of loss among organizational members, to which I turn next.

Therapeutic Leadership of Change

All too often we speak of helping organizations to adapt to change rather than helping the people whom they comprise. Consequently, we overlook the necessity to move beyond structural reorganization and procedural change. In order to accomplish genuine and authentic organizational renewal, participants must deal directly with the human experience of change as loss (Marris, 1986). Whether the change is imposed from inside or outside the organization, members must learn to cope with it. If structural and procedural transitions are to be more than a "facelift" or superficial reorganization, organizational change and development must be approached from a psychodynamic point of view.

Successful organizational change ultimately rests with a reconciliation of the psychological issues of "attachment and separation" (Bowlby, 1982). Early in life, human infants attach themselves to nurturing caretakers (parents and others), producing an affectionate bond. During the course of cognitive and emotional development, infants begin a process of separation and individuation that initiates the emergence of a *core self*—a person. The core self is the most primitive recognition of self from other, what is called *differentiation*. Human development entails object loss as a central feature of change. The term *object loss* refers to dispossession and bereavement of familiar relations, and in organizations that involves the divestment of roles and patterns of interacting. Ultimately, it is experienced by the individual as loss and only later, after working through the feelings, as liberating. So that they may develop cognitively and emotionally, infants have to let go of their attachment to and total dependency on parents. Then they can explore the world on their own (relatively speaking) and, in so doing, find themselves. Separation anxieties are reignited among adults in changing organizations.

As I have noted throughout this book, emotional issues surrounding attachment and separation do not conclude with infancy or early childhood. Rather, they are central relational themes throughout the course of one's life, which underlie strivings for autonomy, freedom, and independence and thereby constitute the psychological bedrock of political, social, organizational and interpersonal relations.

Reframing, as a consequence of change, one's social reality and relinquishing the tendency to censor new, opposing beliefs and assumptions involve emotional loss that sets in motion unconscious processes associated with separation. Organizational change depends upon the collective working through of feelings and thoughts associated with change. This is a group process, best facilitated by consultants and managers as *transitional leaders*. This includes an examination of organizational history and a mapping of where the organization is now, where it is going, and how it plans to get there. But, most importantly, it must involve leadership in assisting organizational members with grieving and loss.

Grief, according to the experts, comprises four phases: (1) numbing—a sense of shock and outrage; (2) yearning—a search for what is lost; anger and disbelief that it has occurred; (3) disorganization and despair—a discarding of old patterns of thinking, feeling, and acting, and a redefinition of oneself; and (4) reorganization—a reshaping of one's internal world and a reframing of social reality (Bowlby, 1980: 85). Therapeutic leaders of change can help their staff work through these phases of grieving. Regular staff meetings should be held to explore and discuss the process and experience of loss.

In organizations, the *numbing phase* is a near-paralysis of operations and a general state of confusion. The *yearning phase*, in which members act as if the change has not occurred, follows. Suppression and denial are common defensive reactions, as is a nostalgic orientation to the past. These defenses conceal the underlying anger and outrage among staff.

When members are able to confront their anger and sadness over the loss of old routines and procedures, they experience the *phase of disorganization and despair*. Here, they not only start letting go of old thinking, feeling, and acting so they can incorporate the new, but they feel the despair of helplessness and lack of control. Although their participation and collaboration in planning can aid the process, they must face the reality of a constantly changing environment over which they have little or no control. This knowledge is depressing and precedes reparation and organizational renewal.

During the *reorganization phase* there is a willingness to experiment with new ideas and feelings—problem solving, error detection, and correction are now possible. Organizational reality testing returns to an open system capable of what Argyris and Schon (1978) call *single- and double-loop learning*. That means organization members are capable of making changes, even when they include reexamining beliefs, norms, and rules and acting on certain values. They respond to shifts in their environment by reflecting upon and making public their underlying operational assumptions and the associated behavioral consequences. Moreover, they can do so, in part, as an effect of acknowledging their psychological resistance to change and loss.

At the individual level, this ability for critical self-reflection evolves from ego strength, and at the organizational level the systemic capacity for double-loop learning rests with what I call *organizational resilience*.

ORGANIZATIONAL RESILIENCE: A ROUSSEAUIAN REBIRTH OF HUMAN COMMUNITY

In this section, I present the concept of *organizational resilience* (OR) as the organizational equivalent of self-cohesion.[9] OR stands for a minimally defensive social system of collaborative and therapeutic leadership capable of responding to change. In fact, it is the intended outcome of the therapeutic leadership of change—the product of exploring resistance and grieving the loss caused by change. OR is the result of what Melanie Klein calls *reparation*, a term that stems from Kleinian object relations and describes the healing process of psychodynamic psychotherapy, when the patient is in the *depressive position*. The individual patient psychically repairs himself or herself by psychologically joining otherwise split internal images of self and others—distortions of self and others. These distortions are internal perceptions of oneself and others as part objects, good and bad, accepting and rejecting. Reparation is the process by which fragmented perceptions and experiences of others become whole again.

Leaders who foster critical, reflective thinking and adaptation to change perpetuate a culture of OR, which arises from a shared sense of mastery and competence in the talents, skills, and values of organizational members. Successful leaders manage institutional boundaries in a manner similar to their management of self-other boundaries—noting the importance of clarifying mutual authority, responsibility, roles, and tasks. Their individuated sense of self is critical to their ability to separate their feelings from others', and others' feelings from their own, which, in effect, enables them to deal more effectively with system boundaries. Such leaders are adept at balancing public pressures with private desires, organizationally and individually.

Leader-follower relations that are minimally defensive and not authoritarian are necessary. Leaders share information and decision making with staff, and, in turn, staff are willing to give and receive critical feedback and take responsibility for their actions. Both supervisors and subordinates feel affiliated with the same system and are committed to the common mission. Many organizations lacking resilience are characterized by insecure and compulsive human relations in which individual members have only a partial comprehension of the total system and its public. Consequently, they are alienated and disconnected from the greater whole of the system, and their efforts are viewed as having little significance.

In practice, OR requires trust and mutual respect among organizational members, which stand or fall on their "collective esteem."[10] OR leaders and followers relate primarily on the basis of consciously shared meaning and purpose, rather than unconscious emotional needs. While they care about one another as fellow human beings, they are not driven to each other psychologically by compensatory and narcissistic motives. Despite being under the pressures of stress and the uncertainty of constant change, each leader's sense of self is adequately integrated and does not require constant aggrandizement by the staff and the public. OR leaders do not attract subordinates who are driven primarily by emotional deficiencies—indeed, such leaders may promote greater self-worth among those with low self-esteem.

To promote OR, organizational leaders must be aware of self and other boundaries in their interpersonal relationships at work. They cannot have a pressing emotional need to displace bad feelings onto others and must be aware of the tendencies of others to do the same to them. Unconscious displacement and projection of bad feelings are more common under stressful conditions. Thus, organizational leaders able to manage interpersonal boundaries and minimize defensive tendencies will foster healthier and more productive interactions with and among their staff. These leaders of resilient organizations are aware of the unique character, talents, and skills of individual staff members. Hence, individuality and interdependence are values consciously stressed and intended to counteract the regressive pull of homogeneity and uniformity.

SUMMARY

People join organizations with unconscious needs and expectations. All of us have tendencies for mirroring, alterego, and persecutory relationships. The Hobbesian climate of many organizations, however, may promote such propensities. Members of organizations with unstable organizational identities feel fragmented and split apart by the perceived absence of organizational continuity and meaningful work. Psychological regression and unconscious narcissistic fantasies distort superior-subordinate relations among them. Repairing conflicted organizational identity requires an organization with many of the characteristics of the Rousseauian therapeutic community (Glass, 1989),

capable of public grieving and acknowledgment of regressive proclivities under stress. Using Hobbesian and Rousseauian political theory
as metaphors for organizations, I have attempted to describe collaborative and therapeutic leadership actions that can produce organizational resilience in place of organizational defensiveness.

The character of leader-follower relationships can most usefully be
pointed out to individual organizational members by an outside consultant
in a nondefensive and nonjudgmental fashion. The consultant uses anec-
dotal data collected from one-on-one interviews and group problem-solving sessions with the membership at large. He or she empathically repeats
to the participants in a given relationship the descriptions of behavior
collected in interviews and observations and offers to the involved parties
a description of the interaction of the leader and follower(s). The consultant
then requests their confirmation or refutation of the data and their interpretation. In *Lost in Familiar Places*, Shapiro and Carr (1991) point out
that meaningful explanations are what they call "negotiated interpretations"—some meaning the consultant and clients reach together. Hence,
testing the validity of data with the participants concerned, presenting it
in a typological form, helps them to change, if they wish, the character of
their work relationships.

So the reader may better appreciate my point of reference, I conclude
with a discussion of the role of the psychoanalytic organizational theorist
as consultant.

ORGANIZATIONAL PSYCHODYNAMICS AND CHANGE: ORGANIZATIONAL THEORIST AS CONSULTANT

Understanding organizational psychodynamics involves the acquisition
of reflective knowledge.[11] This is derived from attempts at illuminating,
by working with organizational participants, the structures of interpersonal
feelings and needs that an organization's identity comprises. Transference
phenomena, which include mirroring and idealizing, persecutory, and
twinship (or alterego) dynamics, represent the core of organizational
identity. Awareness of organizational identity, and the place of one's role
identity in it, is necessary for the assumption of personal responsibility and
claimed action on behalf of individual organizational members and their
desire for change. The consultant functions as a "reteller of narration" who
surfaces the participant's "disclaiming of actions" (Schafer, 1983). The
disclaiming of and discomfort with actions alert the consultant to inauthenticity: a retreat into the external world that consequently "relieves one

[the public manager or administrator] of personal responsibility"
(Chessick, 1986: 87).

The fundamental intent of the psychoanalytic enterprise is that of
unlocking meanings (G. S. Klein, 1976: 48), while the concepts of function, purpose, and meaning of experience and behavior make up psychoanalytic theory (51). Moreover, it deserves highlighting that "what endows
words and other symbolic structures with significance is the communication of affects" (Modell, 1984: 173). Psychodynamically oriented organizational consultants, in contrast to other consultants, know that
"interpretation can be effective only when there is, in Strachey's terms, a
'point of urgency,' that is to say [when] affect is genuine and communicated" (90). This is consistent with the emphasis upon the analysis of
critical incidents as a strategy for reaching feelings otherwise screened off
by repression and denial.

In organizational psychodynamics, the units of analysis are intrapsychic, interpersonal, group, and organizational; the language is that of
activity and relationships; and the transmitter is that of feelings. The
psychoanalytic organizational consultant/researcher helps to make sense
of the intersubjective structure of organizational life and its impact upon
organizational identity and action.

A case in point is that of the department director, discussed in Chapter
8, who requested a consultation to resolve an ongoing conflict between
two of his assistant directors. The director, you may recall, described his
(rational) role as that of managing organizational boundaries between his
department and the (operating environment) public. He complained that
his two assistants constantly quarreled and were unable to manage the
activities of their departments effectively. Coincidentally, he was rarely in
the office himself and spent most of his time in the field. His actions were
perceived not only by the consultant but by his two assistants as flight from
a threatening situation that persisted unresolved (role identity = one who
flees from conflict). Moreover, his two assistants avoided surfacing the
issue with each other and with the director himself. The organizational
consultant's work consisted of paying attention to this flight theme (defensive theme of organizational identity) and helping the three managers
to acknowledge their responsibility for the situation and admit their shared
avoidance. Once that was accomplished it was possible to investigate the
reasons and motives for their past actions so they could learn. This meant
exploring feelings, underlying assumptions, and attributions about each
other and their mutual roles.

I believe the psychoanalytic organizational consultant assists participants, who share a common organizational history, in elaborating and

consensually validating their interpersonal experience. He or she literally helps them come to terms with the psychic or affective base of their relationships. The complex role of consultant is, therefore, that of combined *participant-observer* (Sullivan, 1953; Havens, 1976; Diamond, 1985b; Hirsch, 1985) and *coauthor* (Schafer, 1983) of organizational stories (and metaphors). This interpretive role requires the establishment of a working alliance (Greenson, 1978) with organizational participants to reach, by way of interpretation, some clarification and mutual understanding of interpersonal experience in present organizational life. In the preceding case, the consultant offered the interpretation that regardless of their individual differences and disagreements, the three executives shared a tendency to avoid conflict. They had constructed an organizational identity characterized by mutual flights. This was responsible for the poor coordination of tasks among them and their staff.

Organizational consultants participate in and observe distinctive interpersonal configurations that produce and perpetuate organizational identities. Psychoanalytic consultants assume that (prereflectively) unconscious (Atwood and Stolorow, 1984) actions of organizational members are primarily responsible for producing organizational identities. If not for the consultation, organizational members would remain unaware of the meaning and consequences of their actions and decisions and, therefore, lack the necessary information for change.

One of the objectives of psychodynamic organizational research and consultation is the discovery of organizational identity. Organizational identity is the outcome of the repetitive structures of intersubjectivity located in human interactions that are affected by both conscious and prereflectively unconscious thoughts, feelings, and perceptions that, in turn, influence decisions and actions.

Organizational identity is a structural solution (or compromise formation) to contradictory aims, motives, wishes, and desires among organizational participants. It comprises the intra- and interpersonal needs of organizational members (located in the transference of emotions) in the context of hierarchical arrangements. The mix of social structure (authority, position, and status) and personality (ambitions, ideals, talents and skills, unconscious fantasies and conflicts) helps shape the self-esteem and performance of organizational members. Ambitions, ideals, fantasies, and conflicts of organizational members are surfaced in continuous observations and in-depth conversations about mutual expectations and career objectives between supervisors and subordinates. Talents and skills are evaluated by examining personnel policies and training procedures for employee orientation and by searching for mentoring relationships between supervisors and subordinates.

In sum, awareness of organizational identity is necessary for the assumption of personal responsibility and claimed action by organizational members, which is crucial to initiating intentional change in the status quo. The three managers mentioned previously could not make a change and resolve conflicts without a common handle on the organizational paradox. The interpretation provided by the consultant offered them an opportunity to share in the responsibility and take collective action to correct conditions.

Organizational identity is most accessible to interpretation through the analysis of transference phenomena between organizational subordinates and superordinates, researchers and their subjects, consultants and clients. Unconscious narcissistic expectations are transferred to interpersonal relationships within the organizational setting. Here, the organizational image replaces the parental object. Frustrations of self-other needs stimulate transference dynamics between organizational members that influence the pattern of interactions constituting the organizational identity. Understanding organizational identity offers a glance behind the organizational curtain of complexity where personal motives and reasons for action reside.

NOTES

1. It is important to note that while my work as a consultant in the past ten years has been predominantly with public/government organizations of various sizes, I have been a consultant for several large private companies as well. Although there are clear differences in their strategies and missions, they often have similar problems in coping with change and tend equally to hold on to defensive and bureaucratic routines. Thus, my perception of business manager and worker experiences, while based on fewer consultations, fits more closely the Hobbesian metaphor than the Rousseauian.

2. To ensure anonymity, I do not provide the name of this company.

3. I use the notion of *internal object relations* to refer to the organization of one's experiences with significant others, experiences that are internalized over time and come to influence the individual's expectations and desires of others as well as her or his object choices—what Atwood and Stolorow (1984) call the *intersubjective structure* or *structures of subjectivity* that the personality comprises.

4. The idea for this originated with Benjamin's (1988) book *The Bonds of Love* and was originally suggested by my good friend and colleague Ralph P. Hummel, after he read an earlier draft of this book.

5. *Basic assumptions*, a term invented by W. R. Bion (1959), represent the unconscious expectations people carry with them into groups. These wishes may be understood by observing authority relations within the group setting. According to Bion and as discussed in previous chapters, there are three basic assumptions: dependency, fight-flight, and pairing. In any work group one of these assumptions may predominate at any given time

in a relationship between leader and followers. For Bion, every group consists of at least two groups: a task group and a basic assumption group.

6. Reality testing is a "process postulated by Freud which allows the subject to distinguish stimuli originating in the outside world from internal ones, and to forestall possible confusion supposedly fundamental to hallucination" (Laplanche and Pontalis 1973: 382).

7. See Chris Argyris's (1985; 1990) work for the cognitive side of defensive routines that obstruct organizational learning.

8. For the strictly cognitive view of reflective learning among professionals see Donald Schon's (1983) work.

9. See Glass, (1976: 166).

10. Some may wish to think of collective esteem as an alternative term for organizational morale; it differs in that it views the emotional integrity of the institution as based upon the preconscious images individual members hold of the organization and its purposefulness.

11. See Schon (1983) for the cognitive side of professional learning for practice.

BIBLIOGRAPHY

Allaire, Y., and Firsirotu, M. E. (1984). "Theories of Organizational Culture." *Organization Studies*, 5(3): 193-226.

Allcorn, S. (1992). *Codependency in the Workplace.* Westport, Conn.: Quorum Books.

Allcorn, S. (1991). *Workplace Superstars in Resistant Organizations.* Westport, Conn.: Quorum Books.

Argyris, C. (1990). *Overcoming Organizational Defenses.* Boston: Allyn and Bacon.

Argyris, C. (1985). *Strategy, Change and Defensive Routines.* New York: Putnam.

Argyris, C. (1976). "Leadership, Learning, and the Status Quo." *Organizational Dynamics*, 4(3): 29–43.

Argyris, C. (1970). *Intervention Theory and Method: A Behavioral Science View.* Reading, Mass.: Addison-Wesley.

Argyris, C. (1957). *Personality and Organization.* New York: Harper and Row.

Argyris, C., and Schon, D. (1978). *Organizational Learning.* Reading, Mass.: Addison-Wesley.

Argyris, C., and Schon, D. (1974). *Theory in Practice.* San Francisco: Jossey-Bass.

Argyris, C., et al. (1985). *Action Science.* San Francisco: Jossey-Bass.

Atwood, G. E., and R. D. Stolorow. (1984). *Structures of Subjectivity: Explorations in Psychoanalytic Phenomenology.* Hillsdale, N.J.: Analytic Press.

Barnard, C. (1938). *Functions of the Executive.* Cambridge, Mass.: Harvard University Press.

Baum, H. S. (1990). *Organizational Membership.*Albany, N.Y.: State University of New York Press.

Baum, H. S. (1987). *The Invisible Bureaucracy.* New York: Oxford University Press.

Baum, H. S. (1983). "Autonomy, Shame, and Doubt: Power in the Bureaucratic Lives of Planners." *Administration and Society*, 15(2): 147–84.

Benjamin, J. (1988). *The Bonds of Love.* New York: Pantheon Books.

Bion, W. R. (1970) *Attention and Interpretation.* New York: Basic Books.

Bion, W. R. (1959). *Experiences in Groups.* New York: Basic Books.

Blits, J. H. (1989). "Hobbesian Fear." *Political Theory*, 17(3): 417–31.

Bowlby, J. (1982). *Attachment*. New York: Basic Books.

Bowlby, J. (1980). *Loss*. New York: Basic Books.

Bowlby, J. (1979). *The Making and Breaking of Affectional Bonds*. London: Tavistock Publications.

Bowlby, J. (1973). *Separation*. New York: Basic Books.

Burke, W. W. (1982). *Organization Development: Principles and Practices*. Boston and Toronto: Little, Brown.

Chessick, R. D. (1986). "Heidegger for Psychotherapists." *American Journal of Psychotherapy*, 40(1): 83–95.

Collinson, D. L. (1988). "Engineering Humour: Masculinity, Joking and Conflict in Shop-Floor Relations." *Organization Studies*, 9(2): 181–99.

Crozier, M. (1964). *The Bureaucratic Phenomenon*. Chicago: University of Chicago Press.

De Board, R. (1978). *The Psychoanalysis of Organizations*. London: Tavistock Publications.

Denhardt, R. B. (1987). "Images of Death and Slavery in Organizational Life." *Journal of Management*, 13(3): 529–41.

Denhardt, R. B. (1981). *In the Shadow of Organization*. Lawrence: University of Kansas Press.

Diamond, M. A. (1991). "Treating the Parataxic Organization: A Case Example of Intervention Strategy." *Administration and Society*, 23(4): 61–80.

Diamond, M. A. (1988). "Organizational Identity: A Psychoanalytic Exploration of Organizational Meaning." *Administration and Society*, 20(2): 166–90.

Diamond, M. A. (1986). "Resistance to Change: A Psychoanalytic Critique of Argyris and Schon's Contributions to Organization Theory and Intervention." *Journal of Management Studies*, 23(5): 543–62.

Diamond, M. A. (1985a). "Psychological Dimensions of Personal Responsibility for Public Management: An Object Relations Approach." *Journal of Management Studies*, 22(6): 649–67.

Diamond, M. A. (1985b). "The Social Character of Bureaucracy: Anxiety and Ritualistic Defense." *Political Psychology*, 6(4): 663–79.

Diamond, M. A. (1984). "Bureaucracy as Externalized Self-System." *Administration and Society*, 16(2) 195–214.

Diamond, M. A., and Allcorn, S. (1985a). "Psychological Responses to Stress in Complex Organizations." *Administration and Society*, 17: 217–39.

Diamond, M. A., and Allcorn, S. (1985b). "Psychological Dimensions of Role Use in Bureaucratic Organizations." *Organizational Dynamics*, 14(1): 35–59.

Diamond, M. A., and Allcorn, S. (1984). "Psychological Barriers to Personal Responsibility." *Organizational Dynamics*, 12(4): 66–77.

Duncan, W. J., and Feisal, J. P. (1989). "No Laughing Matter: Patterns of Humor in the Workplace." *Organizational Dynamics*. 17: 18–30.

Eagle, J., and Newton, P. M. (1981). "Scapegoating in Small Groups: An Organizational Approach." *Human Relations*, 34: 283–301.

Eco, U. (1976). *A Theory of Semiotics*. Bloomington: Indiana University Press.

Erikson, E. (1968). *Identity, Youth and Crisis*. New York: W. W. Norton.

Erikson, E. (1966). "Ontogeny of Ritualization," in R. Loewenstein et al., eds., *Psychoanalysis—A General Psychology: Essays in Honor of Heinz Hartmann*. New York: International Universities Press.

Erikson, E. (1964). *Insight and Responsibility.* New York: W. W. Norton.

Erikson, E. (1963). *Childhood and Society.* New York: W. W. Norton.

Fairbairn, W. R. D. (1952). *Psychoanalytic Studies of Personality.* London: Tavistock Publications.

Freud, A. (1966). *The Ego and the Mechanisms of Defense.* 2nd Ed. New York: International Universities Press.

Freud, A. (1936). *The Ego and the Mechanisms of Defense.* New York: International Universities Press.

Freud, S. (1963). *Character and Culture.* New York: Collier Books.

Freud, S. (1905/1960). *Jokes and Their Relation to the Unconscious.* New York: W. W. Norton.

Freud, S. (1923/1960). *The Ego and the Id.* New York: W. W. Norton.

Freud, S. (1926/1959a). *Inhibitions, Symptoms and Anxiety.* New York: W. W. Norton.

Freud, S. (1921/1959b). *Group Psychology and the Analysis of the Ego.* New York: W. W. Norton.

Freud, S. (1933). *The New Introductory Lectures.* New York: W. W. Norton.

Freud, S. (1928). "Humour." *The International Journal of Psychoanalysis,* 9(Pt.1): 1–6.

Freud, S. (1915). "Repression." in Gay, P., ed., *The Freud Reader,* 1989. New York: W. W. Norton.

Fromm, E. (1941). *Escape from Freedom.* New York: Holt, Rinehart and Winston.

Frosch, J. (1983). *The Psychotic Process.* New York: International Universities Press.

Gay, P., ed. (1989). *The Freud Reader.* New York: W. W. Norton.

"Getting Down to Funny Business." (1985). *Nation's Business,* 73(11): 44–48.

Glass, J. M. (1989). *Private Terror/Public Life.* Ithaca, N.Y.: Cornell University Press.

Glass, J. M. (1976). "Political Philosophy as Therapy: Rousseau and the Pre-Social Origins of Consciousness." *Political Theory,* 4(2): 163–84.

Goldberg, A., ed. (1983) *The Future of Psychoanalysis.* New York: International Universities Press.

Grady, D. O. (1989). "Economic Development and Administrative Power Theory: A Comparative Analysis of State Development Agencies." *Policy Studies Review,* 8: 322–39.

Greenacre, P. (1959). "Play in Relation to Creative Imagination." *The Psychoanalytic Study of the Child,* 21: 193–212.

Greenberg, J. R., and Mitchell, S. A. (1983). *Object Relations in Psychoanalytic Theory.* Cambridge, Mass.: Harvard University Press.

Greenson, R. (1978). *Explorations in Psychoanalysis.* New York: International Universities Press.

Grolnick, S. A.; Barkin, L.; Muensterberger, W., eds. (1978). *Between Reality and Fantasy: Winnicott's Concepts of Transitional Objects and Phenomena.* Northvale, N.J.: Jason Aronson.

Grotstein, J. S. (1983). "Some Perspectives on Self-Psychology," in Goldberg, A., ed., *The Future of Psychoanalysis.* New York: International Universities Press.

Guntrip, H. (1969). *Schizoid Phenomena, Object Relations and the Self.* New York: International Universities Press.

Hamilton, N. G. (1990). *Self and Others: Object Relations Theory in Practice.* Northvale, N.J.: Jason Aronson.

Havens, L. (1986). *Making Contact: Uses of Language in Psychotherapy.* Cambridge, Mass.: Harvard University Press.

Havens, L. (1976). *Participation Observation.* Northvale, N.J.: Jason Aronson.

Heidegger, M. (1975). "What is Metaphysics?" in Kaufmann, ed. *Existentialism from Dostoevsky to Sartre.* New York: New American Library.

Heidegger, M. (1927/1962). *Being and Time.* New York: Harper and Row.

Hirsch, I. (1985). "The Rediscovery of the Advantages of the Participant-Observation Model." *Psychoanalysis and Contemporary Thought,* 8(3): 441–59.

Hirschhorn, L. (1988). *The Workplace Within.* Cambridge, Mass.: MIT Press.

Hobbes, T. (1651). *Leviathan.* Edited by C. B. Macpherson, 1968. Harmondsworth, England: Penguin Books.

Horney, K. (1950). *Neurosis and Human Growth.* New York: W. W. Norton.

Hummel, R. P. (1991). "Stories Managers Tell: Why They Are Valid as Science." *Public Administration Review,* 51(1): 31–41.

Hummel, R. P. (1977/1982). *The Bureaucratic Experience.* New York: St. Martins Press.

Ingersoll, V. H., and Adams, G. B. (1992). *The Tacit Organization.* Greenwich, Conn. and London: JAI Press.

Jacobson, N. (1978). *Pride And Solace.* Berkeley: University of California Press.

Janis, I. (1982). *Groupthink.* Boston: Houghton Mifflin.

Jaques, E. (1955). "Social Systems as a Defense Against Persecutory and Depressive Anxiety," in Klein, M.; Heimann, P.; and Money-Kyrle, R. E., eds., *New Directions in Psychoanalysis.* New York: Basic Books.

Jaques, E. (1951). *The Changing Culture of a Factory.* London: Tavistock Publications.

Kafka, J. (1983). "Challenge and Confirmation in Ritual Action." *Psychiatry,* 46(1): 31–39.

Kahn, W. A. (1989). "Toward a Sense of Organizational Humor: Implications for Organizational Diagnosis and Change." *The Journal of Applied Behavioral Science,* 25(1): 45–63.

Kernberg, O. (1980). *Internal World and External Reality.* Northvale, N.J.: Jason Aronson.

Kernberg, O. (1979). "Regression in Organizational Leadership." *Psychiatry,* 42: 24–39.

Kets de Vries, M. F. R. (1980). *Organizational Paradoxes.* London: Tavistock Publications.

Kets de Vries, M. F. R., ed. (1984). *The Irrational Executive.* New York: International Universities Press.

Kets de Vries, M. F. R., and Miller, D. (1984). *The Neurotic Organization.* San Francisco: Jossey-Bass.

Kets de Vries, M. F. R., et al. (1991). *Organizations on the Couch.* San Francisco: Jossey-Bass.

Klein, G. S. (1976). *Psychoanalytic Theory.* New York: International Universities Press.

Klein, M. (1975). *The Psychoanalysis of Children.* New York: Seymour Lawrence/Delacorte Press.

Klein, M. (1959). "Our Adult World and Its Roots in Infancy." *Human Relations,* 12: 291–301.

Klein, M., and Riviere, J. (1964). *Love, Hate and Reparation.* New York: W. W. Norton.

Kohut, H. (1984). *How Does Analysis Cure?* Chicago: University of Chicago Press.

Kohut, H. (1977). *The Restoration of the Self.* New York: International Universities Press.

Kohut, H., and Wolf, E. (1978). "Disorders of the Self and Their Treatment: An Outline." *International Journal of Psychoanalysis*, 59: 413–25.

Kris, E. (1952). *Psychoanalytic Explorations in Art*. New York: International Universities Press.

Kris, E. (1940). "Laughter as an Expressive Process: Contributions to the Psychoanalysis of Expressive Behaviour." *The International Journal of Psychoanalysis*, 21: 314–41.

Kris, E. (1938). "Ego Development and the Comic." *The International Journal of Psychoanalysis*, 19: 77–90.

Kuhlman, T. L. (1984). *Humor and Psychotherapy*. Homewood, Ill.: Dorsey Professional Books.

Kushner, M. (1990). *The Light Touch: How to Use Humor for Business Success*. New York: Simon and Schuster.

LaBier, D. (1983). "Bureaucracy and Psychopathology." *Political Psychology*, 4(2): 223–44.

Laing, R. D. (1966). *The Divided Self*. Harmondsworth, England: Penguin Books.

Laplanche, J., and Pontalis, J. B. (1973). *The Language of Psychoanalysis*. New York: W. W. Norton.

Larcon, J-P., and Reitter, R. (1984). "Corporate Imagery and Corporate Identity." in Kets de Vries, M. F. R., ed., *The Irrational Executive*. New York: International Universities Press.

Levenson, E. (1983). *The Ambiguity of Change: An Inquiry into the Nature of Psychoanalytic Reality*. New York: Basic Books.

Levinson, H. (1981). *Executive*. Cambridge, Mass.: Harvard University Press.

Levinson, H. (1972). *Organizational Diagnosis*. Cambridge, Mass.: Harvard University Press.

Levinson, H., and Weinbaum, L. (1984). "The Impact of Organization on Mental Health." in Kets de Vries, M. F. R., ed., *The Irrational Executive*. New York: International Universities Press.

Levinson, H., et al. (1962). *Men, Management, and Mental Health*. Cambridge, Mass.: Harvard University Press.

Lifton, R. (1986). *The Nazi Doctors*. New York: Basic Books.

Maccoby, M. (1976). *The Gamesman*. New York: Simon and Schuster.

McGhee, P. E., and Goldstein, J. H., eds. (1983). *Handbook of Humor Research*. Vol.1. *Basic Issues*. New York: Springer-Verlag.

Macpherson, C. B. (1977). *The Life and Times of Liberal Democracy*. New York: Oxford University Press.

Mahler, M. S.; Pine, F.; and Bergman, A. (1975). *The Psychological Birth of the Human Infant*. New York: Basic Books.

Marris, P. (1986). *Loss and Change*. London: Routledge and Kegan Paul.

Mayo, E. (1933). *The Human Problems of an Industrial Civilization*. New York: Macmillan.

Meek, V. L. (1988). "Organizational Culture: Origins and Weaknesses." *Organization Studies*, 9(4): 453–73.

Menzies, I. E. P. (1960). "A Case in the Functioning of Social Systems as a Defense Against Anxiety: A Report on a Study of the Nursing Service of a General Hospital." *Human Relations*, 13: 95–121.

Merriam-Webster Dictionary. (1974). New York: Pocket Books.

Merton, R. (1963). "Bureaucratic Structure and Personality." in Smelser and Smelser, eds., *Personality and Social Systems*. New York: Wiley.

Merton, R. (1940). "Bureaucratic Structure and Personality." *Social Forces*, 18(4): 560–68.

Mitchell, J., ed. (1986). *The Selected Melanie Klein*. New York: The Free Press.

Mitchell, S. A. (1988). *Relational Concepts in Psychoanalysis*. Cambridge, Mass.: Harvard University Press.

Mitroff, I. (1983). *Stakeholders of Organizational Mind*. San Francisco: Jossey-Bass.

Modell, A. H. (1984). *Psychoanalysis in a New Context*. New York: International Universities Press.

Moore, B. E., and Fine, B. D. (1990). *Psychoanalytic Terms and Concepts*. New Haven, Conn.: Yale University Press.

Morgan, G. (1986). *Images of Organization*. Beverly Hills, Calif.: Sage Publications.

Parsons, T. (1964). *Social Structure and Personality*. London: Collier-Macmillan.

Reik, T. (1946). *Ritual: Psycho-Analytic Studies*. New York: International Universities Press.

Rice, A. K. (1969). "Individual, Group and Intergroup Processes." *Human Relations*, 22(6): 565–84.

Rice, A. K. (1965). *Learning for Leadership*. London: Tavistock Publications.

Ritti, R. R., and Funkhouser, G. R. (1977). *The Ropes to Skip and the Ropes to Know: Studies in Organizational Behavior*. Columbus, Ohio: Grid.

Rothstein, A. (1980). *The Narcissistic Pursuit of Perfection*. New York: International Universities Press.

Rousseau, J. J. (1762/1976). *The Social Contract*. Edited by Earnest Barker. New York: Oxford University Press.

Roy, D. F. (1959, 1960). "Banana-Time: Job Satisfaction and Informal Interaction." *Human Organization*, 18(4): 158–68.

Rycroft, C. (1968). *A Critical Dictionary of Psychoanalysis*. Harmondsworth, England: Penguin Books.

Sandler, J., ed., (1987). *Projection, Identification, Projective Identification*. New York: International Universities Press.

Sands, S. (1984). "The Use of Humor in Psychotherapy." *Psychoanalytic Review*, 71(3): 441–60.

Schafer, R. (1983). *The Analytic Attitude*. New York: Basic Books.

Schafer, R. (1976). *A New Language for Psychoanalysis*. New Haven, Conn.: Yale University Press.

Schein, E. (1990). "Organizational Culture." *American Psychologist*, 45(2): 109–19.

Schein, E. (1985). *Organizational Culture and Leadership*. San Francisco: Jossey-Bass.

Schon, D. (1983). *The Reflective Practitioner*. New York: Basic Books.

Schwartz, H. (1990). *Narcissistic Processes and Organizational Decay*. New York: New York University Press.

Schwartz, H. (1982). "Job Involvement as Obsession-Compulsion." *Academy of Management Review*, 7(3): 429–32.

Sederberg, P. (1984). "Organization and Explanation: New Metaphors for Old Problems." *Administration and Society*, 16(2): 167–94.

Segal, H. (1988). *Introduction to the Work of Melanie Klein*. London: Karnac Books.

Sennett, R. (1981). *Authority*. New York: Vintage Books.

Shapiro, E., and Carr, W. (1991). *Lost in Familiar Places*. New Haven, Conn.: Yale University Press.

Shulman, G. (1989). "Metaphor and Modernization in the Political Thought of Thomas Hobbes." *Political Theory*, 17(3): 392–416.

Siggins, L. (1983). "Psychoanalysis and Ritual." *Psychiatry*, 46(1): 2–15.

Slater, P. (1966). *Microcosm*. New York: John Wiley.

Smircich, L. (1983). "Concepts of Culture and Organizational Analysis." *Administrative Science Quarterly*, 28: 339–58.

Smith, J. H. (1983). "Rite, Ritual, and Defense." *Psychiatry*, 46(1): 16–30.

Spence, D. (1982). *Narrative Truth and Historical Truth*. New York: W. W. Norton.

Sperling, O. (1950). "Psychoanalytic Aspects of Bureaucracy." *Psychoanalytic Quarterly*, 19: 88–100.

Srivastva, S. et al. (1983). *Executive Mind*. San Francisco: Jossey-Bass.

Sullivan, H. S. (1954). *The Psychiatric Interview*. New York: W. W. Norton.

Sullivan, H. S. (1953). *The Interpersonal Theory of Psychiatry*. New York: W. W. Norton.

Theodorson, G. A., and Theodorson, A. G. (1969). *A Modern Dictionary Of Sociology*. New York: Barnes and Noble Books.

Waldo, D. (1984). *The Administrative State*. 2nd ed. New York: Holmes & Meier.

Weber, M. (1947). *The Theory of Social and Economic Organization*. New York: The Free Press.

White, J. (1986). "On The Growth Of Knowledge In Public Administration." *Public Administration Review*, 46(1): 15–24.

Wicker, F. W.; Barron, W. L.; and Willis, A. C. (1980). "Disparagement Humor: Dispositions and Resolutions." *Journal of Personality and Social Psychology*, 39(4): 701–9.

Winnicott, D. W. (1971). *Playing and Reality*. London: Tavistock Publications.

Winnicott, D. W. (1965). *The Maturational Processes and the Facilitating Environment*. New York: International Universities Press.

Wolin, S. (1960). *Politics and Vision*. Boston: Little, Brown.

Zaleznik, A., and Kets de Vries, M. F. R. (1975). *Power and the Corporate Mind*. Boston: Houghton Mifflin.

Zaleznik, A., et al. (1965). *The Executive Role Constellation*. Cambridge, Mass.: Harvard University Press.

Zuesse, E. M. (1983). "The Absurdity of Ritual." *Psychiatry*, 46(1): 40–50.

INDEX

About the Author

MICHAEL A. DIAMOND is Professor and Chair of Public Administration at the University of Missouri-Columbia. His extensive writings, bridging psychoanalytic thinking and organizational behavior, have appeared in various scholarly journals, including *Administration and Society*, *Human Relations*, *The Journal of Management Studies*, *Political Psychology*, and others. He is a practicing organization development consultant to government, not-for-profit, and business organizations.